William C. Norris
Portrait of a Maverick

James C. Worthy

International Standard Book Number: 0-88730-087-1

Library of Congress Catalog Card Number 87-1808

Printed in the United States of America

Library of Congress Cataloging-in-Publication Data

Worthy, James C.
   William C. Norris: portrait of a maverick.

   Bibliography: p.
   Includes index.
   1. Norris, William C., 1911- . 2. Control Data Corporation—
History. 3. Computer industry—United—History.
4. Businessmen—United States—Biography. I. Title.
HD9696.C62N689 1987 338.7'61004'0924 [B] 87-1808

ISBN 0-88730-087-1

William C. Norris

"Whenever I see everybody
going south, I have a great
compulsion to go north."

William C. Norris

To my daughter,
Joan Barr Tullis, of whom
I am very proud.

Contents

Acknowledgments

I received invaluable help from a number of people in writing this book. Notable among these was William C. Norris himself, who spent many hours with me tape recording his recollections and his accounts of critical events in his own life and in the building of Control Data Corporation. I especially appreciate his willingness to answer frankly all questions put to him and the readiness with which he made available materials from his personal and company files.

Other members of the top management staff were equally cooperative. Much of the information that I found most useful came from my several long interviews with Norbert R. Berg, for many years Norris's closest associate within the company and the person best informed about his years at Control Data. Robert M. Price, who held responsible positions under Norris for the greater part of the company's history and who succeeded Norris as chief executive officer, was likewise helpful in elucidating many of the facts behind critical events in the Control Data story.

A book which is at once a biography of William C. Norris and a history of Control Data Corporation must necessarily deal with many scientific and engineering subjects, and I greatly appreciate the counsel given me on both technical and business matters by John W. Lacey, a senior vice president who joined the company at an early stage and who is well informed on all major aspects of Control Data's growth.

Others whose assistance was of special value were Thomas G. Kamp, Paul G. Miller, Lawrence Perlman, Dr. Walter H. Bruning, and Albert A. Eisele. Frank C. Mullaney, Roger G. Wheeler, and

Marvin G. Rogers, former officers who played key roles during important stages in the company's history, provided information and insights that could be obtained from no other sources. Dr. Donald L. Bitzer, director of the Computerized Education Research Laboratory of the University of Illinois, gave generously of his time in explaining the origin of the PLATO system.

In addition to these, many different people both inside and outside the company supplied information on significant points within their areas of knowledge and expertise; these I have recognized in references throughout the book and take this opportunity to thank.

In the accompanying Note on Sources, I have given credit to the Control Data Archives whose voluminous materials have been invaluable for my purposes; here, I wish to thank Patricia Utterberg and historical archivist Scott Jesse for their aid in making these resources available to me. I am particularly indebted to Jesse for his assistance in researching various special points, for his cooperation in compiling the Bibliography, and for his many hours of tedious labor in verifying references to the numerous source materials I have cited. J. Donald Flanagan of the public relations staff gave research support on several points, and for this I am most grateful.

Some of the most timely help I received came from Karen Ray, secretary to Mr. Norris, who on numerous occasions identified and located documents I needed. I am also indebted to his former secretary, Ursula Wlasiuk, for her aid at various critical stages.

I was especially fortunate in having as my independent editor Pamela Lee Espeland, whose keen editorial skills aided greatly in organizing and presenting the complex materials that comprise this book.

Finally, I thank my wife, Mildred Leritz Worthy, for her understanding and patience during the two years this writing required.

Prologue

I first met William C. Norris in the fall of 1967, a little over ten years after he founded Control Data Corporation. At the time, I was a partner in the management consulting firm of Cresap, McCormick and Paget and had been invited to Control Data headquarters in Minneapolis to discuss a possible consulting engagement. I was given a general description of the work to be done and escorted to Norris's office, where I found a man of slight build, greying hair, and friendly manner.

Following preliminary pleasantries, Norris informed me that he already knew something about our firm, having had dealings in the past with Dick Paget, one of our senior partners. I settled back to listen to what I assumed would be a polite little story—the sort that people tell one another to break the ice and get acquainted. (I was to learn later that Norris never makes small talk, and always has a purpose in any anecdotes he tells.)

It was toward the end of World War II, Norris recounted. He was a commander in the navy, and as the war came to an end he and a group of fellow officers formed a plan to start a private business so they could continue working for the navy when hostilities ended. He took the plan to Admiral Lewis Strauss, on leave from the prestigious investment banking house of Goldman Sachs & Co., in the hope of securing financial backing.

After hearing Norris out, Strauss told him of an able young captain, head of the navy's Office of Management, who had had a great deal of peacetime business experience and in whose judgment he had confidence. He would have Captain Paget critique the plan before making a decision.

Nothing wrong with that, Norris thought—until Paget turned in a negative report and his dreams of gaining the support of Goldman Sachs went out the window.

As Norris finished his story, a puckish grin on his face, I had a sinking feeling. Years ago, Paget had stood in his way, and there I sat, representing the firm Paget had helped to found after the war. It hardly seemed an auspicious start to what I had hoped would be a fruitful relationship and an important one for our firm.

An uncomfortable silence followed, one that Norris obviously enjoyed. Then he went on to surprise me again. Paget's report, he said, and the Strauss decision based on it, had proved fortunate for him and his small group of budding entrepreneurs. In retrospect, it was clear their plan was flawed, and had they proceeded with it they likely would have failed. Instead, he and his associates went back to work and came up with a better plan that proved eminently successful.

Leaving me unsure whether to be wary or relieved, Norris got down to the business of the day. It was his feeling, he said, that Control Data Corporation had reached a point where it had to begin thinking systematically about the future. Up until then he and his colleagues had focused on the day-to-day tasks of running the business and keeping it solvent. What Norris now wanted was an objective study of corporate organization and an independent evaluation of potential candidates to eventually succeed him as chief executive officer. He was then fifty-six years old; the company he had founded was not yet in its teens.

This initial engagement was followed by several others. In 1972 I retired from Cresap, McCormick and Paget, and subsequently Control Data called on me from time to time to do individual consulting. In 1975 I was named a director of Commercial Credit Company, a wholly owned Control Data subsidiary. There was some discussion of my also joining the Control Data board, but nothing came of that for a while because of scheduling conflicts with another board on which I had served for many years. When I retired from that board in 1979, I became a director of Control Data Corporation.

Thus I have been closely involved with William C. Norris, his senior associates, and Control Data for nearly twenty years—two-thirds of the life of the company. During that time I have had a unique opportunity to become well acquainted with Norris himself and to witness his management style and the development of his thinking. At the same time, my role and relationships have been sufficiently detached to allow me to preserve a degree of objectivity. The events recounted in this book, therefore, are told from the perspective of an insider who is also able to take an outsider's view.

The task of any biographer is a difficult one. He must accurately report the character of his subject, yet he must also be rigorously selective because there is no need to record everything about another person. He must communicate to present and future generations the significance of his subject's life and accomplishments, while placing these facts and observations within the larger context to which his subject belongs.

I have chosen to focus on Norris's business and public life and to deal with his personal life only to the extent it has influenced his work. The story I want to tell is that of a founder and preeminent leader of the computer industry whose character has been profoundly shaped by that industry but whose influence extends well beyond it. This requires that I deal at some length with the origins and growth of Control Data Corporation. Data processing is essentially the management of information, and much of what is most significant about Norris's work has been the extension of information management technology to broader fields and applications.

The accident—for that is what it was—of Norris's finding himself in what became the computer industry was one of those chance events that shape the course of history. He and the industry matured together during a time when the flow of information essential for the conduct of human affairs had reached a volume and complexity verging on the unmanageable. In fact, it would have proved unmanageable had it not been for the advent of the computer. Norris played a key role in devising means for applying the new technology to the needs of science, engineering, industry, and society. In the process, his own thinking developed along distinct lines. That is why I have found it necessary to devote a large part of this book to my subject's industrial milieu—which, as I discovered along the way, is replete in itself with human interest and drama.

Unlike my previous biography of General Wood and Sears, Roebuck, the subject of this biography is still alive and well at age seventy-five, we continue to be actively associated, and we are good friends. These circumstances complicate matters for me. I make no secret of the high regard in which I hold Norris; I admire and respect him as a person, as a business leader, and as a concerned, responsible citizen. But I also know him well enough, and have worked with him long and closely enough, to be fully aware that he has his share of faults and foibles. He may be a pillar of industry, but he is also a human being and I have tried to portray him as such. To do otherwise would not only falsify the picture but do injustice to Norris himself. I have too much esteem for him and what he has done to gloss over his shortcomings or ignore his mistakes. He deserves to be presented as he is—not as some contrived and idealized figure. Any good portrait includes shadows as well as lights; it is the two together that convey character. Oliver Cromwell instructed his portraitist to paint him "warts and all." Norris deserves as much and would want no less.

I want to make it clear that this is in no way a commissioned book. Writing it was my own idea, and the result is wholly my property. Although Norris and Control Data gave me full cooperation, I received no fee for the task and no one told me what to put in or what to leave out. I was assured complete editorial freedom in an exchange of letters as well as in more than one conversation. I have checked various sections of the manuscript with Control Data executives and some with Norris himself, but only for the purpose of verifying facts. I am solely accountable for the materials contained herein and the interpretations placed on them.

Naturally it has been necessary to temper my independence with a measure of self-imposed discretion and restraint. Because I am a director of the company, I am not as free to discuss certain matters as I might be if I were totally an outside observer. I also realize that my professional status with Control Data imbues anything I write with a degree of official authority. In no instance, however, have I allowed these considerations to distort what I have to say. My goal throughout has been to tell an important story in an honest and responsible way, and it is my earnest hope that it will be so perceived.

CHAPTER 1

Celebration

It was not a typical corporate anniversary celebration. There were no giant birthday cakes, no nostalgic recollections of modest beginnings and early struggles, no parade of old-timers or toasts to a bright future. Instead, it was a thoughtful two-day conference, sponsored jointly by Control Data Corporation and the American Academy of Arts and Sciences, at which more than 200 business, government, religious, and academic leaders from around the world gathered to discuss the significance of Control Data's strategy of addressing unmet social needs as business opportunities.

It was September 1982, the twenty-fifth anniversary of the company's founding. Featured speakers included management philosopher Peter F. Drucker, Harvard economist John Kenneth Galbraith, Jamaica Minister of Education Mavis Gilmour, and Sir Charles Villiers, chairman of British Steel. Other speakers and guests included heads of national religious organizations, mayors of cities, distinguished scholars, educational administrators, and heads of major U.S. and foreign corporations. In preparation for the conference, the American Academy of Arts and Sciences, aided by a grant from Control Data, had undertaken a probing study of "the potential for and the limits to an expanded role for corporations in meeting social needs, and of the possibilities for new modes of public-private cooperation." This study provided a framework for the conference and was reported in a subsequently published book, *Public-Private Partnership: New Opportunities for Meeting Social Needs.*[1]

There were other ways the company might have chosen to commemorate its first quarter-century. It had a lot to celebrate, including growth in revenues from $626,000 to well over $4 billion, and in employees from a dozen to nearly 60,000; its position as builder of the world's most powerful computers and as pioneer and world leader in scientific and engineering data services; and its domination of the independent market for data storage devices. Any one of these achievements would have been ample cause for self-congratulation.

Instead, William C. Norris, founder, chairman, and chief executive officer, chose to use the conference as a forum for exploring means by which corporations in pursuit of their *business* goals might help solve some of the most vexing problems of modern society. Seventy-one years old, white-haired and of medium build, he mounted the podium to deliver the keynote address. He read from a typewritten text whose main points were projected on a screen behind him, a practice he had followed for many years when he had an important message to communicate.

In his address, "A New Role for Corporations," Norris summarized his business philosophy and described Control Data's success in establishing plants in poverty areas, converting the culturally deprived and physically handicapped into productive workers, encouraging new business and new job creation, strengthening the educational system, revitalizing decayed inner city areas, reversing the deterioration of small-scale agriculture, and other subjects rarely discussed at business conferences and never before at corporate anniversaries. Throughout, he emphasized that Control Data had developed programs to deal with problems such as these not as objects of philanthropy but because they made good business sense.

He cited concrete examples of what business can do, given the courage and the imagination to venture into new and untried fields. The problems of modern society, he maintained, are simply too great to be dealt with by relying solely on traditional means. Unless the economic and managerial skills of business are brought to bear, he warned, the problems will remain unsolved and will in time destroy the business system itself. And because business cannot do the job alone, he called for broad-based cooperation among government, business, religious, civic, and philanthropic institutions.

Norris then proceeded to sketch the outlines for a system of "public/private sector partnerships" and to describe the kinds of governmental policies needed to stimulate their formation and support their work. For such partnerships to be successful, he argued,

William C. Norris Delivering Keynote Address at Twenty-Fifth Anniversary Conference, September 1982 (*Source*: Control Data Corporation)

the financial participation of business would have to be in the form of *investments* rather than charitable donations. He reiterated the credo he had stated on many previous occasions: that major unmet societal needs are prime sources of business opportunity and potentially lucrative markets. Control Data, he pointed out, had demonstrated the practicality of this approach, and he urged other companies to explore means by which they might do likewise.

===

Although the invited audience that day was largely sympathetic, the logic presented had not found much support in business circles generally, where Norris was often scoffed at as a "do-gooder." Control Data under his direction had been described as "a strange corporate animal, as much a social laboratory as it is a business."[2] Financial analysts and professional investment advisors had long been uncomfortable with his business policies and frequently criticized Control Data for "dampening its profits" by allocating "substantial sums for good works." A typical advisory from a prestigious investment banking firm in 1981 observed that while it was not proper for them "to pass judgment on how appropriate it is for Control Data to spend large amounts of money" on "social" undertakings, "[the] fact remains that the cost of these projects is preventing operating profits from the business to flow through to the bottom line."

Although no one at the anniversary conference was heard to make snide observations such as these, Norris himself could not resist chiding his fellow business leaders for being "inordinately influenced by stockholder pressures to deliver short-term earnings," or needling the investment fraternity for its "myopic vision" and "overconcern for the short-term" as opposed to the long-term interests of business and society.

As a matter of fact, over the years Norris had taunted his business peers unmercifully, dismissing many of them as "predatory," "rapacious," and "indifferent to societal needs." In a bylined article published in *Business Week* in 1980, he castigated our "risk-avoiding, selfish society" and pointed the finger of blame at academia, organized labor, private foundations, and government as well as business. "Perhaps the best one-line summary of our society today," he concluded, "can be summed up in the question, 'What have you done for me lately?'"[3] According to him, the typical executive's low level of interest in social problems is equaled only by his lack of personal knowledge of them. "The average corporate executive, hell, he's never been to Woodlawn in Chicago, or the Bronx, or Liberty City in Miami. They read about it, but they read a lot of other horror stories that go in one ear and out the other."[4]

During the conference, these themes were muted because the aim, after all, was to gain converts rather than further alienate unbelievers. Nonetheless, in its unorthodox theme the conference was an authentic expression of Norris's personality and career. Both are revealed in one of his most widely quoted sayings: "Whenever I see everybody going south, I have a great compulsion to go north." He may not choose a course of action *because* it differs from what others are doing, but he needs a stronger reason for doing what he does than the fact someone else is doing it. This tendency to push through the crowd and head in the opposite direction has won him many labels over the years: maverick, Don Quixote, pioneer, noncomformist, iconoclast, visionary, dreamer, willful, stubborn. What emerges is the picture of an uncommon man with an uncommon sense of individuality, self-confidence, and public service.

In the course of the anniversary conference, these characteristics were referred to frequently and, appropriately for the occasion, eloquently praised. He was called an "extraordinary man heading an extraordinary company," "one of the broadest and deepest thinkers in America," and "a doer and leader with a clear image of what our country ought to be." He was commended for his "vision," his "wisdom and foresight," his "fortitude in the face of adversity," his "empathy for the unfortunate," his "courage in moving into untried areas." Special note was taken of his dreams of "ridding the country, and eventually the world" of the nagging problems of poverty, unemployment, and hunger, and of his exemplary sense of corporate social responsibility. Norris is not an unduly modest man; he takes pride in what he has accomplished and genuine pleasure in its recognition. On the occasion of the twenty-fifth anniversary of the company he founded, he basked in the encomiums heaped on him.

The special ambience of an anniversary event aside, there can be no doubt that William C. Norris has written a special chapter in the annals of U.S. business history. Starting in 1957 with a handful of employees and meager resources, he built in a few short years one of the great corporations of the world in an industry from which giants like General Electric, RCA, Xerox, and Bendix had retired in defeat.

He took the measure of his archrival, IBM, in a lengthy and costly lawsuit, after which one of Big Blue's own attorneys described Control Data as perhaps "the most spectacularly successful corporation in the United States today."[5]

These achievements, impressive though they were, told only part of the story. As few social philosophers and even fewer businessmen before him, Norris grasped the possibility of applying the entrepreneurial creativity and managerial skill of business to solving some of society's gravest problems. He was not the first businessman to be concerned with such problems, but he was the first to see on any broad scale the fact that, with imagination and courage, many could be converted into profitable business endeavors, thereby not only ameliorating the problems themselves but relieving society of much of the burden of carrying them.

He saw, furthermore, that approaching such problems under the discipline of the balance sheet could provide more effective use of scarce economic resources, to the benefit of all concerned, including business itself. He had spent much of the decade before the anniversary conference in efforts to spread this gospel, devoting a large share of his time to making speeches before a wide variety of audiences, granting interviews to journalists, publishing brochures and articles in magazines, testifying before legislative committees, and serving on government committees—in short, by all means at his disposal.

His efforts attracted wide attention but few converts, but his resulting disappointment (and irritation) did not discourage him or sway him from his course. Nor can it lessen the significance of the concepts he introduced into social thought and business practice. Future debates on the problems of human deprivation and the role of business in the modern world must of necessity take into account the contributions Norris made.

Norris retired as chairman and chief executive officer of Control Data Corporation in January of 1986, but he continues to serve as a director of the company and as chairman of the board emeritus. He also chairs a newly created board committee on Innovation and Long-Range Opportunity, and in that capacity he is actively engaged in developing further some of the ideas that were features of his years in office. Not surprisingly, he continues to exhibit many of the characteristics that were distinguishing marks of those fruitful years.

For example, his heterodoxy is not limited to his notions about the true function of business.[6] He is a man of many contradictions.

Almost painfully retiring in social situations, for many years he has made an incredible number of speeches and public appearances. A thoroughgoing capitalist, he insists on the importance of cooperating with the nations behind the Iron Curtain for our good as well as theirs. Despite his conviction that "the most experienced and effective management resides in the major business corporations of the world," he has long argued that "without government support there will not be technology to meet all of society's needs." A big businessman, he is convinced that most new ideas and economic progress come from small business. An innovator, he opposes experimentation, maintaining that "if you build a model before making a full commitment, it will only show you all the problems and probably scare you off."

From early in his career he displayed a strong bent for marketing, yet he often cited as "one of the good things about our company the fact that we don't waste money on market research." Shy and unassuming in his personal relationships, he is stubbornly aggressive in pushing his social policy views and is inclined to be snappish when they are questioned. In his strong sense of confidence in his own judgment, he is the epitome of the psychologist's "inner-directed man."

While a man of contradictions, Norris is highly consistent in many ways. His daily routine follows a set pattern, except when he is traveling. Even in "retirement," he continues to maintain an awesome work schedule. He still rises early and works an hour or two every morning before leaving for the office the company provides him in Bluff House, a guest facility on company premises directly across the street from corporate headquarters; his only concession to his new status is to arrive half an hour later than was his former custom.

During most of his years as head of the company, Norris was the first to arrive at work, and it was common knowledge that he worked longer and harder hours than any of his associates. (He remembers learning as a boy on the farm that the harder he shoveled, the faster silage came down the chute and the sooner the job was done.) He always followed, and still adheres to, a tight schedule. During his years as chief executive, he had little contact with other than a few top aides, an occasional distinguished visitor, and journalists seeking to probe "the Norris mystery." He usually ate a simple lunch alone in his office, a book or report propped before him and notepaper in easy reach. No one can recall ever having seen him in the executive dining room or the employee cafeteria.

Except for the fact it was larger and better appointed, his office on the fourteenth floor of the headquarters building looked more like that of a college professor than of a big business executive. There was an oversized bookcase filled with books on a wide variety of subjects. On the table behind his desk were more books and piles of papers, government reports, and other documents dealing with subjects in which he was interested. Fishing trophies decorated the walls. In one corner was a bust of the philosopher Plato, symbolizing his commitment to the PLATO system of computer-based education that became a preoccupation of a large share of his business life. In retirement, all this has been transferred to his present office in Bluff House where he continues essentially the same routine he has followed for many years.

While still in active service, every afternoon promptly at 2:30 he took an elevator to the third floor and walked up eleven flights of stairs back to his office on the fourteenth floor; since retiring, he walks across the street to the headquarters building at the same time every day and continues this regimen, although in deference to his seventy-five years he now walks up only ten flights of stairs, from the first to the tenth floor (these days, he rarely appears on the fourteenth executive office floor). During his years in office, two well-packed briefcases accompanied him home at the end of each day, and he spent the greater part of every evening and weekend reading and making notes. (When his family was young he would work sitting on the couch with the children crawling over him, seemingly unbothered by the clamor.) The car in which he was driven to and from the office—a luxury he allowed himself only in recent years—was equipped with a telephone, a table, and reading lights so he could make productive use of his commuting time.

He has never carried office worries home with him. He discusses serious problems with his wife in an objective fashion, but doesn't dwell on them. "They don't keep him awake at night," his wife reports. "He's asleep five minutes after his head hits the pillow." To this day he walks from two to four miles every evening, carrying a notebook in which he makes frequent entries. He keeps a pad of paper beside his bed and another on the sink in his bathroom, and wakes at night or pauses while shaving to jot down an idea or a reminder. He reads widely and voraciously; according to a long-time associate, he is "always reading, reading, reading, and thinking, thinking, thinking, storing things away in his mind—he has more things in his memory than one of our mass storage drives."

He is an extremely private man who to this day has few personal friends and fewer confidants outside his family. He mixes socially only rarely, preferring small dinner parties over larger gatherings. On those occasions when it is necessary to entertain for business reasons (usually at a hotel or the nearby Decathlon athletic club), he likes to seek out someone he feels comfortable with and spend most of his time talking to that person. He does not belong to a country club or the elite Minneapolis Club, membership in which is practically *de rigueur* for men of his position. And he never became "one of the boys" in top Twin Cities business circles. Many of his peers were uncomfortable with his ideas, and he himself was ill at ease with people he did not know well.

His business associates learned early that his business and personal lives were completely separate. Few were ever invited to his home, and most did not even know where it was. Those who were privileged to cross the threshold entered a structure as individualistic as its owner. Earth-sheltered, it is built into the side of a hill and more below ground than above. It is powered by solar energy and a ninety-foot windmill that produces more electricity than he needs; the local electric company buys the surplus from him.

As idiosyncratic in his managerial style as in his business policies and private life, Norris never fit the stereotype of the big-business executive.

Personal financial gain was never one of his primary drives. When I made my first study of Control Data's top management in 1968, I was startled to find that Norris was paying himself a salary of only $40,000 a year. I protested to him that I didn't care how spartan an existence he chose for himself, but whatever salary he put on his own job placed a lid on what he could pay his subordinates, and in the late 1960s salaries lower than $40,000 were simply not enough to hold the caliber of executives and technicians needed to run a major high technology company. As a matter of fact, by this time he and most of his early associates were wealthy men, at least on paper, because the

Control Data stock they had purchased in the beginning had since appreciated greatly. More recent recruits, however, did not enjoy this advantage and there was an obvious need for a more immediately available system of financial rewards.

Norris agreed, but only reluctantly, to raise his own salary, thus making it possible to establish more realistic rates for his lieutenants. Later, when the company had grown substantially larger and a variety of incentive plans had been introduced to help attract and hold high grade technical and managerial talent, Norris declined to participate in a number of substantial stock option plans and bonus distributions in order that more stock and bonus money would be available to divide among members of his staff.

Norris is well known for his heated opposition to hostile corporate takeovers, many of which are mounted by financiers interested chiefly in quick and easy profits. One reason he feels so strongly on the subject is because he has never been able to understand why anyone would do something just to make money. For his part, he is interested in *what money can do*, not in money itself.

His executive style was autocratic. Those who worked for him soon learned one of his maxims: "If the chief executive says, 'we're going this way,' that's the way it's got to be. The boss's word has to be final." One long-time associate recalls, "Bill runs a democratic show as long as he has his way." And another: "When Bill Norris makes up his mind, he doesn't let anything stop him." It was often said of him that "he has the tenacity of a bulldog," that he was "single-minded," "bullheaded," "obstinate."

"Bill never believed in just putting his toe in the water," one associate says. "His idea always was: Jump in. Do it. Get it done." He frequently admonished those who worked for him that "it's more important to make the decision right than it is to make the right decision." He was impatient with people who wanted to be sure of how a project would turn out before taking the first step. "The important thing is to get started," he would insist. "You don't have to know all the answers before you begin. You can learn as you go along." "If something goes wrong," he often told his associates, "you can reassess. There's nothing wrong with making a mistake, but don't stop, don't back up. Learn from the mistake and make it right."

A large part of Control Data's history has revolved around accomplishing goals that Norris set. Control Data people like to tell an apocryphal story to illustrate the point. Supposedly, Norris was speaking to a large gathering that included members of Congress, United Nations delegates, and representatives of the foreign and domestic press. Control Data, he told them, was about to announce a new super-product that would keep you cool if you were warm and warm if you were cold; it was biodegradable, cost little to produce, and could be made into dresses, draperies, parachutes, and many other useful commodities. As he fielded questions, two top company officials were kneeling behind the curtain pushing two silkworms toward each other and pleading, "Mate, damn you, mate!"[7]

Norris did, in fact, have a disconcerting habit of talking publicly about things as if they were already accomplished when they were still in the process of development or in the early idea stage. According to a close associate, "You've got to be careful telling Bill something you're thinking about because the first thing you know you'll hear him telling someone we're doing it."[8] When he saw where he wanted to go, he was likely to ignore the difficulties of getting there and to leave the details to others. He freely admits that he was always more interested in "long-range planning" than in "operations."

Part of this may have been unconscious, a habit of mind, but another was deliberate—a management technique he continued to use because it worked. By taking results for granted before they were actually in being, he put tremendous pressure on those responsible for seeing them through. According to deputy board chairman Norbert Berg, "He starts you with an end point and then makes you sweat to get there. It's an interesting form of managerial genius."[9]

Berg likens this to the story of a king who was fond of boasting about a beautiful tree that grew in a far corner of his kingdom. One day he let it be known that he would soon take his courtiers to see this marvel. His faithful retainers, aware that there was no such tree in that particular part of the kingdom, went to great lengths to transplant one there; when the king and his party arrived, they found exactly what he told them they would find.

Norris's "retainers" assert that he was equally difficult to work for. Although he mellowed in his later years, he had the reputation of being "a very demanding man." One associate says, "There's something intimidating about Bill, and some people are afraid of him. He has a way of turning up the level of gruffness in his voice that nobody can mistake." Others describe him as "very rough." In answer to the question, "What's it like to work for Norris?" an aide replied, "It's kind of like a religious experience—it scares the hell out of you."

Berg, who is closer to Norris than anyone else in the company, explains: "His tolerance for error is zero. I mean *zero*. I don't mean he's intolerant of entrepreneurial error or of opinion, but if you lay something in front of him it had better be right. . . . He sort of speaks in shorthand: A, L, R, Z—that's the alphabet. He doesn't think he has to go A, B, C—through all twenty-six letters." Subordinates did not always understand this, and because they often felt uncomfortable in Norris's presence they hesitated to ask enough questions to grasp exactly what he wanted. Given Norris's tolerance for error, this led more than one person into trouble. Berg again: "He doesn't want excuses. He wants you to do whatever it takes to get a job done. He doesn't want to know how hard it is. He just wants it done, and he's damned annoyed when it doesn't get done or doesn't get done right."[10]

Despite his formidable exterior, Norris is a genuinely caring man who built a company noted for its fairness and concern for human values. The image people have of him reflects his impatience, his driving will, his confidence in himself, and his iron determination to accomplish his goals regardless of obstacles in his way. Though he was never easy or comfortable to work for, he enjoyed the respect and loyalty of his staff; they held him in awe, but they also recognized his strength and did their utmost to accomplish the tasks he set for them. He steered the company through some hard times, and quite a few people achieved considerable success under his wing. When the twenty-fifth anniversary celebration dawned, they were more than willing to give him the credit that was his due.

What no one realized at the time was that Control Data's anniversary represented not only a height but a pinnacle. By 1985 the company would have experienced disastrous reversals. Many would blame Norris personally for the company's misfortunes and assume that these were responsible for his retiring early in 1986.

In fact, the company reached its earnings peak in 1981 with $289 million, a figure that slipped to $229 million in 1982 and then dropped to $214 and $140 million over the next two years. In 1985 it nosedived to a catastrophic *loss* of $567 million—only slightly less than the *combined earnings* of the three preceding years.

The supercomputer business that Control Data had pioneered suffered severe competition from Cray Research, founded by one of its own former employees. Data storage devices and other peripheral products, where Control Data had once ruled the roost and which by 1980 had grown to be the company's largest producer of revenues, began to lose ground in 1981 and by 1984 were a serious drain on corporate assets. Data services, where Control Data was once the world leader, ran into serious problems in Europe and was slow in adapting to the desktop computer. A severe cash-flow crisis led to default on banking obligations in mid-1985, and the worsening business outlook forced the cancellation of a badly needed issue of new securities a short time later.

The financial community, which had long looked askance at Norris's forays into social problem-solving, united in a chorus of "we-told-you-so's," ascribing the company's difficulties to its meddling with things better left to government and charitable institutions. The policies for which Norris had been lauded so highly were attacked as unbusinesslike and unsound. "Visionary" became a term of condemnation rather than praise, and the encomiums of 1982 had turned to finger-pointing by 1985.

Control Data's troubles attracted avid press attention, with a marked tendency to link them to Norris's unconventional policies and idealistic efforts to address social needs as business opportunities. *Fortune* magazine, reviewing his 1983 book, *New Frontiers for Business Leadership*, labeled him "a business genius who unfortunately thinks he's a social philosopher," an entrepreneur who built a $5 billion company and then proceeded "to talk like a Naderite."[11] Jabs in a similar vein were now voiced with increasing frequency. In 1983 a survey of Wall Street analysts and corporate directors had rated Control Data one of the most admired U.S. companies; a similar survey late in 1985 placed it among the *least* admired and dead last in terms of long-range investment value.[12]

Few critics understood that Control Data's troubles did not arise from Norris's quixotic ideas but from the bread-and-butter components of the business: computer systems, peripheral products, and data services. Actually, the company's unconventional undertakings were doing fairly well. But they were attractive targets, and detractors, including some inside the company, could not resist the temptation to point accusing fingers at them and their author.

As the crisis deepened, it became increasingly clear to concerned observers that what was at stake was not only the fate of a company or of a man, but the fate of an idea. Norris had given a new and broader meaning to the role of business in American life. If economic adversity forced the abandonment of the notion that business could contribute significantly to ameliorating social ills while pursuing its *business* goals, its credibility could be gravely and perhaps fatally compromised. Given Control Data's prominence on the contemporary corporate scene, it could take a generation or more before anyone dared broach the idea again. The loss to the country and the world would be great.

At the time of the anniversary celebration, however, no one knew what lay ahead. It was the fall of 1982, all was well, and the next quarter-century seemed bright with promise.

CHAPTER 2

Preparation

Control Data Corporation first opened for business in 1957 with a handful of employees in rented warehouse space in St. Paul, Minnesota. It had taken twelve years of preparation to arrive at these modest beginnings. Norris, then forty-six years old, had played a pivotal role at each stage leading up to this event.

During World War II he had been a commissioned officer in the U.S. Naval Reserve, assigned to a unit engaged in super-secret cryptological warfare. Toward the end of the war he and a group of his fellow officers, with encouragement from the U.S. Navy Department, had formed a small private company to continue to develop some of the technology that had begun to emerge from their wartime work and would be of importance to the peacetime defense establishment. Engineering Research Associates, popularly known as ERA, was later acquired by Remington Rand and became part of Sperry Rand's Univac Division. Norris and some of his close associates were not happy with this arrangement, and in due course they left to start their own business. Within a few short years Control Data, with Norris at its head, was one of the world's leading multinational corporations.

It was a meteoric rise for a former Nebraska farm boy. Born on July 16, 1911 in the south-central part of the state on a cattle, hog, and corn farm that had been homesteaded by his grandfather in 1872 (and is still owned by the Norris family), William was one of four children. First came a boy who died in infancy, then an older sister, and then William and his twin sister Willa, whose parents considered her a "bonus" and named her after a budding author in nearby Red

Cloud, Willa Cather, whose work would come to characterize the pioneer spirit of the American midwest.[1]

William and Willa and their older sister attended a one-room country school with seven or eight other students—an experience on which Norris would come to place great value. "I knew who Bill Norris was," he told a reporter years later. It wasn't like being "thrown into a big city school where you don't have any identity. You learn to cope at an early age in a very constructive way." Other advantages included the close student/teacher relationship and the practice of older students helping younger ones—the "sense of all working together." Norris would also credit his farm background with having contributed to his coping skills: "On a farm you have to be creative. You can't call up the repairman and have him come over in ten minutes and fix something. You have to figure out how to fix it yourself. You have to improvise." All in all, he recalls, "It was a hell of a nice life."[2]

In high school, Willa got better grades than her brother, but only because "he didn't have to apply himself," she says. In physics, his favorite subject, "Bill knew more than the teacher." He had been fascinated with radio and things electrical since early boyhood, and enjoyed taking the family's electric vacuum sweeper apart and putting it back together. He built his own radio sets from mail-order parts and in the process developed an abiding interest in the new field of electronics. He became an avid ham radio operator. His sister remembers that his room was "always terribly messy" with vacuum tubes, copper wire, various other pieces of equipment, and copies of *Popular Mechanics* magazines scattered about. The walls were plastered with the call letters of ham operators with whom he maintained frequent radio contact.

He went on to study electrical engineering at the University of Nebraska. In the spring of 1932, a month before he was due to graduate, his father died unexpectedly. Working furiously for a few days to complete the work needed for his degree, he hurried home to take over management of the family farm.

With the country in the depths of the Great Depression, 1932 was not an auspicious time to launch an engineering career, and farming was hardly a lucrative occupation. Norris began supplementing his family's meager income with a part-time job in the local office of the Agricultural Adjustment Administration, a key feature of President Roosevelt's New Deal. Helping dole out aid to farmers hit both by

Willa and William Norris, Eighth Grade Graduation, 1924 (*Source*: Willa Norris)

the Depression and the first "dust bowl" storms in 1934 affected him deeply, and from that time forward he would feel a sympathetic attachment to the trials of the family farmer.

Things were not easy on his own farm. One experience in particular sticks in his mind: He had driven a herd of cattle to market, hoping to get a fair return. Instead, he listened in shocked disbelief at the price he was offered. When he protested, the buyer replied, "Sonny, if you don't like that price you can take your cattle right back home." Young Norris walked away, perched himself on a rail fence, and pondered bitterly. Then he went back to the buyer and curtly accepted his offer. On the way home, he vowed that he would never again be put in a position where he had so little control.

But there were some events he could control. His twin sister Willa was elected Queen of the May in her senior year in college and needed a new dress for her coronation. Bill promptly sold a steer to raise the cash. Willa never forgot.

It was during this period that what became known in Control Data lore as the "Russian Thistle Incident" occurred. Feed for cattle grew scarce as the winter of 1932-33 approached, and many farmers had to send their livestock to market prematurely because there was not enough grain and hay to see them through until spring. Faced with the same problem and determined not only to avoid selling at distressed prices but also to keep his breeding stock intact, Norris decided to feed his cattle Russian thistles, a variety of tumbleweed. He had noticed that they occasionally grazed on it even when good alfalfa was growing nearby; since modest amounts seemed to do no harm, perhaps a steady diet wouldn't either. Because the weed was in such plentiful supply, Norris took an even greater chance and added to his herd. His neighbors were appalled; "everyone knew" that Russian thistles were unfit for cattle and would eventually kill them. But Norris's herd survived to reach the stronger spring market in good health and fine breeding form. Many years later, research would find tumbleweed to be high in protein, able to produce more forage per inch of rainfall than most conventional crops, and "a natural for drought periods."[3]

At the peak of Norris's career this story would be repeated many times as early evidence of his independent bent. In 1982, twenty-fifth anniversary celebrants would see him presented with a bronze casting of a Russian thistle, a gift from his Control Data associates.

During that long-ago winter, however, he had no way to tell what the outcome of his decision would be. He knew he was taking a risk, and while he had grounds for confidence there was no guarantee that his cattle wouldn't die. "I couldn't help thinking about what the neighbors would say if I was wrong," he recalls. "But I decided, well, okay, whatever they say they'll say." When spring came and it was clear that his plan was a success, "it was damned stimulating. There was a lot at stake, but I had taken the chance and it worked. That added greatly to my sense of self-confidence."[4]

This trait was further strengthened during the war when, as a member of the naval intelligence unit engaged in deciphering enemy radio transmissions, Norris was given responsibility for a critical project. The technical theory on which he decided to proceed indicated that his idea might work, but there was also a strong possibility that it might not. "Having lived through the Russian thistle experience," he explains, "I felt a lot more comfortable about taking the risk. I remember saying to the fellows working with me, 'Well, what the hell, if it doesn't work it doesn't work. There'll be some name-calling and accusing, but so what? On the other hand, if it does work, we'll all be heroes.' As a matter of fact, it worked." The lesson, he concludes, is that "Once you make up your mind that you can handle adverse remarks, that makes it easier to go what you think is the right way to go, even if it involves a lot of risk."[5]

Since then Norris has taken numerous risks and has had plenty of practice handling adverse remarks. Even when things have turned out badly and the remarks have been scathing, his determination has not wavered. Much of his ability to withstand (some say ignore) criticism grew out of his experiences as a young man—experiences that were important to the formation of his character.

After seeing the family farm through the two worst years of the depression, Norris was hired by Westinghouse Electric Company as a sales engineer. He quickly demonstrated a flair for salesmanship that would serve him well in his later life work. (He considers himself, in fact, "a hell of a good salesman."[6]) He was on his way to a promising future when the Japanese bombed Pearl Harbor in December 1941. Norris applied for and secured a commission in the U.S. Naval Reserve; he was thirty years old.

———

In a decision that would profoundly affect his future, and for reasons Norris never really understood, the navy assigned him to the unit engaged in super-secret cryptological warfare—codebreaking.[7] One of the most serious problems facing the navy was the need to pinpoint the location of enemy submarines. To this end, German and Japanese radio transmissions were intercepted, analyzed, and decoded, and this involved recording and processing enormous quantities of electronic data.

At the beginning of the war, punched-card tabulating equipment and hand-operated calculating machines were the only tools available for this massive task. But they were far too slow; by the time a given set of transmissions had been processed, the submarine was long gone. Better means had to be found, and fast.

Norris was assigned to a group within the unit that was charged with developing speedier processing devices. Their first efforts resulted in large, rotating electromechanical devices with commutators—a definite improvement, but still not good enough. Electronic circuitry, then in its infancy, seemed to hold promise, and a crash program backed by unlimited funds was launched to convert the new technology into usable equipment. The group was led by Captain

Lieutenant William C. Norris, USNR, 1943 (*Source*: Jane Norris)

Howard Engstrom, who before the war had been an associate professor of mathematics at Yale. Engstrom, Norris recalls, was a very creative individual who personally knew many important scientists whom the navy, at his direction, quickly recruited for him.

Norris was deeply impressed by the men he worked with—in his words, an "almost unbelievable assemblage of talent" including mathematicians, physicists, and engineers from leading universities, some already with international reputations. He learned to recognize and appreciate superior technical gifts and to set standards that would serve him well when he came to build his own organizations. He also developed a high tolerance for idiosyncratic behavior, and that, too, would prove useful in attracting and holding exceptional talent.

Some of the characteristics that became apparent in his later career had their roots in his navy wartime experience. One was the ability to break a problem down into its many different parts, see them individually, grasp how they were interrelated, and then concentrate on solving the problem as a whole—in other words, to put together a *system* for dealing with it. Another was willingness to proceed without knowing all the answers in advance. He developed confidence in his ability to find solutions as he went along, believing that at some point everything would come together.

He learned that creative people need resources to work with. "We were able to get everything we needed to do the job," he remembers, and from then on he always sought to provide strong support to those on whom he depended—a trait his later business associates would call "clobbering a problem with resources," financial and otherwise. He formed the habit of doing whatever was necessary to get a job done and persevering regardless of difficulties.

In addition to creating its own group to address the problem of processing vast streams of data, the navy placed contracts for similar purposes with National Cash Register Company, Bell Laboratories, and International Business Machines. It also drew on significant breakthroughs in cryptology achieved by a group of British scientists working at Bletchley Park near Oxford. It wasn't long before navy commanders had at their disposal vital information on enemy movements, as well as greatly enhanced decoding and encoding capabilities.

Many years later Norris would comment on these collaborative arrangements, which cut across a multiplicity of institutional lines. "That was really my first exposure to cooperation on a grand scale, and it worked," he says. "There was none of this business of hiding results in order to get credit. Everybody was working on a common goal and they were very open—that is, within limits of security—in sharing results. And they were fantastic results."[8]

The work in which Norris was engaged is reported to have carried a higher security classification than the building of the atomic bomb,[9] and even today he will discuss it only in broad generalities. There is a story (which he refuses to confirm or deny) that he "did something pretty remarkable to speed the code-breaking process." What we do know is that he was involved in designing several of the technologies that led to the development of the electronic digital computer, whose incredible possibilities he and some of his fellow officers began to realize even before the war was over.

In 1944 he married Jane Malley, a WAVE lieutenant j.g. whose mother had died when she was eleven months old. She had been raised by her grandmother in Parkersburg, West Virginia and worked her way through the University of Cincinnati. On enlisting soon after

Pearl Harbor, she became a member of the first group of WAVES to be admitted to officers' candidate school. She was posted to Washington, D.C. and became administrative assistant to the head of one of the navy sections with whom Lieutenant Norris had frequent dealings. They met, began dating, and in due course were married.[10] From that time on she played a critically important role in his life and his career, providing him with the strong home and family support he needed.

As the end of the war drew near, it was apparent to all in a position to know that the emergence of the digital computer was revolutionizing cryptology. The navy was gravely concerned about the impending dissolution of its prized cryptological unit; the guns might soon be silent, but there would be no letup in the struggle for intelligence, and the essential technologies were lodged in the minds of men who would not be in uniform much longer. When they were

Jane and William Norris on Their Wedding Day, September 12, 1944 (*Source*: Jane Norris)

approached with the possibility of working as civil servants in a government laboratory, they were not interested.

Discouraged at the prospects of keeping the group together by other means, the idea began to emerge that perhaps the only practical way for doing so would be to form a business organization that could continue the work on a contract basis. Part of the navy unit was stationed on the premises of National Cash Register Company in Dayton, Ohio, and inquiries were made of that company's possible interest in taking over the group. But the company had other plans and was anxious to regain possession of the space it had leased to the navy to get back to its peacetime cash register business.

The notion of starting a new company grew increasingly attractive. All of the men in Norris's group had been absent from their prewar jobs for several years, and any ties they had with their old employers were tenuous. Besides, they enjoyed working together and were still caught up in the excitement of what they were doing. Highly placed officials within the Navy Department readily accepted the idea, since it seemed like the only practical means to achieve their goal of keeping the group together.[11]

Leaders among the group—including Captain Howard Engstrom, unit chief; Lieutenant Commander Ralph Meador, principal interface with NCR and Bell Laboratories; and Commander Norris—began holding discussions over lunch and during off-duty hours. A major supporter within the navy itself was Admiral Joseph Wenger, who played an important role in working out the subcontracting arrangements that would make it possible for the new company to operate successfully.

First, however, the group had to secure the financing needed for even a modest business venture. The officers, who had been living on military pay for several years, had few resources of their own, and it was hard to interest investment bankers in a company whose work would be so highly classified that its sponsors could not even tell anyone what it was. The dilemma was solved by bringing in a small group of investors headed by John E. Parker, an Annapolis graduate and Washington, D.C. resident with connections in political and military circles. In the arrangements that were eventually hammered out, ownership was divided equally among "insiders" and "outsiders," with 100,000 shares going to each group at ten cents per share for a total original equity of $20,000. Parker and his associates also underwrote a $200,000 line of bank credit.

Engineering Research Associates (ERA) opened for business in St. Paul in 1946. The reason for locating there was simple: Parker, among other things, was president of Northwestern Aeronautical Corporation, whose St. Paul plant had produced gliders during the war and was now standing idle. As a result of this almost casual decision, the Minneapolis-St. Paul area would grow within a few short years into one of the world's great digital computer manufacturing centers.[12]

Parker became president of ERA with responsibility for financial matters and overall management. Initially there were three vice presidents: Engstrom for engineering, Meador for manufacturing, and Norris for marketing. Others in the startup group included a mathematician, some ten or twelve engineers and technicians from the navy, and a few people carried over from Northwestern Aeronautical.

Within a year there was trouble at the top. Parker placed Norris in overall command of operations in St. Paul, Engstrom headed a small research group in Washington, and Meador left. From this point on, except for the minor activities in Washington and Parker's control of finances, Norris was the man in charge.

Because ERA was a new company with no record of business performance, its initial contracts were limited to those between the navy and Northwestern Aeronautical, with the latter subcontracting to ERA. Because the work to be done was developmental, contracts were cost-plus-fixed-fee. Prudence called for close supervision of work conducted on that basis by an untried organization, and for that purpose the navy created the Naval Computing Machine Laboratory. Physically located on ERA's St. Paul premises, staffed with navy personnel, and charged with handling all phases of contract administration, the laboratory was in direct and continuous contact with everything being done. An important function was enforcement of the tight security required by the highly sensitive nature of the work.

Another key figure in ERA's early history was Joseph M. Walsh. A former member of the navy's cryptological unit, he had joined ERA as controller and assistant to Norris on being released from service. Given the young company's limited financial resources, cash flow was a major problem. Under the cost-plus-fixed-fee arrangements, ERA billed the navy for labor, material, and overhead on a biweekly basis; working with the company treasurer, Walsh set up a project control and cost-accounting system under which costs were accumulated quickly by individual project, thus facilitating the billing process. Thanks to Admiral Wenger, the navy paid its bills promptly. To further accelerate cash flow, Parker worked out a plan to assign invoices on issuance to the First National Bank of St. Paul so ERA could be reimbursed immediately. Walsh, who later became a director of Control Data Corporation, recalls that "It was a high-speed act. We had to do the work, accumulate the costs, make the billing, take it to the bank, and get the money. That made the business exciting."[13]

Under Norris's leadership a qualified technical staff was recruited to supplement the founding core group, and ERA soon developed into a disciplined cost- and schedule-conscious supplier of exotic electronic hardware to the navy. Hobbled by the strict compartmentalization imposed by security constraints, it nevertheless enjoyed the considerable advantage of working for a client with plenty of money and access to much of the advanced computer work going on elsewhere in government and private laboratories. Before long ERA had established a reputation for designing and delivering innovative, high-performance, specialized digital components, high-speed data-handling equipment, and large-scale storage devices.

Working at the state of the art, ERA often experienced technical problems. For one, there was a new machine that repeatedly fell behind schedule. Each time the navy asked about it, the answer was, "It's coming, it's coming." The device was code-named "Amber," after the heroine of the currently popular (and risqué) novel, *Forever Amber*.[14]

From the time Parker placed Norris in charge of the St. Paul plant, his leadership was accepted as a matter of course. James E. Thornton, who joined ERA immediately on graduating from the University of Minnesota in 1950 and later was instrumental in the development of the big computers that would become Control Data's first claim to fame, remembers him as "the unquestioned boss, a friendly man but not a mixer." Although he "had great persuasive powers to encourage people when they ran into problems, he was not a plant-walker and stayed pretty much in his office." He had a "kind of father image to the people who worked for him, and for his part played something like a father role. He called me 'Jimmy,' and I always felt I could count on him."[15]

Initially ERA contracted with the navy to build a variety of electronic devices, including components that proved critical to the emerging digital computer industry. For many of these the group had to develop the technology along the way. Besides modular devices, the company built special-purpose computers for solving difficult cryptographic problems. This was before the days of programming as it is now known; back then, programs were "hard-wired" into the machine, and to perform a new function either a section of the machine had to be rewired or an entirely new machine had to be built. In 1947 Norris proposed to the navy that ERA design a general-purpose computer whose programs could be *changed*. The contract was signed in 1948 and the machine was delivered in 1950. Code-named *Atlas* after the mental giant in the comic strip "Barnaby," this high-speed, general purpose computer was far superior in performance and reliability to anything else then in existence.

A modified version of the Atlas was designated *1101* (thirteen in binary notation) because it was originally developed as Task 13 for the navy. The first 1101 was delivered in 1950, followed by models 1102 and 1103. By the end of 1952 it was estimated that ERA had designed and built more than 80 percent of the installed value of commercially available electronic computers in the United States at the time.[16]

The new company did well financially. In its first year of operation, it had revenues of $1.5 million and a profit of $35,000. Although severely handicapped by undercapitalization, ERA continued to grow; in five years Norris built a workforce of some 1,500, many of whom were professionals and skilled technicians. Several of them would subsequently help to build Control Data Corporation.

ERA was soon doing work for other federal agencies as well as the navy; new clients included the U.S. Air Force and the Civil Aeronautics Administration. Equipment designed and built by ERA found its way into the BOMARC missile program (the predecessor of the SAGE continental defense system) and other advanced military and civilian applications. As word of ERA's spectacular technical accomplishments spread beyond the tight confines of military security, interest in its capabilities grew among elements of the infant computer industry.

James Rand of Remington-Rand was one of the first businessmen to sense the commercial possibilities of electronic computers. In 1949 he established the RemRand Laboratories in Norwalk, Connecticut and hired General Leslie R. Groves of Manhattan Project fame. In 1950 he acquired the Eckert-Mauchly Computer Corporation, a small company that grew out of wartime work calculating artillery trajectories for the army. Located in Philadelphia, Eckert-Mauchly became the nucleus of Remington-Rand's Univac Division.

Interested in further strengthening his company's position in the rapidly forming computer industry, Rand approached John Parker in the fall of 1951 about the possibility of acquiring ERA. Although profitable and growing, ERA was still badly undercapitalized; Parker estimated that at least $5 million and perhaps as much as $10 million would be needed if the company was to have any hope of entering the computer industry in a big way. Rand's offer seemed like the right one at the right time. After hard bargaining, Parker agreed to terms of sale equivalent to $1.7 million, eighty-five times the original investment the founders had made only five years earlier. This figure was reached by multiplying 340 (the number of ERA's engineers) by $5,000, "one of the few times since the Civil War that individuals have been sold by the head outside the professional sports world."[17]

Parker was happy to take his handsome profit, but Norris objected strongly. He feared that he and his bright group of young engineers would lose their creative freedom in the bureaucracy of a large organization whose principal experience was in office equipment, electric shavers, and typewriters—hardly the environment they had in mind.

"This is the wrong decision," Norris insisted, but Parker was adamant and Norris finally agreed to go along for two years. When Parker tried to console him with the assurance that when a large company buys a small one "the guys in the little company [often] wind up on top," Norris responded, "Well, John, I used to work for Westinghouse. When I want to work for a large company, I'll go back to work for one directly. I don't have to work up through the acquisition route." As Norris recalled much later, "John was rather prophetic in what he said. After a couple of years I was made general manager at Univac and Johnny Parker ended up working for me."[18]

To this day Norris contends that if ERA had not been sold, and if it had been able to secure the financing it needed, it could have changed the whole structure of the computer industry. "We had enormous technology, and we were much more advanced than any other company. IBM at that time was still a small outfit, and didn't have the advanced knowledge we had in ERA. It was the chance of a lifetime, and we missed it when Johnny Parker sold out to Jim Rand."[19]

Because Parker had firm financial control, there was little Norris and his associates could do. They took some satisfaction from the fact that at least they were allowed to remain in St. Paul and operate with considerable autonomy. The bad feelings remained, however, and when Norris distributed Remington shavers to his staff the following Christmas, instead of turkeys as he had done in previous years, the irony was lost on no one. His longstanding antipathy to unwanted corporate takeovers traces back in part to this early experience.

With the acquisition of ERA, Remington-Rand had assembled the strongest array of technical computer talent in the world. International Business Machines, Burroughs, and others—even National Cash Register, which had missed its chance for a long head start—had developed nascent capabilities in this area, but none could begin to match the resources James Rand had put together.

Unfortunately, Rand's managerial capacities were not equal to his strategic foresight. The three computer units, plus a fourth created for marketing purposes and headed by John Parker, reported to different corporate headquarters departments and operated as uncoordinated, fiercely independent entities. Eckert-Mauchly in Philadelphia continued to concentrate on commercial applications while ERA in St. Paul strengthened its position as a major supplier to the military; both ignored the Norwalk laboratories, and the New York marketing unit went its way with little regard for delivery schedules or the readiness of essential supporting services. Combined, all computer-related work represented less than 5 percent of Remington-Rand's total business, and it received about that much of top management's attention.

Left largely to their own devices, the individual operating units accomplished important technical breakthroughs. The Eckert-Mauchly group produced the Univac (for *Univer*sal Automatic Computer) system, which gained wide public notice by predicting the outcome of the 1952 presidential election early on election night. Univacs I and II, installed in the U.S. Census Bureau in Suitland, Maryland, greatly speeded the tabulations of the 1950 population census and the 1954 business census. Meanwhile the ERA group pioneered several new techniques in its area and produced the fastest and most reliable hardware in the industry.

Operations under Remington-Rand were further handicapped by the fact that much of ERA's work was so secret that its nature could not be disclosed even to corporate headquarters. When at one critical point ERA obtained navy clearance to bring out a civilian version of a high-speed computer originally developed for military use, corporate officers were amazed to learn about some of the things that had been going on and how far the state of the art had advanced. This particular piece of equipment was a descendant of the earlier Atlas and represented ERA's first major venture into the nonmilitary market. For its time, it was notable for its ability to process great masses of data at high speed and low cost at a level of reliability unprecedented in the civilian experience. Despite these significant breakthroughs, ERA continued to be handicapped by being part of an organization that lacked central direction and coordination.

In 1955 the Sperry Corporation acquired Remington-Rand to form Sperry Rand, and James Rand moved into semiretirement. One of the new management's first moves was to consolidate the several disparate computer units under the Univac name and put Norris in charge as vice president and general manager. At long last the company had a single, unified computer business entity incorporating research, engineering, manufacturing, and marketing under strong central leadership. The future looked promising.

But the going was not easy. Although James Rand was out of the line of authority, he remained a source of trouble and annoyance. Leroy Stutzman, a professor of engineering from Northwestern University whom Norris had hired as head of research and development, later recalled, "You couldn't keep the old warrior out of things. He would periodically come out, and when he did everything was stirred up. He was a rough businessman." While John Mauchly in Philadelphia was cooperative and worked well under the new arrangement, friction quickly developed between Norris and Presper Eckert, two strong personalities who had little liking for each other. General Groves also caused problems. From his base as head of Norwalk Laboratories, he tried to take over the entire operation. Norris successfully blocked the effort, but relations between the two men were never good. Things went smoothly, of course, on Norris's old turf, ERA in St. Paul.[20]

Norris got on well personally with General Douglas MacArthur, who served as chairman of Sperry-Rand from 1955 to 1964, but the famous general contributed little to the developing computer business. Once a month Norris, frequently accompanied by Stutzman, traveled by train to Philadelphia, New York, and Norwalk in a largely fruitless effort to coordinate the work of the three centers of activity. On some of these trips they called on MacArthur at his headquarters at the Waldorf-Astoria Hotel. Stutzman later described these very formal occasions: "General Whitney, who was MacArthur's personal aide when he was in the armed forces, still acted in that capacity with Sperry-Rand. He would come in and, essentially, ask us to come to attention, although not literally, and then MacArthur would make his entrance."[21] Following some general conversation on how the business was going, MacArthur would spend the next couple of hours reminiscing about his campaigns and commenting on various military personalities he had known; "Eisenhower," he once allowed, "was a fairly good aide."[22]

Norris had great respect for MacArthur and on one occasion told him how much he had taken to heart a statement the general had made in an address some years before: "There is no such thing as security in this world. There is only opportunity." MacArthur responded that he could not remember it, "but it sounds like something I would say."

Although the general, according to Stutzman, "ran meetings very well," he did not have much to do with day-to-day operations and, in fact, was little involved in major corporate decisionmaking. Thus he was of little help to Norris, who could deal with difficulties at the operating level but not with roadblocks at corporate headquarters.

One of Norris's biggest frustrations had to do with his reporting relationships. The president, Charles Green, to whom he reported initially, was in poor health and soon left. James Rand then managed to have Norris report to Rand's son, Marcel, whom Norris considered "a complete nonentity. He couldn't communicate. He didn't understand the business. I would meet with him and he wouldn't respond. I thought at first that he was just quiet and reserved, but I soon learned he didn't know what was going on and didn't want to expose his ignorance."[23] Norris simply went around him and worked directly with Henry Vickers, then chief executive officer.

Norris urged that Sperry-Rand use its substantial lead to become the world's principal manufacturer of computers. As late as the early

1950s, still mesmerized by the long-standing success of its punched-card tabulating machines, IBM under the elder Thomas Watson had been slow to grasp the significance of the new technology, and the way was briefly clear for Univac to become what IBM in fact became.

Vickers responded by encouraging Norris to think and plan big. "He told me that he wanted to move rapidly and not to worry too much about the cost because he didn't want to be second, he wanted to be first," Norris recalls. At the time ERA was the only part of the company's electronics business making any money, and Norris warned Vickers that "We can't carry out the kind of program that you have in mind and stay profitable."

"Aw, hell," Vickers replied, "don't worry about that. A few hundred thousand dollars at this point in time is nothing. What I want is to be number one. Whatever it takes to be number one, we will finance it."

Norris took him at his word, and though he later confessed that he was "a damned fool to believe him," he launched a larger program that put his operation in the red, as he knew it would. His worst fears were realized: The heads of the old-line divisions—typewriters, shavers, and the like—"went to work on me for losing all that money."

To make matters worse, Norris's critics were at corporate headquarters in Connecticut and had top management's ear on a daily basis. It became increasingly difficult for him to get the kind of R&D money he needed, and in the scramble for allocation of capital resources he fared poorly.[24]

The company was simply not ready to make the commitments Norris knew were necessary. Men brought up in the typewriters and shavers business found it hard to understand the needs or evaluate the opportunities and risks of the emerging electronics industry. In promising to support Norris, Vickers apparently had been thinking in terms of a few hundred thousand dollars; what Norris needed was millions.

While Norris fumed, IBM began to realize the great possibilities of digital computers. Under the younger Thomas Watson, who took over as chief executive officer in 1956, it changed its basic strategy and moved into the new field with vigor and determination. Backed by its enormous financial resources and impressive managerial talents, and with its strongest potential rival shackled by corporate envy and timidity, IBM advanced rapidly to become the dominant factor in the new industry, a position it holds to this day. Years later, Watson told Lois Rice, a Control Data officer and director, that it was Sperry Rand's failure to realize the good thing it had in the group around Norris that enabled IBM to make its big leap ahead in computers.

Norris and his key associates followed the course of events with mounting dismay. "We sat there," he recalled later, "with a tremendous technological and sales lead and watched IBM pass us as if we were standing still."[25]

Among members of the original ERA group, an ever more frequent topic of conversation in the halls became, "Why don't we go off and start a new company and this time do it right?" Norris was reluctant: "I was the general manager and committed to making the damned thing work, so I always told the guys to cool it." But as matters grew worse, he, too, began to find the idea of a fresh start attractive.

"I think the guys could sense that I'd just about had a belly full," he recalls, "and one day a couple of them came in and asked me if I would join them and head up a new company. I said, 'Well, I'll think about it.'" Not long afterward he received a note from his principal aide, Frank Mullaney, saying, "Bill, if you ever change your mind be sure to tell me."

Norris called Mullaney and said, "Frank, I'm getting out of here."[26]

CHAPTER 3

Building The Company

Mullaney was one of twelve Univac defectors who, with Norris, founded the new company, incorporated in July of 1957. They left over a period of weeks. According to one of those remaining at Univac, "It seemed like several times a week we had a farewell lunch for somebody. It reached the point where we said, 'The next guy who leaves buys his own lunch.' "[1]

It was a young group. Norris at forty-six was the eldest and Seymour Cray at thirty-one the youngest. The ages of the remaining ten averaged just over thirty-four.[2] The group was loosely organized with a broad division of labor. Figure 1, the first organization chart, indicates functional responsibilities but no lines of reporting. Everyone pitched in to do whatever needed doing.[3] However, there was never any question as to who was boss; Norris consulted with his associates but made all the substantive decisions himself.

An early one was naming the new company. This was accomplished in a systematic way. One of the founders, Willis Drake, devised a cardboard contraption resembling a three-columned slide rule. The first two columns listed terms common to digital computing, while the third contained generic words such as *company*, *corporation*, and so forth. Sliding these columns back and forth against one another yielded various three-word combinations. *Control Data Corporation* was the one Norris liked best, and that was the one selected.[4]

It was a fortuitous time to start a computer company. The idea of computers as an emerging technology with important commercial potential was beginning to take hold, and venture capital was

Figure 1

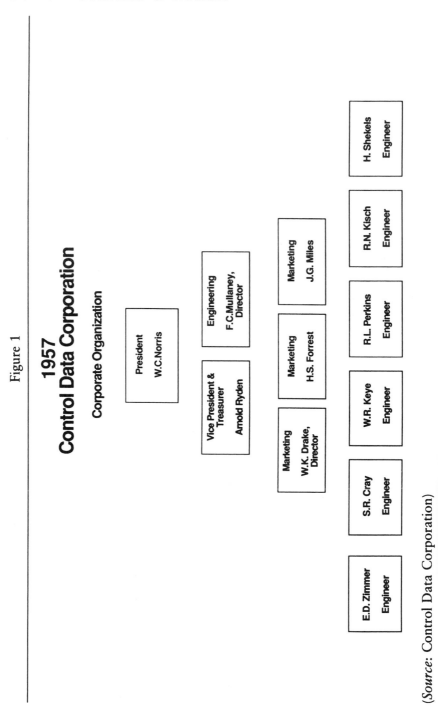

1957
Control Data Corporation

Corporate Organization

(*Source:* Control Data Corporation)

becoming more readily available.[5] The early pioneers in the computer industry were typically bright young engineers who were long on ideas but often short on capital and managerial talents. Many small startups were acquired by major firms that expected to develop and market the new products in much the same way they handled their existing lines of goods. Remington-Rand's acquisition of ERA was one example; other large companies entering the field included General Electric, RCA, Bendix, Honeywell, National Cash Register, and Burroughs. All bolstered their in-house initiatives with acquisitions, but few succeeded in establishing a firm foothold in the business. G.E. and RCA spent hundreds of millions of dollars before retiring in defeat; the Bendix computer operations were subsequently acquired by Control Data.

Initially the new company was financed by the sale of 600,000 shares of stock at $1 a share. It was the first startup company in the digital computing industry to be publicly financed, and it ushered in the dollar stock era in the United States. To save brokerage fees, the principals bought shares themselves and sold the remainder to their families and friends, former colleagues at Univac, and scattered investors intrigued by the glamour of the emerging industry. Norris himself invested $75,000, a physician friend (who grasped only in a general way what the new company proposed to do) put in another $25,000, and the remaining shares were quickly sold to some 300 other investors.[6] Norris, by now the father of six, was quite aware of the risk he was taking, but he and Jane talked things over, scraped together everything they had, and agreed that "if it doesn't work out, we'll just pack up the children and go back to the farm in Nebraska."[7]

Sperry Rand followed the activities of its former employees closely. In August of 1957 a notice appeared on company bulletin boards stating that "certain individuals" who had recently resigned from the Univac Division were attempting to sell stock to finance a new company that planned to engage in some kind of computer and electronics work. The notice warned that while Sperry had no control over what individuals might do, employees should be aware of potential conflicts of interest.[8] Eight months later, in April of 1958, Sperry filed suit in federal court against Norris and six of his associates alleging illegal use of trade secrets, processes, and inventions to which it claimed proprietary right.

William C. Norris in 1957, the Year of Control Data's Founding (*Source*: Control Data Corporation)

Norris turned for help to Robert F. Leach, a partner in the Minneapolis law firm of Oppenheimer, Hodgson, Brown, Baer, and Wolff. Leach, who had earlier handled a private legal matter for Norris, consulted his senior partner, William H. Oppenheimer. "I know Norris," he told Oppenheimer. "I don't know anyone else in the company and I don't know what they've done, but Norris tells me that haven't done anything that's illegal and I believe him. They can't afford very much for defense; that's why Sperry brought the suit." With Oppenheimer's approval, Leach reported back to Norris: "We'll take the case. We'll defend you. You can't pay much, so we'll take our pay down the road and if you're successful we expect to have some business. And if you're not, well, all right, we'll count it as experience."

Leach and his firm succeeded in defeating the Sperry suit. Years later, Norris recalled, "That was a hell of a deal. We won and they only charged us a very nominal amount—$15,000 or some such number. You can almost say it was administering life to us at that stage."[9]

An important further outcome was the cementing of a unique relationship between Leach and Norris. Leach became a member of the Control Data board and Norris's most trusted advisor, one of the few people outside his immediate family with whom Norris ever grew close. Leach's untimely death in 1970 from a brain tumor hit Norris very hard. Years later, he commented quietly, "Hell, even now, I almost cry when I think about it."[10] The Oppenheimer firm still serves as Control Data's outside counsel, and another of its partners, Richard G. Lareau, sits on the board today. But no one has ever taken Leach's place in Norris's mind or Control Data's affairs.

At the outset, the founders had only the broad outlines of a business strategy in mind. In Norris's words: "My decision to leave Sperry Rand was based primarily on my utter distaste for the whole thing. I didn't really have a well-thought-out business plan in mind. I just wanted to get the hell out of there, and felt the field was large, it was expanding, and we would be able to develop a product as we got the company started."[11] One thing the group was sure of: With their limited resources, they wanted no direct confrontation with IBM, which by this time had come to dominate all segments of the office equipment industry by virtue of its impressive marketing and maintenance capabilities. The first prospectus, dated 29 July 1957, was explicit: "Control Data Corporation does not plan to compete directly with the giants of the industry, such as IBM, Sperry Rand, General Electric, Burroughs, etc. . . . Plans are to supplement these major companies as an important subcontractor and as the developer of selected components and equipment which may be used with the computer systems and instrumentation of the major companies."[12]

Norris and his fellows set up shop in warehouse space rented from the Minneapolis Star and Tribune Company, under terms that permitted expansion but required payment for additional space only as occupied. Forklifts trundling huge rolls of newsprint back and forth were a hazard to the unwary. The floor area was divided into office cubicles and work areas by temporary chipboard partitions, which no one ever got around to painting. Work benches were bought knocked down and assembled at night by the engineers using tools brought from home. "It was really kind of fun," Mullaney recalled, "but mighty lean."[13]

———————

One of the most important figures in the history of Control Data Corporation was Seymour R. Cray. He had joined ERA in 1950 after graduating from the University of Minnesota with a degree in electrical engineering, and like Norris had been disenchanted by the Univac experience. He had wanted to accompany the first contingent that left to form Control Data, but Norris had talked him out of it. Cray was engaged in important work at Univac for the navy, and Norris feared that his departure might jeopardize relations with what he hoped would be one of the new company's chief customers.

In September, however, Cray telephoned Norris and told him "I'm ready to come to work." Norris recalls the following exchange:

Norris: Gee, Seymour, does the navy know about this?

Cray: Hell no. I don't have to ask the navy what I can do.

Norris: Boy, this is going to create some problems.

Cray: Do you want me or not?

Norris: Well, of course.

Cray: I'll be at work tomorrow morning.

"We had to scramble around and mend our fences with the navy," Norris remembers, "but they understood Seymour as well as we did, so it wasn't as difficult as I thought it might be."[14]

Cray was already recognized as an authentic genius and a major innovator in electronic technology.[15] He was also a nonconformist who kept odd hours, arriving around noon or later and working at a fast pace far into the night when no one was around to distract him. He wore sport shirts on the job and off and donned neckties only on formal occasions. Former colleagues describe him as "a different kind of guy," "a loner," "a brilliant person who marches to his own tune," a man who "does not tolerate fools gladly." His moods and attitudes were unpredictable; he could be charming or very rude.

He preferred working alone or in small groups. It was an article of faith with him that "success is in inverse proportion to the number of people you put on a task," because "the bigger the group the more people get in each others' way, and the more time you have to spend communicating and explaining." He had a passionate distaste for bureaucracy and administrative detail. His first business plan, submitted only after repeated pressure, was brief:

Five-year goal: Build the biggest computer in the world.

One-year goal: Achieve one-fifth of above.

Cray had absolute confidence in himself and did pretty much what he wanted to do; if he didn't want to do something, he wouldn't do it, no matter who asked him. He was not an easy person to supervise. Years later, when someone grumbled to Norris about a prima donna on his staff, Norris responded, "Don't complain to me about that—I've had Seymour working for me." Cray gave his own subordinates plenty of leeway and intervened in their work only when they were in trouble. In fact, some felt that at times he deliberately let them go up technical blind alleys just so he could move in dramatically to rescue them; those subjected to this treatment described it as being "scrayed." Despite his eccentricities, he was respected and generally well liked.

On rejoining his old colleagues, Cray built a workbench in a corner of the warehouse floor and with two other engineers set about designing a modular circuit configuration that could be used in almost anything digital, including high-speed computers. Like Cray himself, it was an original—and it was fast. Norris quickly grasped its significance and directed that the new company's meager resources be thrown behind Cray and his team. Almost overnight, Control Data embarked on a program to build the world's most powerful computer.

The new company now had a strategy. At the outset, "We didn't really know what we were going to do—at least, I didn't—so we kept the language in the prospectus a little vague," Norris explains. "When Seymour came up with the idea of building a very big computer and the means for doing it, this gave us something to tie into. I kind of felt like shouting, 'Eureka!' "[16]

There was still no desire to take on IBM. Far bigger and stronger companies than the infant Control Data were already locked in costly conflict with the industry giant, struggling for a share of the business market (then thought to represent 90 percent of the new technology's potential). Instead, Control Data targeted the scientific and engineering markets. IBM and the other majors were interested in this field, too, but none of them had Seymour Cray and his high-speed circuitry.

The goal was to build a faster, more powerful computer than anyone had ever built before. It would be called the CDC 1604. In the computer industry, the numbers assigned to products usually have some logic behind them (at least at the start of a series). The ERA 1101, binary notation for thirteen, had been so designated because it had been built as Task 13 under a navy contract. Subsequent models in the series bore the numbers 1102 and (the last) 1103. Because Control Data was conceived by its founders as in a sense a reincarnation of ERA, the idea grew that it should pick up where ERA left off. Therefore, to the number *1103* was added the new company's street address, *501* Park Avenue, and *1604* became a milestone in the history of general purpose digital computers.

The U.S. Navy Bureau of Ships placed the first order for a 1604 in June of 1958 and took delivery in January of 1960.[17] The equipment met all of the customer's specifications and was more versatile, compact, and powerful than competitive models—and, at $600,000, far less expensive.[18] The second 1604 was purchased by the British government for the intelligence agency under whose supervision pioneering protocomputer work had been conducted at Bletchley Park during World War II. Orders from other prestigious customers followed, and Control Data was successfully launched as a manufacturer of large-scale, high-speed computers, the most powerful in the world.

Fully transistorized, the 1604s incorporated the most advanced technology available and were often engineered to the specifications of individual buyers. They were sold with little or no software to customers with professional staffs who could write their own programs and did not need the kind of handholding that new users (such as most business clients) required. The early ones were put together "family style": When a new order came in, space in the warehouse area was partitioned off, a team of engineers and

The CDC 1604, Control Data's First Computer, *Ca*. 1960 (*Source*: Control Data Corporation)

technicians assigned, and about nine months later a computer was ready to ship. The same people who built the machine also tested it, installed it, and taught the customer how to use it.

The company started with a sales force of two: one for everything east of the Mississippi, and the other for everything west. As the business grew, so did the sales and marketing organization. Among the early recruits was Robert D. Schmidt, who would later become vice chairman of the board. Control Data's sales representatives lacked the suavity and polish characteristic of their IBM counterparts; a distinguished scientist at an Eastern university referred to them as "cowboys," and a senior IBM executive once called the rough-hewn Schmidt a "midwest peasant" to his face. "To the IBM types," Schmidt later acknowledged, "we probably looked like peasants."[19]

Over time, the salesmen refined their techniques and developed mutually productive relationships with the people they served, most of whom were well grounded in computer technology. Because Control Data did not yet offer software, it was necessary that the technical staffs of its customers become deeply involved in the buying decision—far more than for the purchase of the business equipment on which IBM had built its reputation and fortune. In competing with IBM, Control Data had a considerable advantage in its chosen market because its giant rival did not yet have a truly large-scale scientific computer, and despite considerable upgrading IBM's general purpose business computers were simply not in the same class as the 1604 for engineering and scientific work. In addition, many engineers and scientists felt more at home with Control Data people than with their IBM counterparts. Some of them resented IBM's aggressive sales tactics and insistence on promoting standardized equipment; Control Data, in contrast, could speak their language and was always willing to adapt its offerings to their special needs.

With its small sales force, Control Data's deliberate strategy was to approach only those potential customers judged sophisticated enough to understand and use the new equipment without too much help from the vendor. The Defense Department, defense contractors, and the Atomic Energy Commission were among the major early customers, and they were soon joined by some of the larger universities. It was clearly a specialized market, and for a time Control Data prospered.

But IBM's corporate pride was stung by the loss of some of its most prestigious accounts to the upstart CDC, and in 1962 it struck back with a tactic known in the computer trade as a "fighting machine"—a standard model with a few changes offered at a sharply reduced price. A month after Control Data sold its fourth computer, IBM announced a modified version of its most powerful machine at one-third less than Control Data's bread-and-butter 1604. This was a severe blow, and Control Data went for many months without taking a new order; in fact, it came within an ace of going under.

Meanwhile, even before the 1604 reached the market, Seymour Cray had begun designing a still more powerful machine. In 1962, to escape what he called "administrative noise," Cray proposed that the company build a laboratory for him on the banks of the Chippewa River in his home town of Chippewa Falls, Wisconsin. Norris agreed, but the decision was not popular. "The move created a bit of a flap within the company," Norris later recalled, "but there was never any concern on my part. Seymour was difficult to see anyway, and the move made him feel more comfortable and he was more efficient."

Norris visited Chippewa Falls every three or four months to have lunch with Cray, but otherwise he left him on his own.[20]

In the tranquility and relative solitude he prized, Cray and a select group of engineers and technicians went to work on the CDC 6600, the world's first "supercomputer." (The derivation of *6600* was aesthetic rather than technical; the stylist designing the cabinet thought those numerals had a flowing character that would look well on the label.) Public announcement in July of 1962 of the 6600's forthcoming availability attracted wide attention. *Business Week* hailed it as a "triumph . . . a machine that will open up a whole universe of scientific calculations that have been impossible to contemplate."[21] IBM chairman Thomas J. Watson, Jr. needled his top management: "Contrasting this modest effort [of Cray in his laboratory] with 34 people including the janitor with our vast development activities, I fail to understand why we have lost our industry leadership position by letting someone else offer the world's most powerful computer."[22]

Seymour R. Cray Holding Example of CDC 6600 Logic, *Ca.* 1963 (*Source*: Control Data Corporation)

While IBM had responded to the 1604 with a "fighting machine," it answered the 6600 with a "paper machine"—one that existed only on paper. Soon after Control Data's announcement, IBM issued a statement that it was working on a computer that would dwarf anything Control Data had on the drawing board. It actually undertook a crash program, but despite enormous effort and great expense the proposed machine proved impossible to build and none was ever delivered. Nevertheless, the phantom IBM machine was enough to freeze Control Data out of the market. When it became apparent that the IBM would be a long time coming (if ever), orders for the 6600 began to materialize, but the experience was costly and again drove Control Data to the verge of bankruptcy.

Angry and embittered, Norris fought back. He instructed his salesmen to report in detail whenever they lost a sale, and also to report any questionable activities they encountered even when they were able to compete effectively.[23] By 1968 enough factual data had been accumulated and organized to file an antitrust suit whose successful outcome five years later marked an important milestone in Control Data's history.[24] The suit was filed in December, the same month the company announced its new and still more powerful 7600. Norris was anxious to avoid repetition of the tactics IBM had used in its efforts to freeze out the 1604 and the 6600, and the strategy worked; the 7600 was launched without having to run the gauntlet that had troubled the introductions of its predecessors. First delivered in 1969, it was one of the most successful computers ever built and enjoyed an exceptionally long run as the world's most powerful.

True to form, Cray was not satisfied. "I've built my last small computer," he confided to friends, and immediately started in on a far more powerful one tentatively dubbed the 8600. He encountered difficulties, however, chiefly because existing circuit technology was not up to his system design demands, and in 1972 he resigned from Control Data in frustration.

The parting was amicable on both sides. In a memorandum to Norris, Cray expressed his appreciation for the support he had had over the years, particularly Norris's willingness to let him operate out of Chippewa Falls. In his estimation, however, his sense of obligation had "slowly been amortized, and I now feel a residual of zero."[25]

After spending about a year collecting his thoughts and regaining perspective on his work, Cray started a company of his own, Cray Research, to be devoted solely to building supercomputers. He was joined by Frank Mullaney, who had left Control Data in 1966 in a disagreement with Norris and now became chairman of the board of Cray Research.

Cray had always been impatient with the constraints working for a large company had placed on him, minimal though they were; even in the relative freedom and seclusion of his Chippewa Falls laboratory it had been necessary to observe a few organizational rules. Also, he had never made any secret of his preference for small organizations. "Seymour thought we ought not to be more than a $40 million company," one company veteran explains. "Once you get beyond that, you get to a point where it's not engineering driving the machine anymore. You're starting to be driven by the needs of customers and stockholders. All kinds of other considerations come to affect your decisions as opposed to making technical decisions."[26]

Cray also felt that Control Data was misguided. For one thing, he was not happy about the emphasis Norris was giving to computer services rather than to computer hardware. According to Mullaney, "Cray wanted a hardware company, as I had, but Bill wanted a

Frank C. Mullaney, Ca. 1962 (Source: Control Data Corporation)

service company, and that had a lot to do with Seymour's leaving."[27] Cray also believed strongly that the only way to sell very large computers was to rely on a relatively small and sophisticated base of customers whose primary concern was performance and who were capable of handling their own software and applications problems. This was the course he planned to pursue in his new company.

Control Data invested over $300,000 in Cray stock to help start him on his new venture; this was later sold for a threefold gain.[28] While Cray Research soon evolved into Control Data's chief rival in the supercomputer field, personal relations between the two principals have remained friendly but not close. Norris is philosophical: "You have to have good competition, and Seymour is good competition—in fact, the best."[29]

Cray was not the first valued employee Control Data had lost, nor would he be the last. Over the years the company has attracted many creative people to its ranks, and it has seen a fair number leave—some to start companies of their own, others recruited by companies looking to strengthen their own position in the computer industry. As a matter of fact, a significant portion of the computer and computer-related industry that is so prominent a feature of the Minnesota economy is staffed by people trained under Norris's aegis. Figure 2 gives some indication of the impact of the three companies he has headed, beginning with ERA.

Norris takes a paterfamilias view of the tendency of some of his best and brightest to depart the fold. "That's life," he says. "Just like your kids, they grow up and they leave home. You're sorry to see them go, but you're kind of proud, too. I always try to part amicably with people if they want to leave because you never know what's down the road. . . . We try to give creative people good opportunities for creativity, but when they reach the limit of what we can provide we're glad to see them strike out on their own, and sometimes help them do it."[30] Not all partings, however, were amicable; some, related to particular circumstances, left lasting bitterness on both sides.

Interestingly, Cray did not remain head of his own company for long. Within ten years it, too, had grown too big for his liking, and he resigned to become an independent contractor working full time for Cray Research but unencumbered by organizational restraints. "I knew when I started that when the company got to a certain size, I really wouldn't want to be participating on a daily basis in the

Figure 2

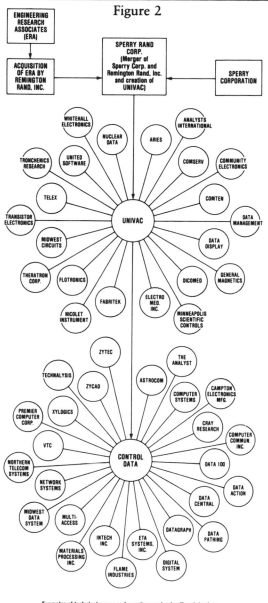

Examples of technical company formations and spin-offs originating
with Engineering Research Associates (ERA) in 1946.

Examples of Technical Company Formations and Spinoffs Originating with
Engineering Research Associates (ERA) (*Source*: *Milwaukee Journal*, 7
October 1980. Revised and Updated by Control Data Corporation)

management," he says. "My interests are really to do the 'thing' part with computers, rather than the 'people' part."[31] In doing the "thing" part, Cray's designs, beginning with the Control Data 1604, have been watersheds in the development of large-scale scientific computers.

Despite Cray's resignation in 1972, Control Data continued its efforts to bring the 8600 project to successful conclusion. Concurrently, however, work was also underway to develop another supercomputer along somewhat different lines from that of the 8600. This task was under the direction of James E. Thornton, whom Norris held in exceptionally high regard. Thornton had worked with Norris and Cray at ERA and Sperry and joined Control Data soon after its founding. He was one of those who had accompanied Cray to Chippewa Falls to build the 6600, but two years later, in 1964, had returned to Minneapolis with Norris's encouragement to work on ideas of his own.

Norris built a laboratory for Thornton and his project, which in due course came to be called the *Star*. Work proceeded for a time on both the 8600 and the Star, but it soon became clear to Norris that he had to make a difficult choice. "We were up to our eyeballs in supercomputer projects," he recalls. "We simply couldn't go full speed ahead on two big computer programs."[32] In 1974, taking into account the basic technology problems of the 8600, he came down on side of the Star. Under Thornton's direction this work continued, scoring important advances in computer technology. Redesigned by stages, the Star appeared in 1980 as the Cyber 205 and helped Control Data maintain its strong position in the supercomputer field.

But in the hypercompetitive environment of the computer business, work had already begun on the next great leap forward, a supercomputer that would far outperform the Cyber 205. For this, Norris adopted a new strategy.

In the course of building a large multinational company, he had never lost his belief in the superiority of small companies in terms of creative and innovative capacity. This led him in 1983 to spin off ETA Systems, Inc. as a separate corporation, comprised initially of 130 Control Data scientists, engineers, technicians, and supporting staff engaged in supercomputer work. Their first task was to design and build a supercomputer capable of performing ten billion calculations per second—hence the name, *ETA-10*. Under the leadership of Control Data veterans Lloyd Thorndyke as president and chief executive officer, Neil Lincoln as chief computer architect, and Anthony Vacca as chief technologist, major breakthroughs in computer technology were accomplished, and as this book goes to press it appears that the first ETA-10 will be delivered on schedule in December of 1986.

The ETA-10 strengthens Control Data's competitive position *vis à vis* its major supercomputer rival, Cray Research. The two companies are now engaged in an all-out effort to dominate the high end of the scientific data processing field. Machines of the two companies differ somewhat in their technical capabilities. For certain kinds of problems, Cray equipment is superior, but for others that of Control Data is still ahead. Both companies are operating at the state of the art, and both are making major contributions to computer science and information management.

_____

The decision made early in Control Data's history to concentrate on large-scale computers was a high-risk strategy. Learning how to build them was in itself a chancy undertaking because state-of-the-art technology—by definition new and untried—carried with it not only the hope of success but the danger of failure. Moreover, at the time Control Data entered the field there was only a limited market for computers of such power. The company's financial resources were thin, and even a minor error in judgment or stroke of bad luck could have been fatal. Good fortune, when it came, helped mightily.

An early and crucial sale was to Lockheed Aircraft for $1.5 million, conditional on the furnishing of a performance bond. But who would write a bond of that size on a company that had yet to deliver its first computer and could afford little more than a nominal fee? Fortunately, through Robert Leach, the people at St. Paul Fire and Marine Insurance Company knew Norris. As Edward E. Strickland, then Control Data's financial officer, later reported, "They really bonded Norris. There was nothing else in the company they could justify writing the bond on. They did it on faith in Bill."[33]

Sole reliance for revenues on a narrow product line of new-generation computers represented a major business hazard. Other computer manufacturers such as IBM, National Cash Register, Burroughs, Honeywell, RCA, General Electric, and Bendix enjoyed substantial revenues and earnings from other well-established lines of business; they had resources to draw on and strong fallback positions should the going prove too rough (as it did, in fact, for several). In its early years, Control Data had to make it with its big computers or not make it at all.

Through ERA and Univac, the founders of Control Data had good contacts with the government and military, and initial efforts were directed at these markets. Bids were made on a number of projects while the 1604 was still in design. According to Mullaney, "We didn't much care how big they were or what they were." Only a few small contracts resulted, and there were major hurdles to overcome. The new company had no tested product, no manufacturing facilities, and only a handful of employees. Its physical plant did little to inspire confidence. "It really wasn't a place you could take the contracting officers or the technical people through and convince them of anything," Mullaney recalls.[34]

Because demonstrable manufacturing capability was essential, one of Norris's first moves was to initiate a search for a compatible small company that might want to be acquired. He found it in Cedar Engineering, Inc., a small local electronics and precision instrument manufacturing company with attractive electromechanical engineering capabilities. Cedar was purchased in November 1957—only four months after Control Data's founding—for 50,000 shares of Control Data stock (at an assigned value of $3 a share) and $400,000 in cash and notes.[35] With 165 employees, electronic and electromechanical assembly operations, a well-equipped machine shop, and an environmental clean room, Cedar provided the manufacturing capability Control Data needed and helped solve its credibility problem. Mullaney again: "It was a plant, there were people sitting at benches working. It was a place to take people through and show them something going on."[36]

The acquisition brought with it other advantages, including a line of urgently needed revenue-generating products. In addition, several members of the top Cedar staff were integrated into Control Data management and played key roles in the company's future; among them were Thomas G. Kamp and Edward E. Strickland. In some ways, however, the acquisition proved difficult to swallow. For one, it immediately soaked up a large part of the new company's meager supply of working capital. In an austerity move, Norris temporarily halved the modest salaries of the management and professional staff. Meanwhile, Allstate Insurance Company provided vital financial support by purchasing a $350,000 issue of 6 percent preferred stock, enabling the company to surmount the first in a series of financial crises.[37]

The kind of high-speed, general purpose computer to which Control Data committed itself is a complex device requiring a broad array of technical skills and organizational resources. At the time it could command only a limited market, and a broader business base was necessary if the company was to be economically viable. Norris's first diversification moves were to enter the military market for specialized digital processing equipment and the more general peripheral products and data services businesses. There were two ways to gain the additional technical and organizational assets needed to support Cray's computer and the ventures into these fields: internal development, or acquisition. Encouraged by the benefits brought to it by Cedar Engineering, Norris chose the latter.

"We were fully aware that our survival in a business already dominated by corporate giants required us to expand quickly," he recalls.[38] Always conscious of the importance of "critical mass," Norris began looking for small companies that would provide Control Data with needed technologies while accelerating its growth. This was not so much a detailed program as it was a sense of direction. "We had some ideas," one member of the group later recalled, "but a certain part of it was happenstance. Things were brought to our attention that seemed to be pertinent . . . there were some that worked and some that didn't, but in the end they all contributed in some way."[39]

This doesn't mean that the company sat back waiting for opportunity to knock, however. As Strickland, who had come with Cedar Engineering and was treasurer of Control Data during this period, remembers, "In those days, I 'had suitcase and would travel.' It was so bad that if I walked in the door of a small company which was publicly held and anyone recognized me, the price of their stock would probably go up, because we actually went out and just made calls on the presidents and told them what we wanted and how we wanted to do it and asked, do you want to become a part of the Control Data team?" Decisions at Control Data's end were reached by a special kind of consensus; according to Strickland, "It was a consensus if Bill could make it a consensus, but if it was not a consensus and Bill thought it was, then it was a consensus."[40]

The company's initial expertise was chiefly in the military field; it had little knowledge of industrial and commercial markets. Through a series of strategic moves, Norris strengthened the company's range of technical competence and market presence, and in the twenty-year period from 1960 to 1979 it acquired eighty-eight companies with a combined value of more than $1 billion. A single 1968 acquisition, Commercial Credit Company, accounted for three-quarters of that total.[41]

Importantly, all of the acquisitions were negotiated on a friendly basis; none was a forced takeover. In many instances the acquired company was in trouble and seeking a buyer for whom its skills, product lines, and markets would be of greatest value and command the best price. For a number of technically sound smaller companies and specialized divisions of larger companies, the preferred buyer proved to be Control Data.

Acquisitions were accomplished by exchange of stock. For a period during the 1960s, Control Data became one of Wall Street's favorite glamour issues. Investors were entranced with almost anything electronic, and Control Data's stock was bid up to levels that gave it considerable leverage in exchange-of-stock transactions. Strickland again: "The price-earnings ratio of [our] stock was very high, so we could always step up the purchase price by 20 percent, as you compute it against the price of the stock, and make the deals. The only problem was, with the volatile stock the price could jump 30 percent, which it did a lot of times, down as well as up, while we were in negotiations. That made it a little more of a challenge, particularly if the stock went down, to hold the deals in bed. But most of the time they held."[42]

Viewed in their totality, the acquisitions added new markets, technologies, staff, and physical plant to the fledgling company. Norris admits there were "dogs" in the lot, but these were few and soon disposed of. Most turned out well, "some beyond our expectations."[43] Many were simply folded into Control Data operations and lost their visibility as separate entities while adding to Control Data's strength.

From the beginning, the military market was important to the new company.[44] In the spring of 1959 a contract was signed with the navy to design and build a special-purpose computer for the fire control system of the submarine-launched Polaris missile. Tied in with other shipboard equipment, this device coordinated such data as the ship's location, true north, and target location, and calculated from these the proper trajectory for each of the vessel's missiles at any given moment. Because much of this data changed continuously with the movement of the ship, it was necessary for the device to have the capability of recomputing all trajectories every few seconds for transfer to the missile guidance system. The navy liked what Control Data delivered, and over the next few years ordered fifty more.

This success, together with the prospect of substantial additional military business, led to the creation of the Government Systems Division in July of 1962. In 1963 a contract was received for a computer that would monitor the flight profiles of missiles after launch to predict continuously the area of impact and to enable the control officer to destroy the missile if it went off course during flight. Although the primary function of the system was safety, it could also be used for immediate postflight computations to facilitate recovery of the spent missile.

Also in 1963, a contract particularly significant for the young company was awarded by the National Aeronautics and Space Administration. This called for the development of a sophisticated system for checking the instrumentation of the Apollo command and service and the lunar excursion modules. Soon thereafter came a contract for a computer to improve the accuracy and reliability of the fire control system of the Talos surface-to-air missile.

Having established its capabilities in these demanding fields, the Government Systems Division was soon deeply involved in developing and building fire control systems for the Poseidon submarine program, airborne computers for the Phoenix program, and other major space and military projects. Revenues from these contributed significantly to Control Data's rapid growth during the 1960s. Equally important were the technological advances generated by the projects, which proved useful in civilian as well as military applications, providing a solid base for the company's worldwide reputation as a leader in the field—and Norris's as a daring and innovative entrepreneur.

Other branches of the business were also growing rapidly, both at home and abroad. Overseas operations became important to Control Data when the second 1604 was sold to an agency of the British government, and they have remained so ever since.[45] The overseas initiative was conceived and pushed vigorously by Norris, who was attracted by the great universities and research institutions of Europe and saw in them the means for significantly broadening the customer base for his narrow product line.[46]

The first overseas office, headed by Edward Strickland, was opened in Lucerne, Switzerland in 1962 with five employees—all transferred from Minneapolis, and none with even a minimal command of any language other than English; in fact, none had ever been outside the United States before. Eventually, subsidiary corporations were established in the principal European countries, staffed with able sales forces comprised of country nationals.

In some ways the company found it easier to penetrate the European market than the one back home. IBM was not yet as firmly entrenched abroad as in the U.S., and it was still limited to selling its general-purpose business data processors. Control Data's reputation as maker of the world's most powerful computers opened doors to its sales representatives. One recalls, "We had a lot more clout than our small size would justify. People, in fact, believed we were much bigger than we really were."[47] Although the typical overseas CDC office was staffed by fewer than ten people during those years, most of the larger European technical organizations soon became Control Data customers. Among them were a Danish research organization; the Technical University of Hanover, West Germany; a Swiss technical institute; Sud Aviation in France; and Phillips in Holland. Other major customers included the defense and intelligence departments of most European countries, and from its outset NATO has relied heavily on Control Data equipment.

Overseas expansion was not limited to Europe; important sales were made early in Australia, Israel, Iran, and in countries behind the Iron Curtain, although business with Eastern Europe was restricted by security considerations. In recent years Japan, Korea, and China have been added to the Control Data roster. International trade has played a vital role in the company's history, and probably will continue to be prominent in the years ahead. As former senior corporate officer and company director Robert Duncan notes, "There's no way Control Data could exist today or in the future if we didn't have a substantial international business."[48]

The rapid growth of the company presented Norris with complex problems of management and control. His prior experience had been confined to relatively small organizations; at the time of its acquisition by Remington-Rand, ERA employed some 1,500 people and had revenues of about $2.5 million, and the Univac division of Sperry-Rand had been about that size when he left it to form Control Data. Eight years later, in 1965, the new company had nearly 10,000 employees and revenues of $160 million; by 1970 these figures had swelled to over 30,000 and $1 billion, respectively. The tasks of shaping, guiding, and energizing what had become a major corporation were greater by orders of magnitude than any he had faced before.

He was strongly supported by the corps of aides he gathered around himself. Several came through acquisitions—Thomas G. Kamp with Cedar Engineering, Paul G. Miller with the Control Systems Division of Daystrom. Two of the most important of this supporting staff were new hires: Norbert R. Berg and Robert M. Price. Berg joined the company in 1959 as a personnel assistant, and Price in 1961 as a computer programmer. In time, Berg was to advance to deputy chairman of the board, and Price was to succeed Norris as chairman and chief executive officer.

Berg became a significant factor in shaping Norris's managerial style. A special relationship developed between the two men that grew in quality and strength as they worked together over the years. Berg probably understood Norris better than anyone else at Control Data, and he gained Norris's confidence to a degree that no other subordinate ever enjoyed. Price, for his part, quickly established himself in Norris's mind as a skilled executive able to get things done without fanfare. As the task of managing the affairs of Control Data grew in magnitude and complexity, he came to depend more and more on Price for day-to-day operations. Of all Norris's lieutenants, Berg and Price were those on whom he relied most heavily.

Needless to say, the company quickly outgrew the original leased warehouse space and the physical plant that came with Cedar Engineering. For a while it bought or leased office, laboratory, and manufacturing space piecemeal at various locations throughout the Minneapolis-St. Paul metropolitan area, but by 1960 it was clear that these would have to be pulled together in the interests of efficiency. Norris assigned Berg the task of finding a suitable site on which to build. His only caution: "Be sure to buy enough land so we won't run short later."[49]

After thoroughly canvassing the possibilities, Berg purchased several contiguous parcels of semirural land totaling approximately 130 acres in Bloomington, a suburb adjoining Minneapolis to the southwest, overlooking the Minnesota River, and only minutes from the Minneapolis-St. Paul International Airport. At the time the site was planted mostly in corn. Bought at prices ranging from $4,000 to $10,000 an acre, this investment appreciated substantially in succeeding years.[50]

The first buildings constructed at the new location were three-story modules, the first two of which ("Mod A" and "Mod B") were occupied in 1962. There was plenty of parking space, and an area in the lot was set aside for company executives. Norris drove a beat-up six- or seven-year-old green Chevrolet. One day Berg walked into his office and said, "For God's sake, Bill, you've got to get a new car. As long as you're driving that thing out there, the other guys are afraid to buy new cars and their wives are complaining." Norris replied, "Well, I guess I can understand that. Go buy me one." Berg bought him a medium-priced Oldsmobile.

Not long after the move to the new location, the representative of a major European electronics company called on Norris and announced, in heavily accented English, "We want to buy you."

"But we don't want to be bought," Norris replied.

"Maybe we buy you anyway," was the response.

Norris walked to the window of his office and invited his caller to join him. Pointing to the adjoining cornfield, he said, "If you do, I'll start a new company right over there. We'll build computers just like we're doing now, and I won't have to look far for all the help I'll need. They're right here. They'll come with me and we'll whip your ass." His visitor soon left, and the matter never came up again.

Additional low-rise buildings were added to Mods A and B in subsequent years, but by the end of the 1960s land values had reached a point where that type of construction was no longer economical. Out for a walk with Norris one day, Berg said, "Bill, we need a lot more space. We need a large new building."

"How big?" Norris wanted to know.

"Oh, half a million square feet."

"How much will it cost?"

"I don't know, but I know what I'm doing."

"Okay," Norris conceded, "but make it the last building on this site. I don't want this place to be an ant hill, with people climbing all over each other."

That was the beginning—and the end—of Norris's involvement in the building of the fourteen-story World Headquarters building, known as the Tower, which was completed in 1971. "One of the smartest things I've ever done," he often said later, "is not get involved in real estate. I've saved a lot of my time, and besides, other people do it better than I can." Of the nearly 8 million square feet Control Data occupied worldwide by 1980, Norris had personally selected none of it. He had helped find the original warehouse space in the Minneapolis Star and Tribune building, but from that point on he had stayed strictly out of the picture.

Norris first set foot in the Tower when Berg took him to see his office on the top floor. On the way he admired the building's spartan, no-frills features; the only thing he was not happy with was the carpeting throughout the building. He had been opposed to it as an unnecessary luxury, but Berg, to his annoyance, had insisted on having it installed on grounds of low maintenance cost.

Norris's office was ready for occupancy, complete with desk, chairs, conference tables, couch—everything, including pictures and his fishing trophies on the walls. He surveyed the scene without comment and walked first to one window and then the other. "Gee," he finally said, "these are nice views. Now tell me, where do I park?"

World Headquarters, Control Data Corporation, Bloomington, Minnesota, *Ca.* 1975 (*Source:* Control Data Corporation)

CHAPTER 4

Broadening The Base

Norris realized from the start that the market for large-scale, general purpose computers was relatively small and specialized and the market for military equipment inherently volatile. He moved early to diversify into broader lines of business, first into the design and manufacture of peripheral computer products and then into data services. These in turn required the building of strong support staffs, which led to entry into the engineering and professional services fields. The financing problems related to leasing large computer systems rather than selling them outright led in 1968 to the acquisition of Commercial Credit Company and expansion into a variety of financial services.

Events confirmed the wisdom of these moves. By the sharp economic recession of 1969–1970, when the demand for computer hardware dropped abruptly, Control Data had gone far beyond its original narrow product line and was able to weather this difficult period in good shape. Significantly, the businesses that kept the company solvent—peripheral products, data services, and engineering, professional, and financial services—were all closely related to (and, in fact, developed from or created to support) its basic business in large-scale computer systems.

The first Control Data computer was delivered to the U.S. Navy in 1960. In 1962 the newcomer to the industry was the fourth largest computer company in the world. By 1964 it had moved into third place, outranked only by IBM and Univac. Markets were developed overseas as well as domestically, with success in both arenas. In the scant span of a decade, Control Data Corporation grew from a small, narrowly specialized company into a multiproduct, multiservice worldwide corporation, thanks to Norris's strategy of growth by acquisition, diversification, aggressive marketing, and physical expansion, as well as the technological innovations he encouraged and supported.

In addition to the central processing unit (CPU), a data processing system consists of a variety of peripheral equipment, chief among which are data-entry and data-storage devices, printers, and monitors. Without the support of peripherals equal to its needs, the high-speed CPU that is the heart of the system is severely handicapped. This was an acute problem in building the 1604, the first of Control Data's powerhouse computers. Most peripheral equipment available at the time had been designed for much slower computers using vacuum tubes and were ill suited to the far more demanding requirements of the transistorized 1604.

As Control Data moved into increasingly sophisticated computer systems for the scientific and engineering market it had elected to serve, it needed peripheral equipment of increasingly higher quality, speed, and power. There was no use in producing a CPU many times more powerful than its predecessors unless it could be served by equally advanced peripherals. Equipment of the quality and reliability needed was available from IBM, but only at prices Norris was unwilling to pay.

Enter Thomas G. Kamp, a young man who had been part of the Cedar Engineering acquisition and was chief engineer of that operation. Norris asked him if he could design and manufacture some of the equipment Cray needed. After study, Kamp reported that he could, but to do so at affordable cost he would have to produce more than Cray could use. He therefore proposed to sell to other manufacturers as well as supply Control Data—in other words, to enter the OEM (*original equipment manufacturer*) market.

Although this was a radical notion at the time, Norris endorsed it. As far back as his ERA days, he had insisted on selling to others (chiefly laboratories and universities) devices originally meant for ERA's own use.[2] He had followed a similar policy at Sperry. Selling to the computer industry seemed to him a logical way of providing Control Data with high-grade equipment at reasonable cost.

But a move into the OEM market would require a major commitment of scarce resources, a course bitterly resisted by those in the company dedicated to the big computer and jealous of diverting resources for any other purpose. This issue gave rise to Control Data's first serious internal controversy. Several of Norris's key lieutenants were against the idea, including Seymour Cray, Frank Mullaney, and the members of the Systems Planning Committee, created by Norris himself to assist in reaching strategic decisions. "There was anger over the peripherals, genuine anger," recalls one insider.[3] The dissidents also objected to giving competitors the benefits of Control Data's innovative technical advances. "They don't have equipment of this capacity," the argument went. "Why should we help them to stay competitive with us in the computer systems business?" "We're selling the family jewels" was another frequently heard complaint.[4]

True to form, however, Norris had decided on the course he would follow and simply overrode the protests. In defense of selling to the computer industry, he said, "If we don't, someone else will." He rightly saw that industry as a major market; as much as two-thirds of the cost of a computer system is represented by peripherals. "We can't just sell mainframes," he argued. "We've got to sell whole systems. . . . Why should we have our sales force going out selling somebody else's stuff, or let somebody else sell stuff we should be selling?" His entrepreneurial judgment proved sound. Other computer manufacturers welcomed this new source of high-quality, reasonably priced equipment for use in their own products.

A new operating division headed by the thirty-three-year-old Kamp was created in the latter part of 1961. The company was now organized into two parts, computers under Mullaney and peripherals under Kamp. There was constant tension between the two divisions, an aftermath of the conflict over entering the OEM market. Competition for resources remained a persistent source of friction. Both businesses required major investments, and their combined demands strained the company's meager financial means. Cray, moreover, was the consummate design engineer, Kamp the consummate manufacturing engineer, and they gathered rather different kinds of aides around them. Cray disliked having his people deal with Kamp's; on one occasion when Norris urged the two groups (who were operating from two locations) to work together on a project, Cray responded,

"I don't want to do that. It demoralizes my people to talk to those guys."[5]

Policy differences were exacerbated by personality differences. Cray was a recluse who avoided personal contacts outside a limited circle, Kamp an extrovert who delighted in dealing with people and took great pleasure from simply walking through a shop to talk with employees. Both made major contributions to Control Data, but it took Norris's strong hand to keep them together in harness.

A distinguishing feature of Control Data's OEM strategy was close and continuing cooperation with potential customers. Plans for new technology were disclosed in advance, while still under development, and components were modified to meet the needs of individual customers. This policy was initiated by Kamp and strongly backed by Norris because it fit with his own belief in the values of cooperation and because he saw it as an effective means of tapping what could become a large and lucrative market.

Control Data's success soon attracted competitors. In a manner characteristic of the computer industry, these maintained tight security on their plans until their new products were ready for market, an attitude Norris scornfully likened to "a virgin afraid of lifting her skirts for fear someone will see what's underneath." So far from exercising secrecy, Control Data arranged tours of its design laboratories for engineers and systems planners of potential customers, and seminars were conducted periodically to review and evaluate impending changes in technology likely to affect their businesses. This policy of openness gave the company a strong competitive edge.

That edge was enhanced by Control Data's readiness, within the limits of the technology involved, to adapt the design of its products to the unique requirements of its customers. In contrast, the typical practice of competitors was simply to offer their standard products at volume prices, a far less attractive alternative from the customer's standpoint.

Powerful impetus was given Control Data's peripherals business by the advent of minicomputers,[6] machines with less power than the big mainframes but selling at substantially lower cost, and later by the introduction of microcomputers that proved enormously popular for home and office use. By this time, companies other than IBM were selling peripheral equipment, but none grasped as quickly as Kamp the great potential represented by these burgeoning new industries. Many were headed by entrepreneurs whose resources and attention were absorbed by the demands of their primary products, and who were quite ready to buy from someone else the supplementary equipment they needed to make their new products more attractive in cost and performance.

Norris viewed moving into the mini and micro markets with mixed feelings. On the one hand, he was strongly attracted by their revenue and profit potentials, but on the other he recognized that manufacturing for these smaller computers would be a definite departure from the original reason for entering the OEM business, which was simply to provide high quality components at reasonable cost for Control Data's own large-scale computers. Building peripherals for minis and micros was quite a different undertaking, and he went along with reservations.

At some point, of course, even this lucrative market had to approach saturation. Kamp remembers that by the late 1960s "there weren't any other major companies, really, to sell to. Most of the dwarfs had gone out of business or we were selling to them." To cover the high costs of new technology and provide a reasonable return on investment, "We needed another route to get volume."[7]

Over two-thirds of all installed computer capacity was IBM, and until then Control Data had restricted its peripherals market to the remaining third. Kamp was intrigued by the possibilities of building disk drives that could be used *with* IBM mainframes—"plug-compatibles," in industry language. Once again, he was strongly opposed by colleagues who worried about the risks of challenging the giant in his own backyard.

Norris, too, was apprehensive, but the prospects were tempting and Kamp persuasive. At the time, this looked like an incremental business. Adapting drives for use on IBM equipment would add little to the costs of designing and developing them for Control Data's established market, and it seemed foolish not to make the modest additional investment that would open up a new and potentially very large market. Risks were nothing new to Norris, who finally put his misgivings aside. According to Kamp, Norris called him into his office and said, "Tom, you've been talking about this plug-compatible business for a long time. It's a big market. Go. And I mean *go*." Kamp adds, "When Bill said, 'go,' he meant like yesterday, and big."[8]

Kamp found a ready market among companies who used IBM mainframes but preferred the lower price of Control Data disk drives and controllers. Partly because of IBM's pricing policy, which provided an umbrella under which its smaller rival fit comfortably, it was possible for the business to succeed. It also helped that IBM's marketing practices were orderly and to a degree predictable; Control Data soon developed considerable skill in anticipating Big Blue's new product introductions. Despite booming sales, however, Norris remained apprehensive and warned Kamp from time to time about the vulnerability of the plug-compatible business.

By 1980 Control Data's peripheral products group was being hailed by the trade press as "turning in the stellar performance on the corporate balance sheet."[9] At the time of the company's twenty-fifth anniversary celebration in 1982, peripherals were a billion-dollar business, and with nearly half of the OEM disk drive market it dominated the peripherals industry.

Still, Norris was not entirely at ease. In his mind peripherals had never been central to Control Data's strategic thrust. Had they not been necessary to the company's own computer systems, Norris recalls, "there would have been no reason for us to go into the business. But that business got profitable and became an end in itself." Even as the money rolled in, he grew increasingly apprehensive of the kinds of troubles that eventually did surface and, by 1985, brought the entire company to the brink of disaster. On that subject he now says, "I'm not trying to duck responsibility because, after all, I was head of the company. I did caution people about having too many eggs in that one basket, but the business was so profitable it kind of lulled everybody to sleep."[10]

The awakening, when it came, was a rude one that occurred simultaneously with other rude mishaps in the company's subsequent history.

═══════════

One of William C. Norris's most distinctive features is his interest in the ways technology can be used to solve practical problems.

As a salesman for Westinghouse in the 1930s, his mind was focused on what X-ray equipment could do to improve the practice of medicine. As an engineer in the cryptological unit of the navy during World War II, his mission was to find ways for using proto-electronic technology for naval intelligence. His work for defense agencies during ERA days was concerned with using the by now rapidly evolving electronic technology for a variety of very practical military problems.

To anyone following his career, it came as no surprise when early in the history of Control Data Corporation Norris should began thinking about how he could put the capabilities of the computers his company was building to problem-solving use. He was interested not only in manufacturing hardware but in finding new and productive ways to use it—a mindset that led naturally to the building of what in time proved to be a continually widening range of computer services.

The first of these was fairly pedestrian. In the spring of 1960, the third 1604 to be completed was installed on company premises for use by customer engineers, programmers, and other Control Data people, and by customers learning to use the equipment they had on order. By the following spring, the efficiency of the operation had improved to a point where there was an excess of capacity, and at Norris's direction efforts were made to find buyers for the unused time. These efforts were successful, confirming Norris's belief that in computer services there was a market that offered attractive opportunities.[11]

There were not many customers for computers as powerful as those Control Data was building: a few government laboratories, the military, some of the larger universities. Even the high-volume engineering and scientific computations of many large organizations could be handled in short periods of time, and equipment of that power was far too expensive to sit idle very long; what was true of many larger organizations was even more true, of course, of their smaller counterparts.

Norris saw that one way to enlarge his market was, in his words, to "sell a little piece of a big computer at a time." Also in his words, he wanted to make the power of big computers "available to the guy who can't afford to invest in one."[12] He was very much aware that many organizations large and small are quite sophisticated technically and have the capacity to use big computers but need them for only limited periods. His solution was to sell them time on one of his big computers. If they needed only a few minutes or an hour or so, he would charge them only for what they used.

He realized, however, that selling time alone would rapidly become a commodity game. There would be nothing to hold a customer if all he was buying was time and he could get that more cheaply by going to his bank and saying, "Run my program on your machine." But if Control Data were also to sell applications—

solutions to customer problems—the customer would have reason to stay with Control Data. Proprietary programs and technical expertise would add value to the time sold. Norris wanted his salespeople to be able to say, "We have the programs you need to solve your problems, and we have the high-speed computers to run them for you."

His plan met with considerable internal resistance and external skepticism. Some of his close associates objected to putting money into services when they felt it could be better spent on hardware. Wall Street thought that Control Data should stick to what it did best: building equipment. The mighty IBM had gone into data services some years before, with indifferent success; how could Control Data expect to do better?

What the investment community did not understand (and some of his own people had trouble grasping) was that Norris had no intention of following in IBM's footsteps. To begin with, he had a very different market in mind: the engineering and scientific communities, rather than the general business community that was IBM's primary interest.

Moreover, he planned to tap a different segment of the engineering and scientific market. Unlike customers who could afford to invest in big computers and were able to provide their own applications programs, many of the smaller customers Norris had in mind were more likely to need help designing programs to fit their special needs. For this purpose, Norris created a new position in the latter part of 1961, manager of applications services, and appointed a promising recent recruit, Robert M. Price. Norris confidently expected that the value added by such programs would significantly enhance the revenue and profit potentials of the service.[13]

The strategy was successful, not least because of what Control Data learned from it. Frank Mullaney later recalled that it "taught us a lot about software and what a customer would and would not put up with because we were selling results rather than a box." More important, it demonstrated in practical fashion the great potential of problem-solving services. "Even in those days, which was by now getting into the mid-sixties, Bill was talking about a very, very large service organization. He was starting to think services as opposed to equipment."[14]

At first the company adapted existing software for customer use—software gained through acquisitions or developed in connection with work for the Atomic Energy Commission, the Lawrence

Radiation Laboratory, the Jet Propulsion Laboratory, oil companies engaged in seismic exploration, and other major clients. A particularly important acquisition in terms of applications expertise was Control Corporation (1960), which brought with it valuable know-how in electrical, gas, and oil distribution control systems. The acquisition of Autocon some years later (1967) added water distribution expertise, and together these became the basis for Control Data's widely used and highly profitable energy management systems. Meiscon Engineers (1963) brought competence in engineering and structural design, and the Control Systems Division of Daystrom (also 1963) afforded entry into the computer process control market.

Other acquisitions, development, and third-party contracts further enhanced Control Data's service and applications resources, enabling it to serve still more industries and special needs. These included seismic exploration, computer-aided design, and stress analysis for bridges, tunnels, and other large construction projects—tasks requiring the manipulation of vast quantities of data. Building the business took time and cost money but proved ultimately profitable, a constantly recurring theme in Control Data's history. In 1969 the data processing service was trade-named CYBERNET, tying it into the emerging Cyber family of Control Data equipment and services.

Processing services are delivered in two ways, by batch and by timesharing. In the batch method, material is processed on an individual project basis. In the early days, materials were carried to and from the processing centers by messenger; today the majority are telecommunicated, greatly expanding each center's area of operation.

The year 1967 saw the introduction of timesharing, a method by which several hundred terminals can be linked by telephone to a central mainframe and each assigned a tiny "time slice" measured in millionths of a second. Special programs switch the attention of the mainframe from one terminal to another, doing a part of each user's program during its assigned "slice" of time and moving back and forth between all of the connected terminals at so high a speed that each user seems to have the mainframe's undivided attention. The technique vastly enhances both the productivity of the equipment and the usefulness of the service for clients.

Meanwhile, in the early 1960s, another Control Data business was beginning to take form: engineering and professional services. By this time, a sizable staff of professional analysts, consultants, and programmers had been recruited to perform various functions. Systems analysts did presale consulting and installation planning with customers and supported the data service operations. Engineers and technicians built the early computers, installed them on customer premises, trained customer personnel in their use, and serviced the equipment; they also provided systems analysis, software consulting, and programming assistance to ensure that the customer would make the most effective use of the equipment.

The acquisition of the computer division of Bendix in 1963 doubled the field maintenance staff from 150 to 300. This was followed by other acquisitions that created the need for a "third party" maintenance service because customer engineers now had to maintain equipment built by other companies as well as by Control Data. In the mid-1960s, additional growth came with the establishment of company branches in western Europe selling equipment that required servicing, and with contracts to maintain computer systems for the Department of Defense outside the United States and for the U.S. Postal Service in this country.

By the early 1970s, engineering and professional services together with CYBERNET had become major generators of revenue and profit, confirming Norris's judgment that services offered great potential for profitable growth.

The outcome of the lawsuit against IBM filed in December of 1968 gave another powerful boost to the services businesses, although that was not the reason the suit was originally filed. Tactics used by IBM in its efforts to keep Control Data's 1604 and 6600 computers from establishing a foothold in the marketplace had almost ruined the company, and Norris was determined to prevent a repetition of similar attacks against the soon to be introduced 7600. In retrospect, it is clear that Control Data could never have established itself in the supercomputer industry if it had been unsuccessful in its attack on IBM. Norris foresaw this clearly and prepared his case carefully.

Backed by a vast array of meticulously gathered evidence, he made repeated efforts to persuade the Department of Justice to initiate antitrust actions. When he did not succeed, he felt that he had no choice but to sue. Later he stated emphatically, "Control Data would never have filed a suit if the government had filed one. This was really an issue the government should have taken up. But they didn't, so in desperation we filed."[15]

He knew the risks involved. Failure or even stalemate could ruin the company. But he also knew that Control Data faced almost certain ruin if a repetition of IBM's tactics blocked the new 7600 from reaching the market. He made sure that he had the support of his management and board. About his Executive Council he later said, "We met and met, and talked and talked, and finally I said, 'This is what we're going to do.' Some shook their heads and some nodded affirmatively."[16]

Taking the issue to his board in a very long meeting, Norris brought with him a group of attorneys, economists, and other experts who reviewed the facts and thoroughly evaluated the pros and cons of filing the suit. John W. Lacey, one of Norris's principal aides and under whose supervision the factual evidence against IBM had been compiled, recalls that "Bill was more careful than I have ever seen him in getting not only consensus but willing commitment from the board." While some directors expressed reservations (one stated bluntly, "IBM will kick the hell out of us"), Lacey remembers that "when we left the room, there was a strong feeling of unity that this was the right thing to do."[17] The petition Control Data filed against IBM demanded triple damages. Then, in an audacious touch, it called for dismemberment of the offending giant.

In the discovery proceedings that followed, Control Data's attorneys examined over 20 million pages of IBM documents, copied over 1 million pages, and added some 500,000 pages (about 150,000 documents) to its already formidable computerized database.[18] Only with the aid of a powerful computer and sophisticated software especially designed for the purpose was it possible to sort, index, retrieve, and summarize this enormous quantity of information. This was the first time high-speed computer technology had been used in a major legal proceeding, and it was a significant factor in Control Data's winning an out-of-court settlement five years later. (Not surprisingly, yet another profitable Control Data business, Litigation Support Services, grew out of the techniques learned in the course of this experience.)

As usually happens in legal affairs of this magnitude and complexity, the suit dragged on interminably. Finally IBM took the initiative in an effort to reach a conclusion. Norris gives an interesting account of what happened.[19]

Overtures started "in the usual way, cocktail talk among lawyers," in which one lawyer said to another, "Let Bill Norris pick up the phone and call [Thomas V.] Learson," president of IBM. Norris sent word back by the same channel: "Hell, no, I'm not going to do that." Three or four months later another message came through: "We might be able to get Learson to call Norris, but he'd never call him at the office." Back went a message from Norris: "You tell those guys if Learson is going to call me at home, I want to know when it's going to be because I don't normally take telephone calls at home." Another month went by before word came back: "He'll call you [on a stated date] between five and six o'clock." Learson telephoned at the appointed time and suggested that the two get together to work things out. Norris replied that he'd "think about it."

One of Norris's advisors told him that if he agreed to a meeting it should be "someplace where you won't be visible because it could destroy the chance of a settlement if the press found out about it." The advisor suggested "somewhere in Nebraska" because "no one would expect you to go there to settle a lawsuit with IBM." Norris decided on Omaha because this would give him a chance to visit his son who was in college there. Norris and Learson met alone in a hotel in Omaha to start the negotiations. Insisting that the case was "much too important to trust to the lawyers," Norris stayed close to the process until its conclusion and made the substantive decisions at all critical points.

At the outset, Control Data's action in tackling the industry giant in a toe-to-toe confrontation seemed foolhardy in the extreme. The conventional wisdom in legal circles was that "this is an unsettleable case."[20] Wall Street and the general business community questioned Norris's judgment; one observer echoed the feelings of many when he said, "Bill Norris has lost his marbles." To inquiries from worried business friends, Norris responded that he knew what he was doing.

In the event, he certainly did. IBM paid a heavy price to get Control Data off its back. By that time it had eight or ten other lawsuits alleging unfair trade practices on its hands, as well as that of the government which had belatedly filed its own suit. The only question remaining was, what would Control Data take to settle?

Negotiations were conducted in greatest secrecy over a period of several months during which Norris used the code name *Bird* and Learson, *Link*. According to Norris, "IBM wanted any settlement it made to look like it was the sleeves out of their vest," or at least something relatively inconsequential.[21] They were anxious to avoid a large cash settlement. But they knew about Norris's interest in data services, and after hard bargaining culminating in a Minneapolis hotel room in December 1972, Norris and Learson finally worked out a deal.

Also present at that meeting were Richard G. Lareau (of the Oppenheimer law firm), Robert M. Price, and John W. Lacey for Control Data, and Paul Rizzo, one of Learson's senior officers, for IBM.[22] Norris and Learson met alone in the living room of the hotel suite and the other four retired to a bedroom, where they struggled lamely to find innocuous things to talk about. At long last they were invited to join Norris and Learson and informed that a settlement in principle had been reached. Many details remained to be worked out, but the framework of an agreement was in place. Its central feature was the lock, stock, and barrel transfer of the Service Bureau Corporation, IBM's subsidiary, to Control Data at a nominal price.[23]

Considering the value of the Service Bureau Corporation and all other cash and noncash elements of the agreement, it was, at over $100 million, the largest private settlement in U.S. antitrust history. Control Data valued the settlement at twice that figure.

The atmosphere in the hotel living room was tense. Lacey later recalled that he "had never seen a man so nervous" as Learson: "He had a book of matches, several books, and as he talked he tore the matches off one by one and threw them in the ashtray, and made all sorts of nervous gestures with his hands." Norris, in contrast, was cool and collected—"poker-faced," according to Lacey. Of the two, Learson was the one most under pressure. He would soon retire as chief executive officer of IBM, and he probably felt an obligation not to leave the lawsuit hanging over his successor's head. Getting rid of the incubus the Control Data action had become seemed a fitting swan song to his years in office, his final contribution to the company he had served so long and well. Norris, clearly the winner, was under no such strain, though he showed no overt signs of satisfaction.

That climactic meeting, like all those that had preceded it, was held in the utmost secrecy. As Norris and Learson were leaving the hotel with their advisors, each group careful to proceed separately, they were startled to find the lobby filled with reporters and photographers. Fearful that their tight security had been breached, they were relieved to learn that the cause of the excitement was "only a fire in the hotel."[24]

During the months of negotiation, bitterness between the parties ran deep. In addition to the formal settlement, Norris and Learson reached a verbal agreement to stop calling each other and each other's companies names in public.[25] In the years since, each party has had occasion to remind the other of this unwritten pledge.

One condition of the settlement was Control Data's agreement to destroy its computerized document index and the analysis sheets prepared by its attorneys. The Justice Department protested bitterly, accusing Control Data of destroying evidence needed for the government's case.[26] In response, Control Data's attorneys insisted that no evidence was destroyed—only the index to the evidence and their own analyses. Norris and his attorneys felt fully justified in this action. Both the index and the attorneys' "work product," which had cost millions of dollars and years of effort to produce, had been paid for by and were the property of Control Data.[27]

Control Data had repeatedly tried to persuade the government to use the voluminous evidence it had so painstakingly assembled and organized; unfortunately the Justice Department had simply not gotten around to it. As matters turned out, Control Data was well served by the government's dilatory tactics. Otherwise it would never have gained the benefits it did from the major concessions of the final settlement.

The government ultimately withdrew its suit. Sixteen more private antitrust suits were filed against IBM between 1965 and 1985; IBM won them all.[28]

―――――――――

The chief benefit of the settlement to Control Data and of greatest interest to Norris was the Service Bureau Corporation with its 1,700 experienced employees and 20,000 established customers.

SBC (as it continued to be known in Control Data for many years) was important to its new parent in three ways. First, it more than doubled the company's data services business, creating the "critical mass" Norris always considered important. Second, it greatly broadened Control Data's business and customer base by adding a strong business services component to an already well-established position in the engineering and scientific fields. Third, and perhaps most important, the Service Bureau brought with it a first-rate management, sales, and technical staff. At the time of the transfer, SBC had not yet reached a satisfactory level of profitability, but IBM had been confident of its prospects and had been putting some of its best people into it. Some years later, Norris commented with satisfaction he did not try to conceal, "They were really loaded with talent." Some of that talent found its way to the highest level of their new company; notable among these were Henry J. White and David P. White (no relation), both now senior officers of Control Data.

Naturally SBC came equipped with IBM computers, which meant that overnight Control Data became one of IBM's largest nongovernmental customers. The company's business data services continue to rely primarily on IBM mainframes, but these are now well surrounded by Control Data peripherals.

Under IBM, the role of the Service Bureau had been conceived primarily as that of pump-primer for selling mainframes. It had been a modest operation for many years, not expected to make much money as long as it helped attract potential buyers for IBM computers.[29] Norris's concept of data services was quite different; he saw them as businesses in their own right, not merely means for supporting mainframe sales.

At the time of the transfer to Control Data, SBC served clients through a nationwide telecommunications network based in an operations center in Cleveland, Ohio and through batch-processing facilities in major cities throughout the country. While offering a limited number of engineering applications through batch and timesharing modes, its work consisted primarily of serving the commercial and accounting needs of its clients.

Under Control Data management, SBC services were expanded worldwide by opening service centers in key cities in the principal industrial nations. Today the Cleveland facility continues chiefly to serve commercial applications on a timesharing basis. Much of the business data it handles for its tens of thousands of customers is critically important, and some is irreplaceable, so extraordinary measures for security have been taken. The facility is housed underground in a massive steel and concrete structure. It is equipped with substantial reserve computing capacity and its own electrical generating equipment that would enable it to continue functioning in the event of a serious natural disaster or civil disturbance. As someone once remarked, "The world could come to an end and Cleveland could run another two days."[30]

Global CYBERNET engineering and scientific services using Control Data mainframes are offered from a central facility in

Rockville, Maryland, just outside Washington, D.C. Through the Ohio and Rockville centers, Control Data's powerful data processing services are accessible through low-cost teletypewriter terminals from virtually anywhere in the world. Clients can easily and economically obtain services that would be inconvenient and prohibitively expensive if they were not available on so massive a scale.

Both data service groups use satellite communications and organize their work by time zones, serving successive areas of the earth as it turns on its axis. This permits workloads to be distributed evenly and operations to go on around the clock. Control Data today is the unchallenged world leader in computer services.

The IBM suit yielded substantial benefits to Control Data beyond the acquisition of SBC. One was IBM's decision in 1969 to "unbundle" its computer pricing. For many years IBM had held rigidly to a policy of including maintenance and software-related services in the price of each computer system it sold, all "bundled" together into a single purchase price. This meant that buyers of computer systems were forced to buy certain software and services whether they wanted them or not—a practice others in the industry, including Control Data, had no choice but to follow.

In the antitrust action brought by Control Data in late 1968, this policy was attacked as an "exclusionary restraint of trade." Bundled pricing, Control Data alleged, had virtually monopolized the computer industry, prevented competitors from vying for the services surrounding the operation and maintenance of large computer systems, and given IBM an unfair and illegal trade advantage. The suit demanded that it be discontinued.

Apparently IBM was already nervous about its bundling practice and had been considering its discontinuance. Actual announcement of a change in policy, however, came only after Control Data's action, a step the IBM unbundling task force attributed to the Control Data suit.[31] Control Data and its attorneys considered this "the first concrete results" of its litigation.[32]

Norris welcomed IBM's action, which he saw as the second truly important development in the computer industry in twenty years— the first being introduction of the transistor. "The ability to sell services without also selling hardware gave our [engineering and professional] services business a big boost," he explains.[33]

Engineering, professional, and data services, like peripheral products, had grown into major businesses by the time of Control Data's anniversary celebration. Between them, services and peripherals accounted for twice the sales and profits generated by the company's original business, computer mainframes.

From the beginning Control Data was chronically short of cash, and rapid growth placed a severe strain on its resources. One source of difficulty lay in the fact that most large computer systems were leased rather than sold outright, an industry practice set by IBM. For Control Data, the debt needed to finance its lease buildup had an unfavorable impact on its balance sheet, as lease payments rather than full purchase price did on its cash flow.

In 1967 Harold Hammer, then chief financial officer, prepared a ten-year projection of the financing needed to cover equipment on lease. He came up with the figure of $1 billion—higher, he joked, than anyone at Control Data could count. It was certainly too high for the company to handle by conventional means, especially when added to the already heavy burdens of rapid expansion and the insatiable demands of research and development required to keep up in an industry characterized by swiftly evolving technology. A possible answer lay in acquiring a finance company whose ability to leverage its equity could be used to advantage in financing the company's leases.

Norris and Hammer began looking about for a suitable candidate for acquisition, but after considering and discarding several possibilities decided that the only practical course would be for the company to create a finance company of its own. Steps were taken to organize CDC Leasing Company as a subsidiary, when by a stroke of sheer good luck for Control Data, Commercial Credit Company of Baltimore became the target of a hostile takeover attempt.

Founded in 1912, Commercial Credit had by the 1960s grown to be the second largest independent finance company in the United States, offering a wide range of credit, insurance, leasing, and related services. During the late 1960s, however, a combination of factors severely depressed the market value of its stock and made it a prime takeover target. The Commercial Credit board was distressed but not surprised when such a move was initiated in April of 1968 by Laurence A. Tisch, chairman of Loew's Theatres, Inc. The board fought back. Knowing how vulnerable it was, it also began seeking another acquirer whose intentions would inspire more confidence than those of Tisch.

Albert Gordon, managing partner of the investment firm Kidder Peabody and a longtime member of the Commercial Credit board, was assigned the task of finding such an acquirer. He put his analysts to work to identify companies whose financial circumstances might make Commercial Credit attractive to them, and Control Data, with its lease-financing problems, emerged as a likely possibility. A member of the Kidder Peabody firm telephoned Hammer, who at the time was in a planning meeting but left to take the call. On returning to the meeting, Hammer passed a note to Norris asking if he would be interested in buying Commercial Credit. Norris scrawled a one-word reply: "Yes."

"But they're awfully big," Hammer wrote back.

"So much the better," scrawled Norris, and beckoned Hammer out of the room to discuss the matter in more detail.[34]

Hammer and Robert Leach were dispatched to New York, where they met with Gordon, his staff, and the top two officers of Commercial Credit, president and chief executive Donald S. Jones and chairman LeBaron Willard. Meanwhile Norris went fishing at his favorite spot in northern Minnesota, where his only means of communication with the outside world was the telephone at a country store some miles away. By this somewhat cumbersome means, he was kept advised of the course of negotiations, and over a weekend the basic structure of a deal was worked out whereby Commercial Credit Company became a wholly owned subsidiary of Control Data Corporation. In this short-order fashion was put together one of the most unusual combinations in American business history.[35]

It was an odd couple. Control Data was a colorful, aggressive company in the highly volatile, fast-moving computer industry; Commercial Credit was a rather staid firm in the relatively stable finance industry (this was before deregulation). Control Data brought to the marriage assets of $350 million and annual earnings of $8.2 million; Commercial Credit's dowry was $3.4 *billion* in assets and annual earnings three and a half times greater than those of its acquirer.

Business Week carried its story of the agreement under the heading, "Marrying for Money,"[36] and there was wide speculation as to how it would work out. Some was frankly negative; the stock market's response to the acquisition was to bid down Control Data's stock by 11 points. Wall Street could not understand why a high-tech, rapid-growth company like Control Data would tie itself to what looked like a stodgy, slow-growth finance company.

There was considerable apprehension on Control Data's home front, too. Members of Norris's own Executive Council recognized the positive short-term advantages but feared that Commercial Credit would one day be a drag on earnings. Norris listened to the objections, then went ahead anyway. One of the council members later admitted, "Maybe we were a little more arrogant than we should have been."[37]

Despite great cultural and economic disparities, the match proved a good one on the whole for both parties. Commercial Credit realized an immediate benefit: avoidance of an unwelcome takeover. To preserve credibility in the financial community, it retained its corporate autonomy and its own board. Control Data had a solution to its leasing problems: For the first time in its history, it had ample means for financing this important part of its business.

From 1968 through 1985, Commercial Credit added $733.7 million to Control Data's earnings and paid its parent $448.3 million in dividends.[38] During three periods of serious financial stringency— 1969–70, 1974–75, and 1984–85—Commercial Credit's earning power helped enable its parent to survive sharp downturns in the computer industry.

At first Commercial Credit management, led by Jones and Willard, expected that the two companies would continue to operate more-or-less independently—as a computer company headquartered in Minneapolis and a finance company in Baltimore—with the principal change being that Commercial Credit would have a single stockholder instead of thousands. (Someone joked that CCC would now be able to hold its annual shareholders' meetings in a telephone booth, in the style of Superman.) Norris, however, had different ideas. "We're not going to run that company like a conglomerate," he said, meaning that he wasn't about to let it run itself even if it continued producing satisfactory results.

He saw many more possibilities in the merger than relief from his financing troubles alone. He formed an ad hoc committee composed of senior executives from both companies and charged them with working out strategies, methods, and amounts by which Commercial Credit could support the Control Data lease base and otherwise integrate its business activities with those of Control Data. The committee usually met in Chicago—"neutral territory" that was easily reached from both Minneapolis and Baltimore.

In the beginning it was evident that Jones and Willard were very uneasy. They feared that unless they took care to protect Commercial Credit's assets their company would be plundered by its acquirer. Banks and other sources of funding for Commercial Credit were apprehensive as well; they had to be convinced that adequate safeguards had been erected between the two companies to prevent an irresponsible upflow of financial assets.

John W. Lacey, a member of the committee and at that time head of the Control Data long-range planning function, worked closely with Jones and Willard in advance of the meetings to convince them that financing Control Data leases was a better-than-ordinary business opportunity, not a threat. He pointed out that the lease base was made up of prestigious accounts such as government agencies, major universities, large companies, and other creditworthy customers that could afford Control Data's big scientific mainframes. When Lacey reworked Hammer's original $1 billion estimate of Control Data's needs, he reduced the figure to a more realistic $500 million. This was still a great deal of money, but it did not seem excessive in terms of Commercial Credit's assets, which at the time were in the $4 to $5 billion range.[39]

Control Data enjoyed the leasing flexibility that resulted from the acquisition. Arrangements could now be worked out cooperatively between Control Data, Commercial Credit, and the customer to tailor leases to the customer's needs—a significant selling aid. It was understood that Commercial Credit would evaluate the customer's creditworthiness, uninfluenced by the fact that Control Data was a party to the transaction. All dealings were strictly at arms' length.

Norris saw numerous opportunities for synergism between the two quite dissimilar companies; in his mind, it was "the marriage of the century." Members of the Control Data board and some of its top officers became directors of Commercial Credit, and vice versa. There was likewise an exchange of executives, to the benefit of both organizations. Norris found, however, that corporate cultures are extremely difficult to change.[40]

Justifiably or not, Norris felt that Commercial Credit had fallen into a rut and was missing many opportunities for growth. One of these was in international operations, and his first major effort was to urge that Commercial Credit broaden its scope by going overseas. For Norris, it was an article of faith that for a company to be viable today it had to be international. Commercial Credit management resisted, but when it became clear that Norris was not going to back down, it reluctantly agreed to an international venture. Early results were mixed, but in time this became Commercial Credit's most profitable operation. Even so, some old-line executives remained bitter at having been forced to do something they did not want to do.

Norris also saw the possibility of using computer technology to improve the efficiency of Commercial Credit's consumer lending business. He appointed a group with expertise in both credit management and data processing to study how this might be done. The result was CYBERLOAN, a computerized system that analyzed loan applications to determine the creditworthiness of the customer, generated the documents for the loan agreement, created and maintained the records of the account, followed up on delinquencies, and produced all necessary management reports. The system served the needs of Commercial Credit's consumer finance business very well, but was never adapted successfully to its business finance operations.

Because all consumer lending institutions—banks, credit unions, savings and loans—follow very similar procedures, it was clear in Norris's mind that a sizable external market could be developed for CYBERLOAN. Responsibility for this applications service was transferred to what is now the General Business Services unit of Control Data's data service operations. It has since been built into a profitable business, and Commercial Credit is one of its major customers.

Norris was an early proponent of electronic funds transfer. He believed that financial institutions would soon have to rely much more heavily on electronic information systems, and that much of their business, both internal and external, would be conducted in that way. He was particularly taken with the thought of cooperating with Commercial Credit to develop a service that could be used by Commercial Credit and sold to other financial houses as well. The two companies worked on the project off and on for four or five years, but the idea never got very far.

In Norris's eyes, Commercial Credit was a staid and uninspired organization that seemed content to plod along and lacked the strong marketing orientation needed to move in new directions with greater growth potential. Hoping to remedy that situation, he transferred Paul G. Miller from Minneapolis to Baltimore in 1975. Miller was given the job of heading Commercial Credit and breathing new life into its management. He had been the architect of Control Data's successful computer systems marketing program, and Norris felt that the talents he displayed in that role were precisely what Commercial Credit needed.

One of Miller's first actions was to create a task force to explore the possibilities of expanding Commercial Credit's business into new fields. Of all the options explored, real estate seemed the most promising. Over the next several years, two established real estate organizations, Relocation Realty and Electronic Realty Associates (ERA) were acquired, a mortgage company was formed, and savings and loan charters were secured. The plan looked good on paper but, as Miller recalls, "never blossomed as we thought it would," chiefly because of difficulties encountered in getting the various acquired parts to work together.[41] The effort was eventually abandoned and the acquisitions sold.

By the latter part of the 1970s, Norris was becoming increasingly concerned with the problems of joblessness in the United States and interested in the job-creating potentials of small businesses. He saw a vast potential market for services that could be provided by the combined resources of Control Data and Commercial Credit. Four types of services that could meet the needs of small businesses had already been created by the two companies as discrete operations: small business finance, which Norris had instructed Commercial Credit to strengthen; training programs using Control Data's computer-based PLATO education system and delivered through Learning Centers, for which Commercial Credit had been given responsibility; the batch processing services that had come with the acquisition of SBC, and for which small businesses were already the principal clients; and a nascent retail marketing activity whose functions (other than to serve small business) were not yet clearly defined.

Norris believed that bringing these four separate operations together into an integrated organization would meet the needs of a broad spectrum of the small-business community. Thus was born the Business Centers program, an ambitious one for which Commercial Credit was given responsibility. Norris had originally visualized using local Commercial Credit offices as nuclei for the Business Centers, but this proved impractical. In a vain effort to meet Norris's high hopes, Commercial Credit overshot the mark and began opening new offices that proved far too elegant and overstaffed.

"The Business Centers lost a lot of money," Norris says, "and the whole concept got a black eye. If they had done what I really had in mind, they would have added a few people and a little bit of space [and the Centers] could have been very successful because the market was there and it was just a question of how to serve it profitably."[42]

The Commercial Credit acquisition accomplished its original goals: It solved the problem of financing Control Data's lease base, and it proved to be a profitable corporate investment. It failed, however, to fulfill some of Norris's hopes and dreams. Yet he remained philosophical: "All in all, Commercial Credit served Control Data very well. It's just that we didn't get the maximum potential out of it."[43]

Norris did not succeed in his efforts to make significant changes in Commercial Credit's culture. Even though he put his own men in key positions, it remained essentially the same stable (Norris would say stodgy) financial house it was when it became Control Data's reluctant financial ward. Not surprisingly, Commercial Credit found Control Data's culture equally uncomfortable.

It did not turn out to be "the marriage of the century" after all. But as sometimes happens with marriages of convenience, this one worked out fairly well.

———————————————

Soon after founding Control Data Corporation and starting to build giant computers, Norris began to branch into new lines of business. *Branch* is the right verb. The trunk of what became the Control Data tree was the large-scale computer. *From* that trunk grew the peripheral products business, data services, and engineering and professional services, and *to* that trunk were grafted the financial and related services that came with the acquisition of Commercial Credit Company. In due course he would add educational and training services and a complex array of human and economic development services that would make Control Data Corporation one of the most fascinating enterprises in U.S. corporate history.

CHAPTER 5

The PLATO Story

While Control Data's big computer, peripheral products, and services businesses were developing, another significant technical and business innovation was reaching maturity. This was the PLATO system of computer-based instruction, a sophisticated application of computer technology to the teaching and learning process.

While still in the navy during World War II, Commander Norris had begun thinking about the possibilities of using computers for training purposes. He became acquainted with Edwin A. Link, inventor of the Link Trainer, a device simulating an airplane cockpit during takeoff, flight, and landing used widely during the war and since for training pilots. "He was a nice person," Norris recalls, "but arrogant as hell, like most inventors. In talking with him, I pointed out that [in the cryptological unit where Norris was working] we had some digital circuitry that was coming along and could replace the analog circuitry he was using and make the trainer a lot more flexible. He got quite excited about it," but under the pressure of war work nothing further was done at the time.[1]

After the war, at Engineering Research Associates (ERA), Norris toyed with the idea again, but "on looking into it found it would be grossly uneconomical because the cost of the circuitry was just too high." Nevertheless, the possibilities continued to intrigue him as he moved from ERA to Sperry and finally to Control Data, but because of other pressing matters he pushed it aside.

Then one day in 1960 Harold Brooke, one of his star salesmen, returned from a visit to the University of Illinois where he had just written an order for a 1604 computer. Brooke reported to Norris that some interesting work was going on there directed toward adapting computers to instructional uses. Norris's interest was immediately aroused, and he directed Brooke to follow developments closely and keep him informed. This was the beginning of Norris's and Control Data's long and controversial involvement with the PLATO system of computer-based education and training.

———————

Those at the University of Illinois who named the system obviously thought of the name first and then looked for words for which PLATO could be the acronym. These are somewhat less than memorable: *Programmed Logic for Automated Teaching Operations.* Memorable or not, a more fitting name than PLATO could hardly have been found.

It was certainly better than the one the system had first been given. The screen of the original terminal consisted of two sheets of glass separated by helium gas that was activated by electronic impulses to produce images; literal-minded technicians had dubbed it a "gaseous discharge device." When a secretary in the laboratory pointed out that this phrase had connotations that were not very nice, the search began for a more appropriate name, and PLATO was the happy result.

The idea for what became the PLATO system originated at the University of Illinois in 1959 when Chalmers Sherwin, professor of physics, pointed out to William Everett, dean of the College of Engineering, that with the growing reliability of computers "we ought to be looking at the possibility of using them for teaching."[2] Everett referred the matter to Professor Daniel Alpert, director of the university's Coordinated Science Laboratory, a unit engaged in advanced radar research involving extensive use of computers.

Alpert appointed a committee of professional educators and computer scientists who held a series of fruitless meetings over a period of several months. These sessions were marked by sharp disagreements between the two groups, and Alpert reluctantly concluded that Sherwin's idea, however intriguing, was impractical. But before transmitting his report to the dean, Alpert showed a copy to one of his young assistants, newly degreed Dr. Donald Bitzer, and asked for his opinion.

Bitzer took strong exception to Alpert's conclusion. He told Alpert that he had already been thinking about ways to use old radar equipment as part of an interface for teaching with a computer, and asked Alpert to delay his report until he could test some of the ideas forming in his mind. Assisted by a programmer and a technician, Bitzer went to work.

By ingeniously rigging together radar-scanning and television equipment with various other devices found in the laboratory, Bitzer was able in a few weeks' time to create a terminal capable of interacting with a central computer to perform instructional functions. Although the machine and the program that ran it were crude by later standards, they demonstrated the practicability of the basic concept. Bitzer was given the go-ahead to take it further.

The increasing demands of Bitzer's staff and other units of the laboratory for computer time soon exceeded what the university's existing system could supply. The pioneering but aging Illiac I, designed during the 1940s by U of I scientists, was used by researchers in many different parts of the university. Funding was secured to lease one of Control Data's high-powered 1604s for the Coordinated Science Laboratory's exclusive use. The new equipment was operational by 1961, making it possible to give Bitzer and his group an hour a day of computer time instead of fifteen minutes. This was a substantial improvement, but far short of the group's growing needs. Norris followed these developments closely. Impressed with Bitzer's progress, he made overtures through Brooke to help the young scientist satisfy his insatiable appetite for computer time by providing him a powerful computer for his own use and under his direct control.[3]

As it happened, about that time one of Control Data's 1604 computers was being taken out of service. Norris proposed that it be refurbished and installed rent-free on university premises for the use of the PLATO group. Although not a new machine, its market value was still substantial. The only costs to the university would be those of insurance and maintenance; otherwise, the university's sole obligation would be to share information and technology. The entire transaction was effected by a half-page letter. Thus was launched one of the most fruitful academic/corporate collaborations ever undertaken.

The 1604 was installed in Bitzer's laboratory in 1963 and replaced from time to time thereafter by still more powerful computers as they became available. In the early days of the collaboration, the National Science Foundation provided valued support, but the bulk of the resources supplied came from the university and Control Data.

Although it was clear from at least 1967 on that the PLATO concept was sound, a great deal of time and money were required to get the system fully operational, and it was not until 1975 that it had reached a point where it could be offered commercially. Developing the technology was a common effort shared by both the university and the company, but moving it into the marketplace was Control Data's responsibility.

The technology that emerged from this cooperative arrangement was unique. Remarkably versatile and adaptable, PLATO can handle instructional material from kindergarten through postdoctoral levels. It teaches elementary third-grade arithmetic and higher mathematics with equal ease. Courses are available in all the modern European languages, in medieval English, and in classical Latin. Among its other language capabilities, PLATO handles Pharsi and Japanese and can master other written languages as needed.

PLATO programs include *courseware*, instructional materials for direct use by students; tools for teachers and administrators to use in managing courses; and an authoring program that enables users to modify existing courseware or write their own.

An important feature of the system is its interactive capability. Courseware can be written to require the student and the computer to talk back and forth to each other, with each rejoinder being responsive to the preceding statement. (Note the parallel to the philosopher Plato's Socratic dialogues.) An almost human give-and-take relationship develops between student and computer. The computer can address the student by name, correct gently, and compliment as deserved. Animated graphics can be incorporated as well.

The managing programs (collectively known as CMI, for *computer-managed instruction*) are a critical element of the PLATO system because they facilitate the individualized instruction that is the greatest single advantage of computer-based education. By definition, computer-based education is delivered through computer terminals, which enables it to employ an individualized pattern of instruction because an interactive terminal can be used by only one person at a time. If students move ahead at different speeds (rather than all together, as in the traditional classroom), they must be tested to determine whether they have mastered a course segment before being allowed to move on to the next. And they must be able to take the tests when *they* are ready. Teachers need ways to tell where each student is in the course, how well each is doing, who is having trouble, and the like. Administrators need means for assessing the progress being made in each classroom and in the school as a whole. CMI programs generate this information automatically, relieving the teacher of much of the drudgework of the traditional classroom.

A significant feature of PLATO is that it changes the dependent/ independent variables of the learning process. In traditional education, students attend class for a fixed period of time and the amount of learning that takes place is variable. With PLATO just the opposite is true: The amount of learning is fixed, but how long it takes is variable. Everyone masters the same body of knowledge, but some take longer (or move faster) than others. PLATO's management capabilities are what make this possible.

Many elementary schools are facing a serious shortage of competent math and science teachers; with PLATO's help, a relatively unskilled teacher can handle these subjects effectively. Some schools cannot even consider offering certain subjects; with PLATO, there are virtually no limits. In 1985 the PLATO system based at the University of Georgia delivered over 100,000 hours of Latin instruction to secondary schools around the state, many of which would not otherwise have been able to offer the course.

Some universities, including the University of Illinois, have converted large segments of their curricula in certain fields to delivery by PLATO. Through Control Data facilities, PLATO trains and tests airplane pilots, computer technicians and programmers, managers, and nurses, and administers tests to securities salespeople. The army uses PLATO to train officers and enlisted men. To help meet the current shortage of engineers, an entire undergraduate engineering program, largely PLATO-based, has been designed and is being developed in cooperation with a consortium of seven engineering schools.

What Norris likes best about PLATO is the fact that it allows students to progress at their own rate. His feelings on this score are probably rooted in his own experience in a one-room school, about as far away from high technology as one can get. He attributes the good education he and his sisters received there to the ungraded environment and the time the teachers spent with individual students. With eight children of his own who attended more modern schools, he is acutely aware of the pressures that the graded school system places on students; once a child falls behind or out of step with the class, boredom sets in and the hope of catching up is slim. Norris sees computer-based instruction as bringing back the best features of the schooling he enjoyed.

As late as the early 1970s, however, all this was in the future. There was a great deal yet to learn about how to use the emerging technology in actual teaching processes. For Control Data, this began with internal applications.

One was the training of new employees in Engineering Services. Previously an introductory course in digital computing had been offered by traditional means; in 1973 Norris ordered it converted to PLATO. Other technical and management training programs were reorganized for computer-based delivery, and each successive application enhanced the skill of the conversion process and the effectiveness of the training.[4] But it was the introduction of PLATO to the work of the Control Data Institutes that provided the first significant experience in its large-scale use for educational purposes.

The first Control Data Institute had been established in 1965[5] to train computer technicians and programmers for the industry as well as the company. At the time there was no trained labor pool on which the computer industry could draw, and the schools and colleges offered little in the way of useful technical preparation. The industry had to provide its own technical education, a major operating expense. Norris recognized that here was a significant unmet need that Control Data could help serve by converting its in-house training programs into revenue-generating vocational schools—once again, "selling what we learn."

Control Data's internal training program was modified to meet the broader requirements of the industry as a whole, and professional educators were employed to ensure that state accreditation requirements were met. Two courses of instruction were offered, Computer Technician and Computer Programming and Operations, each requiring 1,000 hours of classroom and laboratory work over approximately a ten-month period. The educational methods used were standard—lectures and discussions, printed texts, the chalkboard, paper and pencil exercises.

From the beginning, the institutes had cost problems, and "it began to surface in the back of [Norris's] mind that if we could get the technology to replace some of the labor...we'd have a leg up." Unfortunately, "it was too early, and the technology was too costly, but it was still an element in my thinking." By 1974, however, the technology had advanced to a point where in Norris's judgment it could be used to advantage in the institutes, and he ordered them to "PLATOize" their instruction, not only to help control costs but "as a means for introducing the computer into the educational process."[6]

There was considerable resistance among the institutes' managers, who had only recently achieved borderline profitability after a long struggle and who feared that the cost of installing PLATO would throw them back into a loss position. One of them lamented that he had just started holding his head up among his peers, and now he was going to have to return to being sensitive about telling people where he worked.[7] Despite Norris's insistence, little progress was made in converting to PLATO until all educational activities, including the institutes, were grouped into the Education Company and placed under John Lacey's direction in 1977.[8]

Even under Lacey's close supervision, "PLATOizing" the institute curriculum still required the better part of two years and the investment of over $1 million in courseware and training. There were two major tasks to be accomplished. Teaching materials had to be converted from written to electronic media, and teachers had to learn to be *managers* rather than merely *purveyors* of instruction.

Neither task was easy. Converting textbooks into courseware involved more than simply translating the written page into images for the monitor screen. Moving from time-based to mastery-based education required that steps in the instructional process be thought through much more clearly, and that the learning objectives of each step be defined much more precisely. Material had to be organized and presented differently to utilize the capabilities of the computer. A PLATO Learning Management system (quickly known as *PLM*) had to be created to facilitate substitution of individualized computer-based instruction for group classroom work.

Meanwhile, institute instructors feared that if PLATO proved as efficient as management claimed it would, many of them would be out on the streets looking for work. They were skeptical of assurances that the result would be to increase enrollments rather than decrease staff. Their concern proved unfounded; enrollments rose, and more rather than fewer teachers were needed. The instructors found they now had more time to spend counseling individual students and would have resisted any effort to return to the old ways.

Conversion to PLATO saved the institutes: Its greater flexibility and cost-effectiveness moved them from marginal to comfortable profitability. A major problem in the past had been the rigidity of traditional instruction. New classes had to start on specified dates regardless of whether all the seats were filled, and empty seats stayed empty until the next new class started ten months later. Prospective students applying late had to wait weeks or months for the next class, and many were lost in the interim. All members of a class finished at the same time regardless of ability.

PLATO changed all that. Newcomers could start at any time, empty seats could be filled as the class went along, and students could complete the course when they demonstrated mastery of the subject matter. For some, this meant starting work earlier than usual; for others, it meant delaying their job search until they were fully prepared and capable.

From the company's standpoint, moving from group to individual instruction, filling seats promptly as new students enrolled, certifying students as soon as they were ready, and relieving teachers of the humdrum chores of drill and practice, testing, and record-keeping made it possible to increase materially the number of students per teacher per class and to boost the productivity of the institutes by some 20 to 25 percent.[9] In states without sharp restrictions on student/teacher ratios, productivity doubled, with significant gains in the quality of learning. By 1979 the institutes were generating a rate of gross profit well above that of the total company. Regrettably, this halcyon period was short-lived.

After converting to PLATO, the Control Data Institutes had the chance to become what one insider calls "the IBM of vocational education." The demand for technical education was on the rise, and Control Data had the means to deliver it. As it turned out, however, further growth was modest, and today the institutes occupy a minor place in the field and enjoy only a modest rate of return.

That Control Data did not realize the promise of the institutes is attributable to a number of factors. Part of the problem was failure to plow back into the institutes enough of the profits they earned to maintain their technological leadership; a disproportionate share of those profits seems to have been used to finance other startup activities in education.

A more immediate problem was a temporary decrease in 1982 in the demand for vocational education and delayed response in shrinking costs accordingly. The costs problem was complicated by the failure of the institutes to grasp the significance of the microcomputer, which made it possible to deliver much of the instructional material locally at far less expense. "They were told about it," Norris said later, "but they didn't do anything about it. Other vocational schools started using microcomputers, and suddenly our labor costs were out of line."[10]

A more intransigent problem, of which costs were a part, lay in the fact that with the coming of keener local competition, the market for vocational education changed and the institutes failed to adapt quickly enough to the new competitive realities. This highlighted one of Control Data's perennial problems: weakness in consumer marketing skills. The company has always done well in marketing computer systems, OEM products, and sophisticated engineering, professional, and business services, but it has never fully mastered the art of selling in retail markets.[11]

Despite these difficulties, Norris insists that "the institutes were not a monumental screw-up. They have a solid base on which to build, and they're coming back strong."[12] Today there are twenty-five Control Data Institutes operating in the United States plus others in Canada, Europe, and Australia. In the past twenty years, they have graduated over 132,000 students, 78,000 in the United States and 54,000 abroad.[13] About 60 percent of all instruction is via PLATO, and Norris thinks "it can go much higher"—about 75 percent is the share he has in mind.[14]

Most important, however, the institutes provided an opportunity to convert PLATO from an interesting laboratory exercise into an effective educational program. It was a rich learning experience that laid solid foundations for PLATO's future.

By 1975 PLATO was ready for the external market, but the market was not ready for PLATO. It had to be developed, and that proved more difficult than anticipated.[15] The problem lay partly in PLATO's parentage: a great research university and a high-technology company. From the university's standpoint, PLATO meant sophisticated, high-level courseware; from Control Data's, it meant large mainframe computers serving remote terminals through long distance telephone lines in the same manner as its well-established data services business. Unfortunately, neither suited the primary and secondary school markets in which Norris was most interested.

It was in these markets that Norris saw the most pressing needs and the greatest opportunities. On more than one occasion he has called attention to the fact that "As a country, we are becoming less and less capable of coping with the rapidly increasing supply of information, and that is impeding our productivity." But the human side of the problem troubles him most. "Underprivileged and disabled persons are being neglected. Gifted students are not being challenged. Many high schools are producing a steady stream of functional illiterates,"[16] a fact he sees as a grave threat to the kind of technology-based society America has become. Norris is acutely alarmed that the United States ranks in forty-ninth place among the nations of the world in literacy.[17] Dr. Walter H. Bruning, who has headed Control Data's efforts at the elementary and high school levels since 1984, reflects Norris's thinking accurately in his statement that "Unless we stem the illiteracy tide now, we are headed toward a society with enormous disparity between the educated wealthy minority and the relatively uneducated poor majority. It doesn't take much imagination to realize the economic and cultural problems such a chasm will create."[18]

Norris was (and is) painfully aware that much of the nation's school system faces serious financial difficulties, and some of it is already bankrupt; that the costs of conventional education are mounting inexorably; and that the quality of education is deteriorating as hard-pressed school boards try to make ends meet. Norris sees in PLATO the effective answer to both the cost and quality problems of the educational system. And he sees in the wide adoption of PLATO the means for greatly broadening Control Data's business base.

Unlike the costs of labor-intensive conventional teaching, those of capital-intensive PLATO have fallen steadily and will continue to drop as computer technologies advance. On the quality side, Norris envisions PLATO taking over much of the monotonous routine of the traditional classroom, freeing teachers for more personal and individualized interaction with students. Regarding both cost and quality, Norris sees PLATO as the means for a quantum improvement in educational productivity. There are those, both inside and outside the company, who agree with him, and those who do not. But before any of this was even remotely possible, Control Data had a lot to learn, and the learning process was long, hard, and expensive.

The first hurdle was the lack of courseware at the elementary and high school level. A great deal of excellent material had been generated at the University of Illinois. Most of it, however, was fragmentary, designed to supplement classroom lectures rather than serve as units of instruction. The bits and pieces were valuable but it was difficult to use them as building-blocks for courses, much less entire curricula.

It quickly became apparent that Control Data would have to write its own courseware, and a staff of professional educators was recruited for the purpose. Writing courseware, however, proved to be quite different from writing either textbooks or standard computer programs, so new sets of skills had to be learned. The lack of agreed-on pedagogy in some areas was yet another source of difficulty. It is fairly easy to determine whether an accounting or scientific program is right; either it works or it doesn't. But there is more than one way to teach spelling, and professionals in the field are in sharp disagreement over which is best. Also, writing courseware is much more dependent on the designer who structures the course than on the programmer who carries out the designer's plans. It is the designer's task to build in the full benefits of PLATO, and this required breaking new ground in pedagogy. Finally, writing curricula for a program extending from elementary school through high school was a formidable undertaking that would take years to accomplish, and it was obvious that a sharper initial focus was needed.

After consulting with William J. Ridley, a professional educator newly hired to help implement the PLATO program, Norris decided to address the dropout segment of the age sixteen to twenty-four population, a disadvantaged group poorly served by traditional education and one for which he had special personal sympathy. Tentative contacts had made clear that the level of computer sophistication among educators was generally low, and that an effort to introduce PLATO into regular schoolwork was more likely to be viewed as a threat than a boon. A program for school dropouts would demonstrate the advantages of computer-based education and could be the means for opening doors into the education system proper.

This involved building a basic skills curriculum covering reading, mathematics, and language arts for grades three though eight and a high school curriculum covering these subjects plus social studies and science for grades nine through twelve. The basic skills portion would bring students to the level of functional literacy; the high school portion would qualify them for the high school equivalency certificate. Training in job-seeking and work-group skills would be added to enhance students' prospects for employment.

In the latter part of 1976, Norris ordered full steam ahead, but because the project met with strong resistance at the operating level he agreed to fund the first year's work from his discretionary "chairman's budget," a fiscal device he had established that enabled him to direct executives to undertake tasks in which he was especially interested.[19] Under Ridley's direction, a staff of competent educational psychologists was recruited. By the end of 1978 the first version of the basic skills curriculum was ready to go; this was followed two years later by the high school equivalency curriculum. Thus, by 1980 Control Data and PLATO were ready with a complete program of remedial instruction for grades three through twelve.

Creating these programs was not easy. Not only was it necessary to learn new skills for designing and writing courseware, but those who were involved with the project also found that important parts of the teaching and learning process were not well understood even in academic circles. Educators were accustomed to relying on textbook publishers to organize teaching materials into logically sequenced learning events. But the experience of those publishers was confined chiefly to printed matter and offered only limited guidance to the task of organizing instruction for effective delivery by *electronic* means. Control Data's staff had to learn mainly on their own, often by trial and error.

The difficulty was not the hardware, which was already well beyond existing capacity to use it to full advantage. Rather, the problem lay in learning how to arrange intellectual materials into a coherent program that interacted, taught, tested, recorded, and moved students on to the next step. The task was completed only by diligent effort—and with constant prodding from Norris.

Both the basic and the high school skills curricula were marketed through the company's Fair Break employment readiness program and its chain of Learning Centers set up in key cities to make the program more readily available to a broader public. Several sales were made to state penal institutions, with dramatic improvements in the quality of education offered to inmates. Despite the demonstrated success of these applications, however, neither the public school community nor the private and parochial schools showed much interest in PLATO.

The chief barrier was cost. Installing PLATO involved buying or leasing several terminals for use by teachers and students, plus monthly long-distance telephone charges to connect the terminals with the central computer in Minneapolis (or Urbana, for schools using the University of Illinois computer). PLATO at that time was simply beyond the means of all but a very few schools.

Norris was disappointed in the failure of his cherished PLATO to gain a foothold in the traditional educational market. He took some comfort in the fact that his staff had learned to organize and present instructional materials in a new way—electronically—and remained confident that sooner or later means would be found to put PLATO into the schools.

One opportunity that looked promising proved abortive through no fault of PLATO or Control Data. Recognizing that developing countries have a special need for vocational education, Norris had his staff survey the field. Iran under the Shah was moving rapidly toward becoming an industrialized nation, but the shortage of technically trained personnel was proving to be a serious obstacle. In 1977 a vocational training institute employing fully individualized instruction was opened in Teheran, and a second was under construction in Isfahan. The ultimate goal was a countrywide network making extensive use of PLATO and capable of turning out as many as 5,000 graduates a year. Before the project could progress beyond this modest but promising start, the Shah was overthrown, and the Ayatollah Khomeini's interests lay in fields other than technical education.[20]

As previously noted, Control Data itself makes extensive use of PLATO for training purposes, the results of which are seen in the company's high level of employee productivity. Through the nationwide network of Control Data Institutes, Learning Centers, Business and Technology Centers, and agro-business dealerships, PLATO is bringing instructional services to hundreds of organizations and tens of thousands of people. PLATO plays a large role in a number of Control Data's most significant current undertakings, such as the Employment Readiness program for the hard-core unemployed and efforts to aid small businesses and family farms, to teach wellness in industry, and to provide meaningful employment to the homebound handicapped. PLATO pervades all of Control Data's businesses and, as such, is an effective selling tool for the company's highest-value products and services. Peripheral product and mainframe customers may have their personnel trained by PLATO. A program for training supercomputer programmers supports the sale of multimillion-dollar installations.

Despite the setbacks, Norris contends that the benefits PLATO has brought to Control Data go far beyond the income it generates from outside education and training applications. Not only has it resulted in a multitude of technology spinoffs; its effects have been felt throughout the entire corporation.

═══════════════════

Over a period of several years, Control Data acquired considerable experience and skill in preparing and delivering computer-based education. Problems, however, remained.

The original PLATO system was based on a central mainframe computer that was accessed by remote terminals via telephone lines. By the late 1970s one mainframe was operated at the University of Illinois in Urbana and served Illinois schools, and others were operated by Control Data in Minneapolis and on both coasts to serve other educational and commercial clients. Systems were also installed at the University of Delaware, Florida State University, the University of Georgia, and the University of Nebraska, each serving its own faculty and public schools in its state, and in May of 1986 Boise State University in Idaho proudly announced that "PLATO has joined our faculty." Another system is operational at the University of Brussels in Belgium.

For school systems and other clients large enough to use them, mainframes could be installed on their own premises and dedicated to their special purposes. Courseware and managing and authoring programs could be stored in the mainframe and called up as needed. There were many advantages to this system; supported by extended core storage (ECS), the capacity of the mainframe was virtually unlimited, which meant that a rich variety and depth of instructional resources could be readily available. But access to a central computer by telephone is expensive, and lease or purchase of a mainframe with the additional storage needed at that time required a major expenditure that few potential users were able or willing to shoulder.

Then came the personal computer, which revolutionized all computer delivery systems by sharply reducing or completely freeing them from their dependence on central mainframes. When first introduced, personal computers quickly became popular, and it appeared that they would enjoy a wide market in both schools and homes. Schools around the country began buying Apples, IBMs, and other desktop equipment at a rapid rate, as did consumers. For some time, it appeared that personal computers would become standard features in a large share of all U.S. households, and that home study, supplementing work at school, would be one of their primary uses. In this event, the primary vehicle for delivering instructional materials would be inexpensive diskettes (the ubiquitous "floppy disks") rather than local terminals connected by wire to distant mainframes.

Attracted by what seemed likely to become a very large combination school and home market for educational materials, Control Data in 1981 brought out a microcomputer of its own, the CD110, and entered into an agreement with Texas Instruments Company of Dallas to market PLATO courseware rewritten in diskette form for TI's stand-alone microcomputers. The choice of TI was based on the merits of its equipment and its presumed strength in the fast-moving personal computer field, a market with which Control Data was unfamiliar. This proved to be a costly mistake. Less than a year later, following the completion of a large part of the courseware conversion process, TI announced its withdrawal from the personal computer field, leaving Control Data high and dry.

Conceding the popularity of Apple and IBM PCs, Control Data mounted a concerted effort to reconvert its courseware for use on these models. But writing, rewriting, and re-rewriting courseware is expensive and time-consuming, and much valuable time had already been lost. Moreover, by 1983 Norris was starting to have grave doubts about the strategy.

For one thing, the large school and home market for educational materials in diskette form had failed to materialize. Schools found that stand-alone computers were much more difficult to use for instructional purposes than they had anticipated, and homeowners proved to be more interested in word processing and spreadsheet analysis than in helping Johnny learn to read.

Also, from the vendor's standpoint, selling diskettes is a highly competitive, low-margin retail business for which Control Data had little appetite or aptitude. And as more than one software company has learned to its sorrow, programs released on diskette are virtually impossible to protect from pirating. Before too much more valuable time had been lost, Norris and his associates reached the conclusion that, for Control Data's purposes, a wiser course would be to concentrate on the *delivery of educational services* rather than rely too heavily on the *sale of educational products*. This was a course for which Control Data had unique experience and capabilities.

By this time it was evident that the opportunity offered Control Data by the microprocessor lay not in marketing its own microprocessor or courseware in diskette form, but in modifying the classic PLATO delivery system to maximize the inherent advantages of the personal computer.

The original PLATO terminals were "dumb"; that is, they were not computers in their own right but simply a means for communicating with a distant mainframe that performed the processing and record-keeping tasks. The microprocessor, in contrast, is "intelligent"—capable of doing much of the interactive instruction—but severely limited in its capacity to store the necessary program material. It can, however, be set up to access a central mainframe as needed. Programs can be downloaded from the mainframe to the PC via telephone line and processed by the PC, and a record of that processing (the instructional exercise and the test results) can be returned to the mainframe for central storage. The long-distance telephone connection is required only intermittently, meaning that costs are significantly reduced. Retaining the mainframe, with all its massive storage capabilities, but capitalizing on the advantage of having an intelligent terminal at the user end, "wasn't all that difficult," Norris says. "It was just a question of modifying the software so that a lot of it resided in the microcomputer."[21]

Computer-based instruction is inherently *individual student*-centered, and every student works at a different rate. Unless the personal computers at which they are working are organized into some kind of network with a central computer, the teacher has no way to monitor individual student progress—and no way to tell whether a student has mastered a particular course segment before going on to the next. For a student to return a diskette and request the next one is no indication that learning has taken place. The benefits of computer-based instruction can be realized only with a central facility for interconnecting student work stations, administering tests, and maintaining individual and group records that the teacher can access at any time. For all their other advantages, stand-alone PCs cannot by themselves provide the classroom management capability that is so valuable a feature of full-fledged PLATO.

Norris was indignant at the fad-like manner in which schools were acquiring personal computers and accomplishing little beyond exposing young people to a few elementary tasks. Other computer companies were offering courseware of varying quality, but none had programs for training teachers or managing the teaching process—or the means for tying the personal computers into a total system. Without these tools, teachers could not make effective use of the hardware, and much of it soon began gathering dust in school closets. Even the computers that continued in use were having little meaningful effect on what happened in the classroom. This fell far short of the revolutionary impact on education Norris had envisioned.

At about the same time the personal computer appeared on the scene, an important advance was made in computer mainframe power, and this, too, had a positive effect on PLATO's marketability. Classic PLATO had been built around the Control Data 1604 and 6600 and, later, the Cyber 70 and 170 machines. All of these were powerful for their time, but they lacked the huge storage capacity required for PLATO, and it was necessary to add memory capacity in the form of extended core storage (ECS)—to the tune of several hundred thousand dollars per installation. The Cyber 180, introduced in 1984, was designed with the needs of PLATO specifically in mind; ECS was no longer necessary because clients could now run PLATO as just another program on their 180 mainframes. With increasing frequency, mainframe purchasers began to buy PLATO as a software add-on, while others chose Control Data hardware over other types on the market because of the availability of PLATO.

Today PLATO systems—central mainframes with networks of microprocessors—are widely used in business and industry to meet the massive training and retraining needs created by the decline in basic industries and the rapid changes in industrial technology. They are used by major airlines to train flight and maintenance crews, and by utilities to train nuclear workers in safety procedures. Other clients include automobile manufacturers, oil producers, pharmaceutical companies, and financial institutions. There are over 7,000 hours of training in PLATO's library of standard courseware, and customized courseware is being developed constantly to meet special needs. PLATO's penetration of the industrial training market has been successful, and the potential for further growth is impressive. Progress is also being made in developing the military training market, where prospects are especially promising because of the growing need for technically competent personnel. This is a huge market in which PLATO has a strong position because no other computer-based training system has PLATO's instructional management capabilities.

The company continues to woo the elementary and secondary school markets, and results are being seen in that quarter as well. The international educational market remains somewhat elusive, however. Adapting courseware for use in other countries requires more than simple language translation. Cultural differences come into play and make the task difficult, though certainly not impossible. There are promising prospects for leaping the cultural barrier through joint ventures with local educational enterprises, such as the one now being formed in Saudi Arabia where King Faud and Sheik Yamani are enthusiastic supporters of PLATO as a means to aid in developing the infrastructure the country needs on which to build a modern industrial economy.[22]

Adapting technical courseware, whether for industrial, military, or engineering purposes, presents fewer cultural difficulties and opens up the possibility of creating a vast worldwide market. The experience of the Control Data Institutes in Germany is illustrative. There are now thirteen institutes in that country, where some 5,000 students are enrolled at any given time, making CDI the largest nongovernmental training facility in the country. Curricula have been broadened to include a wide range of technical education, and Control Data is known in Germany as "the training company."[23] In Japan PLATO is used extensively in both schools and industry.[24]

More than a decade after it was first offered commercially, PLATO shows promise of becoming the ubiquitous training resource Norris has had in view for many years.

As part of a companywide reorganization to focus on markets rather than technologies employed, Control Data in 1984 established a wholly owned subsidiary, United School Services of America (USSA), with Dr. Walter H. Bruning as president, to consolidate in a single unit all educational products and services for the kindergarten through high school market. In keeping with the new market focus, the task of serving university, military, and industrial educational and training clients was assigned to the divisions responsible for designing, building, and maintaining high-speed computers for the engineering and scientific markets, of which the universities, industry, and the military are major segments. USSA began exploring several avenues to the elementary and secondary school field, including the formation of local companies to act as distributors and the possibility of operating local schools on a fee-for-service basis.

Work is also underway to develop systematic programs for training teachers and administrators in the effective use of the technology. Computer literacy is not a problem since today it is no more necessary for users to know how their computers work than it is for drivers to know how their car engines work. Instead, the challenge is to help teachers understand how to use the technology to assess individual student needs and progress through the analytical tools the system provides. Once this is accomplished, teachers will be able to rid themselves of the mundane tasks that now take up so much of their time and go on to establish more personal and productive relationships with their students.

Some reorganization of classroom practices will be necessary. The application of any new technology always requires changes in old ways of doing things. Weaving had been a cottage industry from time immemorial, but the power loom, when it came along, could not be used in the home and the whole system of textile manufacture had to be restructured. Computers could not be used effectively in business or military operations without major changes in business and military practices. The same applies to the classroom. If working with computers is ever going to be anything more than an optional, supplemental activity subject to the whims of teachers and the vagaries of funding, computers will have to be integrated into *central* instructional processes.

Experimental programs are now underway in various parts of the country, in cooperation with local school systems, to work out practical means for achieving this goal. The feasibility of this approach has already been demonstrated in the Control Data Institutes, but experience in public school environments is an essential step in gaining acceptance from the educational establishment.

It is already clear that instead of dehumanizing the teaching/ learning experience, the computer can be the means for *re*humanizing it. In part, this is because the computer itself calls on and greatly enhances human capabilities that might not otherwise be tapped. One of Norris's favorite stories is that of the inner city school in Baltimore where students repeatedly broke into the school at night (through a basement window conveniently left unlocked) not to steal but to get more time on PLATO. And speaking of his frequent visits to the daycare center near Control Data's plant in the northside slum area of Minneapolis, "You have to experience a little black girl, four years old, right out of the inner city, in front of a PLATO terminal and you'll change your mind about technology being inhuman. Even these kids realize that they have at their fingertips a tremendous amount of knowledge. So what could be more human than that?"[25]

PLATO also makes possible a major change in the teacher/student relationship. Spending six hours a day, 180 days a year together during the formative years makes teachers the most important persons in a child's life, after the parents. "Twenty years ago," Norris said in 1978, "the computer was considered the epitome of depersonalization, but it's actually just the opposite. Through the computer you can be much more personal than ever before."[26] Currently much of a teacher's time is spent in drill-and-practice, testing, record-keeping, report-writing, and other dull and tedious work that can be done better and more cheaply by a computer. When teachers are relieved of these chores, they will be free to spend more time with children, dealing with them as individuals and creating new patterns of creative relationships. The ideal of Mark Hopkins on one end of a log and the student on the other seems that much closer to reality.

All of this appears to be coming to fruition at a most opportune time. More and more people are becoming impatient with the public schools and reluctantly taking on the heavy financial burden of sending their children to private schools. Disillusionment with the quality of public education is resulting in a growing demand for higher levels of educational accountability. As of 1985, forty-two

PLATO and Enthusiastic Young User in Action, *Ca.* 1978 (*Source*: Control Data Corporation)

states had introduced or were considering introducing some form of testing to determine the qualifications of teachers for continued certification.[27] The American Federation of Teachers has endorsed the concept of mandating professional standards and performance. Many states—notably those in the West and the Sunbelt—are faced with a serious shortage of qualified teachers. The amount of knowledge that must be communicated is increasing, the resources available are not, and traditional modes of instruction are unequal to the task. The computer makes possible the first significant improvement in educational technology since the invention of movable type 500 years ago.

Computer-based education has come a long way since Norris first learned from Harold Brooke of Donald Bitzer's work on PLATO in 1960 and entered into the cooperative arrangement with the University of Illinois in 1963. From the standpoint of hindsight a quarter of a century later, it is clear that mistakes were made that could have been avoided and money spent that might have been saved. But a vast amount of learning had to take place, and the mistakes, the costs, and the time were part of the learning process.

Education is the last great field for the application of computers. Just as business, government, the military, modern medicine, science, and engineering can no longer function without the computer's aid, the challenges facing education require the support of computer technology. This will shortly be a multibillion dollar market, and Control Data is well prepared to serve it.

This would not have happened without the confidence Norris had in the course he was pursuing, and his stubborn resolve to see it through. And stubborn resolve was necessary, because of all the programs Control Data has undertaken none has drawn as much critical fire as PLATO. Norris himself is at least partly responsible for the adverse attention PLATO has received. On several occasions he has stated publicly that over the 17-year period 1963-1980 the company spent more than $900 million developing computer-based education before beginning to realize a profit. These statements have been widely misunderstood, both inside the company and out.

In the first place, Norris was talking about the *complete system* of computer-based education, for which *PLATO* has become a kind of shorthand. To Norris, there are four essential components to such a system: hardware, software, courseware, and knowledge bases. The hardware, of course, are the computer mainframes, terminals, microprocessors, and audiovisual equipment; the software are the programs for directing, controlling, and recording individualized student instruction; the courseware are the computer-assisted instructional programs and the diagnostic and testing tools to aid in analyzing student needs and progress; and the knowledge bases are encyclopedic bodies of information accessible by computer to support the instructional programs. "I had enormous difficulty, even inside the company, getting people to understand that PLATO is a lot more than hardware," he explains.[28] In fact expenditures on the development of hardware were less than for any of the other components of the system.

Also, Norris's purpose in making such statements was to emphasize the fact that ventures into nontraditional fields may involve substantial costs and take longer than usual to bring to profitability. The effect, unfortunately, has been a marked tendency for journalists and the investment fraternity to question Norris's business judgment.

There has also been a great deal of internal sniping at the program from people scrambling for a share of scarce company resources. But Norris has simply brushed off all criticisms from whatever source and persisted in giving computer-based education his unqualified support.

Besides, the statement about the time and money spent on PLATO, even as a total system, is an oversimplification. The $900 million includes every expenditure made over the period in question that could reasonably be attributed to educational effort, while the revenues thrown against it are only those of the company's training and educational accounts. PLATO so thoroughly permeates all Control Data businesses that the company has a problem accounting accurately for its revenues. For example, if PLATO is sold as part of a computer system sale, credit goes to computer systems and does not show as training or education. It is integral to many of the company's most profitable professional and engineering services, and while with some effort revenues attributable to it could be separated out, from a managerial standpoint there is no practical reason for doing so.

Robert Price once summed the matter in these terms: "[PLATO] is so pervasive through all our businesses that it's very hard to add up all the dollars flowing from it. It's not only the dollars flowing in from direct teaching [and training], but an enormous benefit is that the technology spreads out through all our applications areas. It changes the whole philosophy of how we interface with users. It changes our approach to normal data processing applications to make them more usable and more tutorial. It changes our philosophy on how to support our customers and enables us to provide remote support. There is far more benefit than just the dollars of revenue that can be toted up on the board as education revenues."[29]

For at least the last ten years, Norris has been predicting that education will become Control Data's principal source of revenue and profit. Considering only those services where its contributions can be clearly identified, 1985 education revenues were over $235 million, and for the three years preceding 1985 they grew at an average annual rate of 30.4 percent.[30] This does not include value added by PLATO to programs for use by agriculture, local government information services, job readiness and industrial training, health maintenance, and the like where there is no realistic way of separating out the numbers. It can only be said that without PLATO these programs would not exist at all; in a real sense, they *are* PLATO.[31]

The clearly identifiable training and education market alone is growing by about 25 percent a year. "Nothing else around here," says Norris, "is growing at that rate." He sees an almost unlimited potential in that area. "Unless we screw up," he says, "this will be our largest and most profitable business." He admits that "you can debate whether we will get our share of the 25 percent growth, but given the position we already have in schools, industry, and the military, I can't imagine how we could be that poor in managing."[32]

Despite all the criticism and frustration PLATO has engendered, Norris has never doubted its vast potential. At the press conference in January 1986 where he announced his decision to retire as chairman and chief executive, he was asked what he considered his proudest accomplishment. His unhesitating answer: PLATO.

CHAPTER 6

The Northside Story—
And Its Sequel

Throughout his long career, Norris has always been a sensitive person about people, concerned about fairness in individual and small group matters. However, during his years at ERA and Sperry and his early years at Control Data he showed little overt interest in larger social issues. The interest may well have been there, but the demands of struggling new businesses took priority.

Then, in early 1967, a critical event took place. Norris attended a seminar for chief executive officers at which Whitney Young, head of the National Urban League, was the principal discussion leader. Norris was greatly impressed with Young as a person and deeply moved by his account of the social and economic injustices to which most American blacks were still subject. Young opened Norris's eyes to disturbing realities of American life.

In terms of race relations, the summer of 1967 proved long and hot, and in July there were a series of violent disorders in a number of cities across the country. The savagery and destruction of the riots in the Minneapolis northside area dealt a severe blow to the civic self-image of local leaders who had long prided themselves on the high state of civility of their community. This was the sort of thing that might happen elsewhere, but not in Minnesota! Much soul-searching ensued, during which civic groups earnestly debated the whys and wherefores and sought means to ensure that nothing of the kind could ever happen in their city again. A variety of actions were undertaken and considerable funds were raised to ameliorate some of the more obvious affronts to white middle- and upper-class notions of social dignity.

Meanwhile, Norris took a step of his own. He flew to New York to get Whitney Young's advice. What, Norris asked, can a company like Control Data do to help avoid a repetition of this kind of disaster? Young's answer was simple: Jobs. "Until these young blacks have jobs," he told Norris, "until they have something to look forward to and work for, you're going to have trouble in Minneapolis and everywhere else."[1]

That trip to New York was Norris's Road to Damascus. "All of a sudden," according to Norbert Berg, "Norris was different. It was like he'd had his eyes opened. He had become aware of problems and of his ability to do something about them. I always believed Whitney Young did that. I'm not sure he was as aware of it as I was, watching from the side."[2]

On returning home from his meeting with Young, Norris called his key people together. The idea of hiring blacks was not new to them; from the beginning, Control Data had followed a policy of nondiscrimination in employment. As a practical matter, however, few blacks had actually been hired because from 1960 on the plants with the most Control Data jobs in the Twin Cities had been located on the metropolitan perimeter, far from the inner city where the majority of blacks lived. Shortly after Norris returned from the Whitney Young seminar in early 1967, the company at his instigation had opened a hiring office in the black neighborhood with shuttle bus service to its suburban Arden Hills plant, one of the largest manufacturing facilities in the state. Working with churches and local community organizations, it had succeeded in attracting a few black applicants, but most of them had found the plant's suburban setting unappealing and the arrangement had been dropped.

After talking with Young following the riots, Norris insisted to his staff that as a major employer Control Data had an obligation to start hiring blacks in significant numbers—not as a civic duty, but as a business necessity. "My God," he expostulated, "you can't do business in a society that's burning." He appointed a small task force under Berg, then vice president for personnel and administration, with instructions to find a way to break down the barriers. "I want to see us taking blacks—especially young blacks—off the street and putting them to work," Norris ordered. Berg and his group knew Norris well enough to take him at his word.

The task force studied the problem and concluded that if blacks were to be hired in any significant numbers, the jobs would have to go to them, not the other way around. This meant putting a plant in the heart of the inner city area. When the task force made this recommendation to Norris, his response was brief but telling: "Fine. Make it a new one." With no more detailed directive than this, Control Data embarked on a course that was to open broad new fields of corporate enterprise and give new meaning to the concept of corporate social responsibility.

Norris specified a new plant because he wanted the people in the community to know that the company was serious in its intentions and had come to stay. He also believed that an attractive new plant would become a community landmark that people would take pride in and protect from vandalism—as they were not likely to do for an old, beat-up structure. Because a new plant would take a year to design and build, the company rented temporary quarters (from a firm that had been frightened away by the riots) and began operations in November 1967. Work on permanent quarters was started immediately, and the new, fully modern structure built largely by local minority contractors was occupied in March 1969.

The employment objective was to hire the hard-core unemployed or underemployed of the area. For operational purposes, these were defined as high school dropouts, people who had previously held only part-time or seasonal jobs or no jobs at all, and individuals with prison records including persons currently on parole. A target group deemed especially important was unemployed female heads of households.

Norris and his associates were fully aware that they had embarked on a risky endeavor. Prevailing wisdom in the white business community questioned whether a competent workforce could be built from the kind of labor pool Control Data meant to draw from. Given the hiring objective, prudence might have dictated putting into the plant a product requiring mostly low-skilled workers, one not too vital to the business; if the project failed or the output was not up to standard, the shortfall would not be critical.

The product Control Data put into its new plant met neither of these criteria, but it satisfied others that Norris laid down. He felt that employees should not be given jobs that "just required putting components on a board," but instead should work on a recognizable product, "something they can see that contributes to the company's business, something that they can associate with and take pride in."[3] Furthermore, Norris specified, the product must require enough skill to provide motivation for learning and a realistic basis for career progress—a future. Finally, the product must be critical to the company itself to assure close management attention.

At the time, Control Data had need for additional capacity to fabricate a number of different electronic devices. The one that met all of Norris's criteria was peripheral controllers. A peripheral controller is a complex device that directs and controls the high-speed flow of work between a computer's central processing unit and other components of the system and is a key element in its operation, especially so for the giant computers that are Control Data's stock in trade. Unlike most other working parts of a computer, which are hidden inside the casing, it is a stand-alone device (then about the size of a refrigerator, now much smaller) that can be seen in advertisements as well as in operating computer systems—a recognizable product with which those who help make it can identify with pride.[4] Manufacturing controllers involves an array of skills ranging from entry-level to fairly high, providing incentives and opportunities for advancement.

This choice also satisfied Norris's final criterion: Peripheral controllers are vital to Control Data's business.[5] In a move daring even by Norris's standards, he ordered the company's controller production concentrated entirely in this one plant and made the whole company, domestic and worldwide, dependent on its output. The feelings of the manufacturing staff "were ambivalent, not to say schizophrenic . . . . Some felt, 'My god, this is a dumb idea. We'll never be able to make it work.' "[6]

But it had to work—or else. This was precisely what Norris intended. As his associates had long since learned, he dislikes starting anything on a trial basis. To do something on trial is to admit in advance the possibility of failure, "and if you leave room for failure," he will tell you, "you're very likely to fail." He was determined not to run any such chance with this new venture. He knew there would be difficulties, and he deliberately created a situation that left no room for retreat.

This was fortunate because time and again those responsible for bringing the plant on line and delivering a quality product would have called the project off if they could have. Within a year the early enthusiasm of many of those in management had seriously waned, but they had had no choice but to persevere. No matter how intractable the problem, means for dealing with it had to be found. As Berg emphasizes, "It was a vital part of our business. We had no choice but to make it work or we were out of business as a company."[7]

There were troubles by the numbers. There were productive and creative solutions by the numbers, too—but not by the book; many had to be invented. Not everyone employed at the new Northside plant needed special attention, but enough did to require more than the usual administrative response.

Roger G. Wheeler, then a member of the headquarters personnel staff and later vice president for personnel and public affairs, was given special responsibility for watching over the new plant and keeping top management—specifically Norris and Berg—apprised of all significant developments. Richard Connor and Gary Lohn, two members of Wheeler's staff who later became vice presidents, were assigned to work full-time with plant management in dealing with out-of-the-ordinary problems. They were told that their job was to provide "a direct linkage from the corporate staff to the production floor of the plant" so that "information on problems doesn't have to come up through various divisions and layers of management. . . . You keep us posted on what the problems are and what it's going to take to solve them."[8]

Conner and Lohn reported directly to Wheeler and, through him, to Berg and Norris, which meant that they had immediate access to whatever resources or authority they needed. This in turn brought Norris and his key staff directly into the loop of learning how the new plant worked and what managerial adjustments were necessary to bring it to a satisfactory level of performance.

Berg used his daily morning meetings with Norris to update him on plant developments. "I'd tell him what kinds of problems we were running into and how we were solving them," he says. Whether the solution required money or something else, Norris would "just nod his head, like, of course, if that's a problem that's what you do."[9]

Many adjustments had to be made. For example, it was recognized at the outset that good relationships with local community groups would be more than usually important. With this thought in mind, before any announcement was made of plans to open the plant,

Wheeler and other company executives met frequently with community leaders, many of whom they had come to know through earlier efforts to recruit from the area. Senior management wanted to be sure that the plant would be welcomed, not perceived as an effort on the part of big business to exploit a poverty-stricken neighborhood. They learned from these meetings that people in the community had come to judge the potential merit of a new project by the amount of ballyhoo with which it was introduced by its sponsors—the louder the noise, the more suspect the undertaking. To avoid misinterpretation, Control Data asked the leaders to make the public announcement themselves. The mayor of Minneapolis telephoned Norris in anger because he had not been informed in advance and first learned what was afoot from the newspapers. But the community was reassured.

Management recognized, too, that assistance would be needed in recruiting, as well as advice on dealing with a new and unfamiliar workforce. Based in part on the counsel they received and in part on what they learned as they went along, numerous changes were made in established company practices.

The traditional purpose of the hiring interview is to screen people out; Control Data undertook the far more difficult task of finding ways to bring people in. During interviews, the focus was not on what people had done but on what they might become. To avoid the appearance of making arbitrary judgments about people who had reason to be suspicious of judgments made by whites, hiring was done essentially by order of application, with results the company's sophisticated personnel technicians found surprisingly positive. Aptitude testing was thrown out, record-checking was eliminated, and the application blank was limited to name, address, and Social Security number. The single employment test was the physical examination, a practice retained on advice of local leaders who pointed out that this would be the first checkup in a long time for many applicants.

The problems encountered in bringing the new plant on line were daunting. Because of the highly technical nature of the product, it was necessary to transfer experienced personnel from other plants to manage the new operation. Almost all of these were white, and few were equipped to deal with this kind of workforce. Special aid and counsel was therefore required for the supervisory staff.

Most of the new employees whose work they were to direct had had little or no prior work experience and needed substantially more training than was customary in other company facilities. These out-of-the-ordinary attentions cost time and money. Application was made for government assistance, and a portion of the additional cost was reimbursed under the Department of Labor's job training program.

A unique rule was adopted: A new employee had to fail *three times* before being dropped. After the first failure, an effort was made to determine the cause and the individual was reassigned to a job that seemed better suited to his or her capabilities. After the second failure, the process was repeated. At each stage, trainers worked closely with employees to provide them with whatever assistance they needed. This "three times" rule, together with the "first come, first served" hiring system, meant that there had to be a range of entry-level jobs available so people could be switched promptly from one to another. This worked well and remarkably few people failed entirely; unskilled, untried people were given a chance to succeed, and most of them did.

Many of the jobs required relatively little skill at the outset, but the majority of workers could be upgraded to semiskilled as they gained competence. There were a fair number of skilled positions to which people could aspire, and they were helped to get there. For example, one of the most important units of the plant was the test and checkout section, which was responsible for making sure that all products shipped were in perfect working order. (With peripheral controllers, there is no room for error; they must work right the first time.)

Typically in the computer industry, the only people hired for work of this kind were at least high school graduates, and preferably technical vocational school graduates as well. However, in the labor market from which these employees were hired there were precious few such people available. Berg and Wheeler made a bold decision: only *non*-high school and *non*-technical school graduates would be assigned to test and checkout work. Those selected for these positions were put through a rigorous training program roughly equivalent to what they might have received in a technical high school. The results were eminently satisfactory.

In the nearly twenty years the plant has been in operation, many of those who originally brought no or few job skills to the workplace have advanced to skilled ranks and some into supervision and management; eventually, in fact, virtually the entire original staff of managers, foremen, and lead persons was replaced by people brought up from the ranks of the Northside plant.

There was a fair amount of turnover, but much of it was in the form of "throughput"—people being promoted to better positions in other plants within the Control Data system. Early in 1981 at the beginning of the Carter administration, in a presentation to the White House staff, the "throughput" for the dozen years the plant had then been operating was reported to be *three times* the average number of employees in the plant. Northside, in fact, became a valuable asset to the company as a source of competent, well-trained employees for its own needs and those of other Control Data plants as well.[10]

Northside was never meant to be a philanthropic undertaking. From the outset, Norris insisted that it be measured by the same standards as any other Control Data plant, and that it be held to the same quality, cost, and productivity requirements as its sister plants elsewhere. He was adamant: "If all it does is make jobs that keep people busy and give them some income, it doesn't prove anything. It has to be a business success before it can be a social success."[11] It took longer to reach the proficiency of other plants than had been the company's previous experience—approximately three years instead of the usual one—but there was never any question that it would be other than first-rate in every sense of the term. Today it is one of the most efficient and productive manufacturing facilities in the entire Control Data system.

———

But to reach this goal required overcoming many difficulties other than those encountered in the original hiring and training process. Acquiring new and complex skills was not the only problems faced by many employees. Merely adapting to the culture of a factory was often a hurdle: coming to work on time and staying on the job all day, even in the face of weariness or boredom; observing plant rules; obeying safety regulations—these are learned behaviors, and some had to learn on the job.

Most of the people hired needed more than a job, and in many ways home and personal problems proved more troublesome than those at the workplace. Personal problems that interfered with work were common: liquor and drug abuse, disorganized home life, family disputes, marital troubles, wayward children. Run-ins with the law were everyday facts of life. Many had difficulties managing their personal finances. Not a few were victims of unscrupulous merchants or landlords.

Problems such as these could not be left at home when employees reported for work—if, indeed, they were able to report for work at all. However they might be categorized technically, these were work-related problems and had to be dealt with as such; otherwise, the building of an effective workforce would have proved impossible. It became clear early that a great deal of counseling was necessary to help employees resolve some of the problems that were interfering with their work, and staff was added for this purpose.

Often, the mere opportunity to discuss a problem with a sympathetic listener enabled the employee to think his or her way through to a constructive conclusion, although frequently counselors were able to make suggestions that employees found useful. In many cases, some special help was needed. The staff took steps to gain a thorough knowledge of local community resources to which employees could be referred as necessary. Often, special help was provided by the company itself.

Control Data's 1968 acquisition of Commercial Credit Company provided access to a local Commercial Credit office that helped more than a few employees straighten out tangled financial affairs. Trouble with landlords was common. Arrangements were made with the Oppenheimer firm for one of its young attorneys, Robert Weinstein, to spend the better part of two days a week for more than a year in the plant to be readily available to employees who might need his help. Many of them did, and Weinstein, now a prominent member of the Minneapolis-St. Paul legal fraternity, has many a human interest story to tell. Among other things, he often had occasion to aid employees whom someone was trying to impose upon, and he recalls with amusement how quickly hitherto abusive landlords were likely to become agreeably reasonable on answering their door to find a vested, briefcase-carrying, homburg-hatted caller identifying himself as attorney for his tenant.[12] The young lawyer was able to help employees with various other kinds of legal difficulties as well. Merchants, landlords, and others soon learned that Control Data employees could not be pushed around easily.

One peculiar problem that surfaced early was an abnormally high rate of absenteeism on Mondays. The reason was quickly found:

Over weekends, troubles in the neighborhood often resulted in workers landing in jail. A solution to the resulting absenteeism was devised by the Oppenheimer attorney, who worked out an arrangement with the court and police whereby Gary Lohn could visit the city lock-up early on Monday mornings to bail out any company employees who might have run afoul of the law. The procedure soon became so routine that the court authorized Control Data to print its own bail bond forms, complete with company logo; Lohn's signature was sufficient to gain the employee's release—in effect, into Control Data's custody. The need for this particular form of special assistance gradually faded.

Another class of absenteeism was more serious and intractable. Because a deliberate effort was made to hire women heads of households, many of those in the workforce had responsibilities for young children. It was common practice for the mothers to arrange for childcare with relatives or friends, but it often happened that for one reason or another a relative or friend could not help on a particular day or for a particular period. The mother had no choice but to stay home with the children, and the frequency with which this occurred was serious enough to threaten the viability of the entire venture.

After study, Wheeler concluded that the only answer was an expensive one: a daycare center located in the neighborhood, with adequate facilities and equipment, and managed by professionals. When this recommendation was relayed to Norris by Berg, the response was, "Go do it."[13] Norris's only suggestion was to find other employers willing to participate. Several were found who had employees living close enough to the proposed facility to benefit from it. A modest amount of government aid was secured and a not-for-profit corporation was formed. In the beginning, its board was made up equally of parents and representatives of employers, but control was shifted gradually until the facility became wholly community-owned and managed.

The center opened in temporary quarters while a new building specifically designed for the purpose was constructed. It quickly became and remains a prominent feature in the life of the community, and local residents take particular pride in it. Not incidentally, it went a long way toward solving the plant's troublesome absenteeism problem.[14] Norris took great pride in the Northside plant. He was especially taken by the daycare center and went there frequently to make sure that everything was going smoothly. "He was absolutely enthralled by the children," Wheeler recalls, "and just loved the place."[15]

These were a few of the ways in which Control Data dealt with the many difficulties of starting an inner-city plant and turning it into a smooth-running component of the system. Norris's staff knew from long experience that he expected them to do whatever was necessary to get the job done. Over the years, he had frequently admonished them, "When you come to an obstacle, you don't say you can't do it, you just overcome the obstacle and do it."[16] At no point were problems permitted to serve as excuses for substandard operation.

Almost from the beginning, the morale of Northside's employees was remarkably high. They knew that what they were doing was of critical importance to the company, and they saw themselves as a key component in the organization.[17] For its part, the company was (and is) proud of the plant and often took visitors through it; notable among these were U.S. Chief Justice Warren Burger, Vice President Walter Mondale, and numerous governors, members of Congress, mayors of major cities, church leaders, visiting dignitaries from abroad, and other nationally and internationally prominent figures. Employees were impressed by the pride the company obviously took in what they were doing, and this pride was reflected in their work.

While the Northside plant was still in its early, difficult stage of development, Norris said one day to Berg, "Let's try one in Washington. There are a lot of blacks there who need jobs too." With the proximity of the Congress obviously in mind, a site was selected in a badly run-down area within a few blocks of the nation's Capitol, and a plant was opened there in February of 1969 to manufacture card-reading devices.

Unfortunately, rapid technological advances soon made this product obsolete, and a major contract with the Washington Metropolitan Area Transit Authority on which the company had counted failed to materialize. To keep the plant open, a variety of subassemblies were scheduled, but production runs were too short to achieve efficiency. These problems were overcome in time, but eight years were required to reach normal productivity. At Norris's insistence

The Northside Plant, *Ca.* 1970 (*Source*: Control Data Corporation)

William C. Norris at the Northside Child Development Center, *Ca.* 1976

and over vigorous internal objection, the company persevered, and today the Capitol plant is a highly efficient operation.

In the winter of 1969–70, when Northside was beginning to show progress, Norbert Berg was co-chairman of a biracial committee formed to help increase employment opportunities for minorities in St. Paul. A particularly worrisome problem for the committee was the plight of people urgently in need of jobs but able to work only part time, such as mothers with school-age children and trade school and high school students. Driving home one evening after a meeting of the committee, Berg toyed with a novel idea.

Next morning at his regular session with Norris he said, "Bill, these mothers can't get jobs and these kids can't get jobs. We could organize a whole plant on a part-time basis, four hours a day for mothers after they get their kids off to school, and four hours in the afternoon for teenagers after school. We could even put in a third shift in the evening and work the plant twelve hours a day." Norris's reply was brief: "That's a good idea. You ought to do that."[18]

The Selby-Dale section of St. Paul was chosen for the venture. This was an area of very high unemployment where no new industrial job-producing investment had been made since before the turn of the century.[19] Following the practice that had worked so well in starting up the Minneapolis Northside plant, community organizations were contacted and the advice of community leaders was sought. The response was enthusiastic. Temporary quarters were rented in an old bowling alley, and preparations were begun to establish a light electronics assembly plant.

Unfortunately, at precisely this time the computer industry went into a quick, sharp recession, and Control Data found itself with no need for an additional assembly facility. But discussions with neighborhood groups were already underway and community expectations were running high; with the company's credibility at stake, a search was begun immediately for an alternative use of the space already leased. Herbert F. Trader, whose duties then included responsibility for company publications, suggested a bindery, and this proved to be an ideal solution. Control Data's business requires a considerable volume and variety of manuals, operating bulletins, and other printed materials to be assembled, bound, and mailed, and these functions had previously been contracted to outside vendors. They were now consolidated, brought in-house, and placed in the Selby-Dale facility, which began operations in February of 1970.[20]

The bindery—a success from the start—today employs several hundred mothers and students, all working part time in three four-hour shifts. Selby-Dale handles all of Control Data's bindery work and that of a number of other companies on a profitable contract basis. The converted bowling alley was replaced in 1974 by a modern plant designed for hand-collating and binding operations. Employee morale and productivity are high, and costs are competitive.

In a 1979 interview, Mayor George Latimer of St. Paul described a visit he had made to the plant two years earlier as "inspiring because you could feel the productivity, you could feel the commitment, you could feel the ease with which people related to each other and the pride they took in having a job."[21]

As with the Northside Minneapolis plant, the Selby-Dale facility is the pride of both the company and the community. In the dozen years since the new facility was opened, its attractive exterior has not been marred by a single line of graffiti—this in a neighborhood where graffiti is common. No burglar alarm was ever found necessary. The plant manager, Richard Mangram, likes to tell the story of how, some years ago, the rear door of the plant was inadvertently left unlocked at close of business one Saturday noon. This was discovered that afternoon by employees playing basketball in an adjoining lot. Mangram was telephoned immediately and was assured that the employees would stand guard until he arrived and secured the door. "Dick," they told him when he appeared, "everything is fine. We've been watching it."

Following recovery from the business downturn of 1969–70, Control Data began growing again at a rapid pace, in some years adding as many as a thousand new employees a month and requiring a number of new plants. Encouraged by the progress of the Northside plant and the success of Selby-Dale—and not discouraged by the problems of the Capitol plant—Norris in 1970 laid down a rule that future new plants were to be located in poverty-stricken areas. The policy was not popular with the operating executives who needed new facilities for their expanding businesses, but Berg as head of administration was adamant in carrying out Norris's dictum. "It has to go into a poverty area," he told them, "or you don't get it." Often, Berg continued, "they had to be dragged kicking and screaming, but in the end they always came along."[22]

Shortly after the startup of Selby-Dale, Norris in one of their regular morning meetings said to Berg, "You know, on our next poverty thing, we ought to try some burned out coal mining town somewhere in Appalachia. People there need jobs too."[23]

Berg contacted the Economic Development Agency of the state of Kentucky and told them what he wanted. In due course, a report came back: "We've got a place here we'd like to show you." Berg flew down and found "a very nice little town with a small college and tree-lined streets—it looked like Hometown, USA." Berg told his hosts, "No, you don't understand. This is the kind of town that every other company would like to put a plant in. They don't need us. We're looking for a *poor* town."

In telling the story later, Berg commented, "I'll never forget the way the guy from the development agency looked at me, like he thought I was crazy. But anyway, he said, 'Okay, we'll *show* you a poor town.'" They took him to a small town in a county with the dubious distinction of being the second-poorest county in the contiguous forty-eight states. "We made a quick deal and went into Campton, Kentucky," Berg recalls. Unlike Northside and Capitol, this plant presented no startup difficulties and was successful from the beginning.

Mayor Latimer's 1977 tour of the Selby-Dale bindery had been conducted personally by Berg. At lunch following the tour, Berg told Latimer of Control Data's need for a world distribution center for computer parts. The Mayor responded, "Why don't you duplicate your success [at Northside Minneapolis] and do it right here in this community, Summit-University St. Paul?" Berg told him the amount of land he would need and the date by which construction would have to start: December 15, 1977. "We'll do it," said the mayor.

Latimer went back to his office to call a special meeting (held in the backyard of his home) of all city officials who would be involved in the project. His announcement of what he had committed to do was greeted with "much consternation" and flat statements that it "wasn't possible." But the mayor insisted, "We're going to do it," and that was that. By dint of extraordinary effort, the impossible task was accomplished and Control Data broke ground on December 23, missing the mayor's commitment by only eight days.[24]

Reflecting Norris's interest in energy conservation, the resulting World Distribution Center was a 240,000 square-foot complex, built 40 percent below ground and partially heated and cooled by an active solar system. Although staffed at the outset by personnel from various units whose work was consolidated in the new facility, the policy from the beginning was to fill vacancies from residents of the community, and five years later fully one-third of the 450-employee workforce were from the Summit-University area.[25] This was an enterprise very different from any of the previous inner city plants and with none of the problems these plants had encountered, but it served the purpose of bringing jobs to a community badly in need of them.

Control Data had long had an aggressive affirmative action program, and Berg followed the employment statistics of the company closely. He and Norris were pleased with the progress made in the hiring and promotion of women, blacks, and native Americans but concerned that few Hispanics were represented on the payroll. In 1981, Berg suggested that the next new plant be placed in a Texas city with a large Mexican-American population. Norris said, "Fine. How about El Paso?"

Berg looked into the matter and reported back: "Bill, there are already 50 or 60 electronics firms in El Paso where they operate a split-plant arrangement and have most of their work done by cheap labor across the border. That's a terrible image, and we don't want any part of it." Norris agreed, and Berg instead proposed San Antonio, a city with 54 percent Hispanic population and a very high rate of unemployment. A new plant was established there in August of 1981, and a largely Hispanic workforce was recruited and trained. This was followed in May of 1985 by a Control Data Business and Technology Center.

In June of 1986, introducing Norris as keynote speaker at a meeting of the Texas Association of Private Industry Councils in San Antonio, Mayor Henry Cisneros recalled Control Data's first contact with him five years earlier (when he was a city councilman) about a new plant in his city. "We fully expected them to want to locate in a green grass site in the suburbs . . . . I couldn't believe that a Fortune 500 company would want to locate in a slum area of the middle of town." But this was exactly what Control Data wanted, and another inner city plant was successfully launched. In concluding his introductory remarks, the mayor told his audience, "I urge you while you're here to visit the Alamo to understand the past, and then to visit the Control Data Business and Technology Center to understand the future."[26]

Other ventures into areas of high unemployment were plants in Toledo, Ohio, and Bemidji, Minnesota. With what had been learned from the earlier ventures, they presented no more difficulties than any other new plant startup. A common thread running through the entire experience was providing opportunities for jobs and careers where few had existed before, and doing so in ways that yielded permanent rather than transient benefits—and in the process adding significantly to Control Data's productive capabilities.

From the Northside experience, fortified by that gained subsequently in other poverty-area plants, Norris and his associates learned that it is possible to build competent workforces from labor pools with little prior industrial background, and that it is possible to convert so-called unemployables into capable, motivated workers. They learned that helping employees solve their personal and home problems makes them more productive at the workplace. And they learned that plants with a few hundred steady jobs can raise the quality of life of neighborhoods and stabilize whole communities. The latter made a lasting impression on Norris. Starting from the early days of Northside, his conviction that jobs can be the means for solving a wide range of social woes became a ruling force in his thinking and a significant factor in shaping his business policies.

Some of the personnel practices introduced to deal with the special problems of the Northside plant proved useful in other company operations as well. Skills learned in counseling employees with pressing job, home, and personal difficulties became the basis for the companywide counseling program known as EAR (Employee Advisory Resource). Skills learned in supervising women and minority workers in inner-city plants translated into training programs for supervisors and executives throughout the company. Exposure to the human and economic costs of poor health habits among employees marked the beginning of an interest in employee health which later flowered into the ambitious StayWell program.

The "selling what we learn" theme so prominent throughout Norris's career is evident in the marketable products and services that resulted largely from the Northside and Selby-Dale experiences. What was learned in converting hardcore unemployed into productive workers became the basis for the Employment Preparation Service, which now operates more than fifty profitable training centers on contract with public and private agencies across the country. Several major corporations subscribe to the Employee Advisory Service, an EAR descendent that generates a handsome gross profit. StayWell is available at attractive per capita rates to corporations who want a healthier workforce. Like all the poverty-area plants, each of these programs is designed to serve an unmet or poorly met social need—not as a charitable gesture, but as a profitable business.

Control Data's success in creating job opportunities in distressed areas is a dramatic example of serving a social need. The company demonstrated that it was possible—not easy, but possible—to take a giant step toward meeting this need while at the same time filling vital niches in the company's operations. In some instances, more time and money were required to bring poverty-area plants to acceptable levels of productivity, but Norris saw these as R&D investments. And as good R&D should, they paid off by laying the groundwork for promising new businesses.

CHAPTER 7

Evolution of a Strategy

Nothing about Control Data Corporation has attracted as much attention as its policy of "addressing unmet societal needs as profitable business opportunities." It is this policy that is largely responsible for the frequency with which Norris is described as quixotic, visionary, and impractical, and why he is blamed by many for the serious difficulties in which the company found itself in 1985. Yet it is also this policy that most firmly cements the positions of William C. Norris and Control Data Corporation in the economic and social history of our time.

Norris made two moves that together set his company on a course that would break new ground in corporate enterprise. First, he entered into a cooperative arrangement with the University of Illinois, and several years later he located an important plant in a poverty-stricken inner city area in Minneapolis. Prior to the Northside experience, he had concentrated on developing and applying computer technology in more-or-less standard business and institutional settings. He now saw intriguing possibilities in environments traditionally considered the province of governmental and charitable endeavor. Specifically, he began to explore means by which computers could help serve unmet or poorly met social needs, and among other relevant computer-based technologies he saw in PLATO an especially useful tool. Significantly, he saw possibilities for serving these needs not as objects of corporate philanthropy but as straightforward business markets with attractive potential for profit.

In Control Data folklore, Norris first adopted this strategy as a means for expanding his business. But that's not quite the way it happened.

His first concern was for the needs themselves, which troubled him deeply. But as he considered how these might best be served, he recognized the importance of doing so in ways that would have lasting effect and not require constant replenishment. Gradually he began to realize that some of these areas of unmet needs represented potential markets in themselves which Control Data, in cooperation with government and other institutions, was well qualified to serve, and from this grew the idea of "addressing society's major unmet needs as profitable business opportunities."[1] As time went by, Norris and his associates came to lay greater stress on the "profitable opportunities" than on the "unmet needs," but in the etiology of the concept, the needs came first, with profit the means for serving them.

This sequence is apparent in the Northside experience. Norris was genuinely distressed at the extent of human misery brought explosively to light by the riots across the country and in Minneapolis during the summer of 1967, and he determined to do what he could to relieve the conditions that had led to those events. When Whitney Young helped him to see that the lack of jobs was at the root of most of the problems bedeviling the community, this in turn led to his decision to place an important new manufacturing facility in the rundown Northside area. He insisted from the outset that it be held to the same productivity and quality standards as any other Control Data plant, despite the fact that the labor pool it was meant to recruit from was generally considered to be below par. He also insisted that it be self-supporting, not makework that would last only as long as it was given special support. As an integral part of his strategy, he actively sought aid from federal job-training funds for a portion of the extra costs entailed in bringing the new plant on line, but there was never any expectation that this would be other than partial and temporary.

It would have been easy for Norris to have made a generous donation to any of several philanthropic causes aimed at improving conditions in the Northside community. Instead, he chose a more ambitious and difficult path, one that went far beyond writing a check. The course he followed produced results that were permanent in terms of human as well as economic values and changed Norris's whole way of thinking about Control Data and its place in the scheme of things.

In the spring of 1968, after the new Northside plant was well underway, Norris wrote to Minnesota Governor Harold LeVander, "[We] are in the process of rethinking our business strategies in an effort to come up with the best manner in which we can help with our society's current problems such as poverty and crime."[2] His use of the phrase "*business* strategies" was significant: Norris was already thinking of how solutions to problems such as these could be integrated into the business itself rather than dealt with externally.

An important outcome of the Northside experience was demonstration of the fact that the business of Control Data Corporation could be conducted in ways that would help relieve at least one of the major ills of modern society: joblessness. Norris decreed that future new plants were to be located in areas of high unemployment, and that the disadvantaged were to be given priority in hiring. Furthermore, all company facilities, old and new, were to make special efforts to recruit and train minorities, open better and more challenging opportunities for women, employ the physically handicapped, and help all employees to realize their highest potentials. These objectives were to become integral parts of efficiently managing the business; they were not to be additions to normal costs of operations but means in themselves to increase productivity and lower costs.

Seeing these policies succeed for Control Data, Norris began thinking that some of the things learned in the course of implementing them might be salable to other companies and the government, thus defraying a portion of their cost. In 1971 a group called Human Resource Management Services was organized to market a number of personnel programs developed originally for Control Data's own use,[3] and this gradually evolved into Control Data Business Advisors, incorporated in 1979 as a wholly owned subsidiary. The Fair Break program, first offered commercially in 1975, grew out of learning how to convert marginally employable recruits into a motivated, productive workforce.

These steps were not merely fresh examples of Norris's bent for "selling what we learn." What made them truly significant was the fact that he was moving toward recognizing certain unmet social needs as potential business markets *in their own right*, to be developed as any other business market. This was a milestone in the evolution of his thinking and a radical departure from traditional business practice.

But the need was far greater than the number of people Control Data could hire and train by itself. Norris saw a potentially very large market, with an ever-widening array of possibilities, that Control Data with its Northside experience and its maturing PLATO technology was uniquely equipped to pursue. Finding ways to serve unmet needs as business markets would enable the company to leverage its resources and reach far more people than it could ever serve directly through its own facilities, while simultaneously broadening and strengthening its business base.

By this time ends and means had become inextricably entwined in Norris's mind. A genuine concern for the needs themselves was always high on his scale of values, but so, too, was converting them to markets where business could be done and profits could be made.

In broadening his field of vision, Norris extended to new areas habits of mind developed in his prior experience. His basic strategy for Control Data had always been to identify needs that had previously gone unrecognized or underserved and to fashion means for converting them into profitable business ventures. He had begun with the needs of the engineering and scientific communities for powerful computers to handle computations of a magnitude and complexity that had never been attempted (often not even conceived) simply because machines capable of handling them did not exist. He had then moved to the needs of the computer industry itself for peripheral equipment too costly for individual manufacturers (other than the industry giant) to make for themselves. Next he had addressed the needs of organizations for occasional access to high-powered computers. In each instance, the need existed but the market did not; it had to be created.

Markets were established in all three areas by recognizing and defining the needs and designing means by which they might be served as profit-making businesses. In a fundamental sense, what was involved was a process of product development. The required skills were the ability to recognize the need, the imagination to design the product, and the entrepreneurship to combine the need and the product to create the market. Within a decade of its founding, Control Data had grown from a highly specialized to a broadly based enterprise by creating markets where none had existed before.

Given Control Data's experience with the Northside plant, Norris began to see possibilities for enlarging the concept of computer-based services to include new kinds of unmet needs, specifically those in the so-called "social problems" areas. To him, these simply represented different kinds of needs which fit neatly into Control Data's basic business strategy. Although some of the resulting ventures veered sharply from traditional notions of profit-making activities, in entrepreneurial terms the strategy underlying them did not differ in principle from the one that had brought Control Data into more technical markets. The underlying purpose of both was to broaden and strengthen the company's economic foundations.

Norris did not try to solve all the social problems that plague the country. Rather than tilting at every windmill on the horizon, he was careful to focus on problems that fell within Control Data's areas of competence and fit its basic business strategy. Essentially, those he elected to confront dealt with improving the management of information within specific fields: education and training, health care, small business support, rural and urban revitalization. "We never had any 'social programs,'" Robert Price would later say, "We had *business* projects addressing social problems—social needs—as business opportunities."[4]

In moving into these nontraditional areas, Norris was not breaking with Control Data's established line of development; on the contrary, he was extending that line to its next logical stage. The company's ventures into these new fields were reviewed in some detail at the 1982 Riverwood conference conducted jointly by Control Data and the American Academy of Arts and Sciences for the purpose of planning the company's twenty-fifth anniversary celebration. John Voss, executive director of the Academy, observed that what Control Data was doing "actually turns out on examination . . . to be a very sane and quite imaginative and somewhat daring expansion of your regular business."[5]

Norris's primary interest had always been in the *applications* of computer-based technologies. He now saw in social needs areas the possibility of creating sizable markets for new applications that would not only serve the needs themselves but would also broaden and strengthen the business base of his company. He was acutely aware of the tremendous strength of IBM and the gathering threat of the Japanese, and he foresaw the drastic shakeout that occurred in the computer industry in the mid-1980s. Other companies would soon be scrambling for niches *within* the industry; he was looking *beyond* the industry.

Norris was convinced that computer technology could be applied in many fields where its use was not yet known. He recognized that it would take longer than usual to develop markets in some of these areas, but he was sure that in time they would exceed in size and profitability any of the other markets in which the company was engaged. He was confident that he was aiming Control Data in a strategic direction that would position it strongly for the next quarter century.

Unfortunately, Norris's rationale was not widely understood. Because of deeply ingrained patterns of thinking, people in the business community and elsewhere viewed his interest in these "extraneous" areas with considerable skepticism. At best, they saw his actions as rather imaginative forms of corporate philanthropy; at worst, as the idiosyncracies of an eccentric individual who happened to be in a position to put his offbeat ideas to work. It was not uncommon for people to dismiss Norris's claims that he was pursuing profitable business opportunities as rationalizations or even self-delusions. Perhaps the most prevalent attitude was that Norris (and, by implication, the company's directors) had a sincere and wholly laudable concern for relieving some of the most distressing ills of society and were content with smaller rates of return than they could have realized had they devoted their time and resources to more conventional forms of business endeavor.

In plain words, the business philosophy that Norris preached and Control Data practiced differed so sharply from what most people were accustomed to hearing and seeing that many had difficulty fitting it into familiar categories of business behavior. But Norris was not nearly as unorthodox as he seemed. His initiatives were original, innovative, and unconventional, they moved into areas not customarily considered appropriate for profit-making endeavors, but they were well within the accepted canons of business theory.

The greatest entrepreneurial opportunities always lie in areas where existing goods and services fall most critically short of meeting needs. By this measure, some of the areas in which Norris was interested were among the greatest untapped opportunities the contemporary world had to offer: education, new business and new job creation, retraining of the structurally unemployed, urban and rural rehabilitation, reform of the prison system. Each had grave problems urgently in need of attention; Norris saw these as representing significant business opportunities for Control Data Corporation.

The idea of addressing unmet social needs as business opportunities is not as outlandish as it may seem. In a fundamental and literal sense, *all* business activity is directed to serving social needs, such as the provision of food, clothing, and housing. At bottom, all human needs are social, and serving them is not only a legitimate business purpose but the *only* business purpose that has any moral justification. Finding ways to convert unmet needs into profitable markets is the businessman's prime responsibility. However, a tradition has developed in our culture that relegates the serving of certain kinds of social needs to governmental, religious, and charitable organizations rather than business; the role of business in those areas is restricted largely to philanthropic giving.

Keep in mind the spirit of the times during which the series of events recounted here began to unfold. It was a period of heightened concern for the underprivileged. President Lyndon Johnson's Great Society had established new standards of governmental responsibility for shouldering the burdens of social ills, and Minnesota had long been a leader among the states for its "progressive" social legislation. All things considered, it seemed appropriate to assume that one or more agencies of government would (and should) assume major responsibility for dealing with the festering problems uncovered by the 1967 riots.

Private philanthropic endeavors were also in high favor during these times, and here, too, Minnesotans had long been more than usually active. The Minneapolis-St. Paul business community has an enviable record of providing support to worthwhile causes. It is well known for its "Five Percent Club" of companies that donate that portion of their annual pretax profits to cultural, welfare, and other projects to improve the quality of life in the metropolitan area. (Five percent is about three times the national average of corporate philanthropic giving.)

But the Five Percent Club held only limited appeal for Norris, and in fact he refused to join it, much to the annoyance of his business peers. "[Even] though these efforts are highly laudable," he wrote, "their end results tend to be narrow in scope and small in scale. Meanwhile, major societal needs are left relatively unattended."[6] Moreover, he considered 5 percent grossly inadequate in terms of the magnitude of the needs to be served, especially in view of the fact that the greater part of corporate giving goes to cultural causes such as opera, theaters, museums, and the like. However important these may be to the overall quality of a community's life, they have little relevance to the "major societal needs"—the human underpinnings of the social system—that were the objects of his special concern.

According to Norris, philanthropy can ameliorate social problems but never solve them. "You look at the reports [of corporate and other foundations] and, hell, there are hundreds of little projects, $10,000 here and $5,000 there, and what have they got to show for it? You can see, they're really not accomplishing very much." And again: Philanthropy "makes the boss feel like a white knight for a little while," but even the best efforts are "peripheral to real problems like job creation, urban and rural poverty, and the overhauling of an educational system that has gone to hell."[7]

He was even more critical of government. "The fact that conditions have become steadily worse . . . makes it clear that government has failed [in its efforts to solve social problems] and that fundamental changes are needed in the way we address society's major needs."[8] "Relying mainly on public services for meeting many of our societal needs," he charged, "has driven our country to the brink of disaster," and he cited as evidence "our decaying inner cities, poverty-stricken rural areas, shamefully high levels of disadvantaged youth unemployment, an unresponsive educational system, and an antiquated, overcrowded prison system."[9]

Norris's criticisms were on sound footing. An inherent weakness of most charitable and governmental endeavors, by themselves, is that they are a cost. Hence they are necessarily limited, both in terms of the efforts they can expend and the results they can obtain. We appear to be at or beyond the workable upper limits of taxation for social purposes, and there is little prospect for any substantial increase in levels of corporate or individual philanthropy. Efforts to deal with social problems through any combination of government action and private philanthropy are inherently unequal to the task because the massive resources they would require are simply not available from those sources.

In large degree, charitable and governmental actions *consume* rather than create resources. They are not self-renewing and require constant replenishment. They are deductions from rather than additions to the fruits of productive labor. Even if we consider only the most pressing of social needs, their sum total is far too great to be met by drawing down capital.

If social problems can be converted into markets, however, they become sources of revenue rather than drains on resources. They create capital rather than consume it. Properly managed, they can be equally or more effective than charitable and governmental programs, and they are not subject to budget limitations.

A further weakness of both charitable and governmental efforts is the fact that they are usually able to deal only with the externals of problems, not their internal dynamics. They treat symptoms, not diseases. Norris did not deny that symptoms might need attention, too, but he always saw through them to the causes that would have to be addressed to keep the symptoms from recurring. The hungry must be fed and the homeless housed, but feeding and housing in themselves provide only transient relief unless something is done to help people acquire the means for meeting their own needs. Most often, in our society, this comes down to jobs.

Unfortunately, the job-creating capacity of philanthropic agencies seldom goes beyond temporary makework projects, while those of government are severely limited unless they are closely integrated with industry. Norris acknowledged the importance of the economic environment created by the fiscal and monetary policies of government, but he considered these to be macroeconomic influences. Job formation, on the other hand, takes place in the microeconomic context of the individual company or plant. Content to leave largely to others the problems of the macro environment, Norris concerned himself with the flesh-and-blood human beings who needed jobs.

Norris's focus on jobs led him to recognize the importance of technology to new business and new job creation, and from there to see the need for more effective support for new small businesses. Technology exchange, new business formation, new job creation: to Norris, these were needs that business, in cooperation with government, could serve better than any other institution of society. And if this could be done, the severity of many of the other grave ills would be sharply reduced.

But for business to serve those needs, they would first have to be converted into businesses, for business itself is a social institution subject to logics and disciplines of its own. Specifically, the activities in which it engages must offer the prospect of generating revenues sufficient to cover all costs and provide capital to support continuity and new initiatives. In a word, a business must produce a profit.

In taking this approach, Norris said, "We abandoned the traditional do-gooder concept in favor of one that says we should address society's unmet needs as profitable business opportunities. In that way, we're not worrying about doing good or doing well. We're really doing what needs to be done. And solving social problems is no longer a peripheral (and thus expendable) add-on to [our] real business—it *is* [our] business."[10]

The object of all business effort is the mobilization and management of economically valuable resources for which someone is willing and able to pay—what economists call an "effective demand." Unless there is a chance that a profit can be made, the effort is not a suitable one for business. It might be quite appropriate for a private charity, a religious organization, or an agency of government, but not for a business. If a project undertaken by a private corporation fails to realize a profit, scarce resources have been wasted, capital has been impaired, and the cost of the project has become a levy on the owners of those particular assets, who may or may not be proper bearers of the burden.

A key here, of course, is ability to generate revenues. In the social needs areas, Norris visualized three principal sources of revenues: users of the services, cost-sharing arrangements between industry and government, and third-party financing through purchase-of-service contracts.

Some important services can be sold on a straightforward commercial basis directly to users (for example, Control Data sells its HELP program to hospitals and training programs to manufacturers and the military). Norris contemplated that in some instances arrangements could be made between industry and government to share the research and development costs of needed new services. "The concept of such cost-sharing . . . is not new," he wrote. "[It] has been applied many times to develop needed technologies—computers and satellite communications, to give just two examples. When the viability of the [technologies were] sufficiently established, private industry further developed and pursued them independently as profitable business opportunities."[11] Control Data frequently took this approach in bringing out new military hardware and certain other kinds of scientific apparatus, but found no opportunity to do so in developing services in the social needs areas. Still, Norris felt that industry should be alert to the possibilities of entering into cost-sharing arrangements wherever that might be possible.

It is a hard fact that in many social areas, those who need services do not have the means to pay for them, and recourse must be had to some form of third-party financing. Typically, but not always necessarily, this means an agency of government. However, the purchaser may be a corporation wishing to provide employees with improved health services or homebound disabled workers with special training. It may be a professional society wishing to prepare members for accreditation or an athletic association wishing to provide professional counseling services for its players.

In many cases, however, the source of funds must be a public agency on the sound premise that certain kinds of costs should be borne by the general public through the taxing power of government. This raises an important point: Who is the customer? Is it the disadvantaged youth who needs job readiness training, or the educationally retarded student who needs to acquire basic reading and arithmetic skills, or the convict rotting behind prison walls? Or is it the governmental entity responsible for job training, or the school board, or the state department of corrections? The youth, the student, and the convict may be beneficiaries, but the *customer* in these and many other instances is likely to be an agency of government acting on behalf of the public—which is, in fact, the ultimate beneficiary.

Unfortunately, there is a strong predisposition in many quarters to assume that when public funds are used to meet social needs, the work of serving those needs should be performed by a governmental or other nonprofit agency. There is no such predisposition in the use of public funds to serve a host of other pressing public needs, and vast sums for such purposes have long been appropriated by every level of government. The U.S. Department of Defense does not manufacture its own aircraft, tanks, and ships, or NASA its own computers; state highway departments do not build their own roads; local police departments do not produce their own communications equipment.

These are all public needs served by the use of public money to employ private, profit-making organizations to perform stated functions. A very large sector of the national economy is engaged in providing goods and services on a for-profit basis to agencies of federal, state, and local governments. Norris felt that there is no logical or practical reason why governments should not contract in a similar manner with private sources for the performance of job training, community development, and other useful services such as those he initiated.

The Department of Defense sets detailed specifications for the purchases it makes. By the same token, a governmental agency operating in areas of social needs can specify precisely the services it wishes to buy, the conditions under which they are to be delivered, and the standards that must be observed. And the social agency, like the Department of Defense, can monitor performance on its contracts.

In matters such as these, it is the role of government to make two quite different kinds of decisions: first, *which needs* are to be served by the expenditure of public funds, and second, *by whom and how* the service is to be provided. The fact that a government agency *decides* does not necessarily mean that it must also *do*.[12] Norris believed that in a number of critically important needs—for example, job readiness training—needs could best be served on a purchase-of-service basis.

Government participation is something Norris has long been accustomed to and comfortable with. Unlike many people in business who viscerally display antigovernment biases, Norris not only accepts the notion of government participation in a variety of matters that touch directly on the daily lives of ordinary citizens; he also believes that government should in some cases be *more* active than it is and solicits greater involvement.

His business success has always depended on substantial government involvement. ERA was put together to serve the ongoing needs of the U.S. Navy and other government agencies for powerful electronic data processing equipment, and its revenues were largely drawn from public sources. From its beginnings, Control Data's most important single customer for computer equipment has been the U.S. government. Norris had no qualms, therefore, about soliciting governmental participation when he began looking for ways to expand his business activities into the arena of social needs.

Norris was concerned with accomplishing far more than Control Data could do alone. "Major improvements," he wrote, "will take planning and implementation in which all segments of society, including business, labor, academia, government, and the churches participate. A high degree of interaction will be required because basic change in one segment won't occur without accommodation and support from others."[13]

Although broad participation is essential, he argued, it is up to business to "take the initiative and provide the leadership for planning and managing the implementation of programs meeting these needs."[14] Only through the initiatives and capabilities of business, he held, could the ends he envisioned be attained because "no other sector of society has such capabilities for effectively planning, assembling the resources for, and managing the large and diverse programs necessary today." He went on to point out that "Most government agencies are focused on single fields—labor, commerce, housing, agriculture, or urban development—and lack both the competence and the authority to confront social problems that require multifaceted solutions." Most philanthropic agencies, too, are highly compartmentalized in their interests and programs. Business, he argued, could become the catalyst, coordinating its own efforts with those of other institutions such as government, education, foundations, and other nonprofit institutions to "make essential contributions to broad-scale programs out of their own expertise and authority."[15]

It was an interesting unfolding of thought. First came concern for the problems of unemployment in a disadvantaged community, followed by efforts to provide jobs in ways that would be self-supporting and not require continuing subvention from either the company or the public. Then came moves to sell to others some of the methods developed to help prepare people for jobs, out of which grew the recognition that some important needs could be converted into business markets. Finally, as the magnitude of these needs became apparent, the conviction took hold in Norris's mind that in this direction lay Control Data's best hopes for the future.

The fact remains that concern for the problems came first and continued as a high priority in Norris's thinking. Profits were important, but Norris saw these essentially as the means to enable business to serve the needs and do so on a self-supporting, self-renewing basis. This meant generating sufficient revenues to cover all costs, including the costs of capital, because that was the only way the business could survive and render the variety of services for which it was responsible.

Norris's close associate, Norbert Berg, says of him, "I don't know a thing that Bill Norris does that is just pragmatic and crass and not founded on a fundamental personal belief. Areas of concern that he is pursuing as business opportunities are indeed business opportunities, but they are also solid personal concerns."[16]

For all of his adult life, Norris has had a genuine concern for human deprivation. Much of this grew out of personal experience. He lived through the Great Depression and the rigors of the Dust Bowl and worried about the plight of farmers he assisted as a member of the local staff of the Agricultural Adjustment Administration. Later, on fishing trips to Canada and the Caribbean, he was depressed by the missing teeth and other signs of malnutrition evident in his guides and other local people he came to know, and he has kept some of them supplied with vitamins for many years.[17]

Often when he returned from trips that had taken him to areas such as a coal town in Kentucky, the Bronx, Watts, rural West Virginia, Mexico City, or Jamaica, he would talk to his associates about the abject poverty and human misery he had seen. "It doesn't have to be this way," he would say, "It just doesn't have to be this way."[18]

CHAPTER 8

Serving Society's Unmet Needs

Norris learned from his experiences with poverty-area plants how he could help make things better. Above all, he learned that he could do so within the framework of a business enterprise and accomplish more than customary governmental and philanthropic means. Control Data received some public funds in the form of training subsidies, but these were integrated into the business process in ways that provided lasting benefit and did not require renewal.

Norris found that some social ills could be dealt with in the context of regular business operations, while others could be converted into opportunities for profitable new business ventures. Most important, he started seeing the possibilities of extending to these new areas the *applications* strategies that had served the company so well in technical arenas.[1]

Although Norris has never expressed the thought in so many words, his actions reveal his belief that computers can do almost anything if we only put our minds to it. He now put his mind to this new and broader challenge. As his ideas developed in the course of his wide reading and long evening walks with notebook in hand, two themes emerged as central: technology and jobs. He came to see that some of the ills that most seriously trouble modern society are rooted in unemployment and underemployment and that if the job problem were resolved many of the others would soon disappear or be greatly relieved. To him, technological innovation is the wellspring of new jobs.

From the time of the 1967 inner-city riots onward, the problem of jobs, particularly for the underprivileged, had been of haunting concern to him. "Jobs, jobs, jobs got to be a fixation with Bill," Berg recalls. " 'People don't want handouts,' Norris would say, 'they want jobs,' and he had proof of that in the success of our inner-city plants."[2] Norris himself has written that "no quantitative data can begin to measure the human and social costs of broken families, low self-esteem, futility, anger, and the higher mortality, illness, and crime rates that go hand-in-hand with unemployment. Nor are there figures to represent the billions of dollars in potential production that has been lost forever."[3]

Beginning with the decision to place an important new plant in a devastated area, he shaped the policies of his company to make jobs more accessible to groups whose opportunities are limited, and he achieved a significant measure of success. His task was made easier by the fact that Control Data was growing—at some points during the 1970s it was adding over 1,000 new employees a month. Putting plants in disadvantaged areas did not take jobs away from other places; new jobs created by growth were a net increase in employment, not a transfer. It did not require any flash of insight for Norris to see that the nub of the problem was not just jobs but *new* jobs, and that the means must be found to encourage and facilitate new job creation.

As he considered the matter from this perspective, he came to see more clearly the role of technology. Control Data was able to create new jobs because of its vigorous pursuit of new technologies. The kinds of technologies that are useful for job-creating purposes are those that provide the basis for new products, new services, or new businesses to serve human needs, the satisfying of which call for organized effort and productive employment—in a word, jobs.

Technology is not necessarily technical. Norris defines it as " 'know-how'—[a] way of doing things and organizing actions to achieve desired results."[4] Thus defined, technology may be incorporated in a mechanism or device, or it may simply be knowledge, understanding, skill, or imagination; essentially, it is the ability to do something or make something happen. For a technology to perform a job-creating function, it must be applied. It may be interesting lying on a shelf or incorporated into a drawing or turning over in someone's mind, but to generate jobs it must be put to work, and the work must require human effort. Technology does not stand alone: Innovation is required to invent it, and entrepreneurship to use it. Norris states the relationship slightly differently: "Jobs result from innovation, which is the total process of creating and applying technology."[5]

As he looked about him, Norris came to realize that while much (though by no means all) technological innovation originates in big business, the vital processes of entrepreneurship are far more characteristic of small companies than large. Ours may be a big-business economy and huge organizations may dominate the economic scene, but many of the fruitful ideas and most of the new entrepreneurial efforts emanate from small enterprises. And it is the small-business sector that accounts for the major part of new job formation. Norris concluded that the most effective way to address the country's jobs problem was to strengthen small business, and particularly to foster new small-business formation.

He had learned from his own experience that the creation and application of technologies—innovation and entrepreneurship—are fostered by technology transfer. "One of the world's largest untapped resources," he has often written and said, "is the wealth of information and technology lying dormant or underutilized in the libraries and laboratories of businesses, governments, research institutes, academic institutions, and individual inventors."[6] And: "Vast amounts of underutilized technology exist in industry. Most companies use only a part of their stock in their own commercial activities; the remaining unused technologies may well have commercial applications elsewhere in the economy, and it is likely that technology utilized in one product could be applied to other products in the same or different industries. Yet these technologies are seldom shared due to a long-standing bottleneck: the concern for maintaining a proprietary position."[7] He conceived this resource as potentially of great value to the entire economy, and especially to small business, and a plan to make it more readily available as a key element in a massive job creation program began to take shape in his mind.

In early 1976 Norris sought an interview with Senator Hubert Humphrey, who came off the Senate floor to meet him in his office. Norris presented the Senator with a one-page memorandum titled "Millions of New Jobs Program," aimed at aiding small business by encouraging "more efficient use of the vast amount of technology that exists in the world" by means of "a world-wide computer-based technology service."[8] Norris recalls that "the senator sat there, leaning forward in his chair, his elbows on his knees and this paper in his hands." "Well, I'll be damned," Humphrey said. "Will this work?" When Norris assured him that it would, the senator responded, "I have difficulty understanding this, but you're a credible person, and if you say it will work I'd like to try it." As chairman of the Joint Economic Committee, Humphrey assigned two of its staff members to work with Norris to develop the idea in sufficient detail to provide the basis for drafting legislation.

While this work was underway, Norris had several further meetings with Senator Humphrey[9] and testified before the Subcommittee on Employment Opportunities of the House Committee on Education and Labor in support of the Full Employment and Balanced Growth Act of 1977, popularly known as the Humphrey-Hawkins bill. This bill was generally opposed by the business community, and Norris was the only big businessman to testify in its favor. "I wasn't all that enamored of it," he recalls, "but, damn it, it was at least a start to do something about creating jobs."[10] Unfortunately for Norris's efforts to include in the bill measures to encourage technology transfer and other parts of a job-creation program, "about the time we were really beginning to get somewhere, Humphrey took sick and that was that." Norris tried working with Representative Augustus Hawkins, "but the legislative climate had changed" and nothing came of it.[11]

Although he had hoped originally for federal support, Norris decided to proceed on his own with plans for a job-creation program, two key components of which were Technotec and Worldtech. Technotec, begun in September 1975, was designed as a computerized database for the gathering and storage of many types of technology. Owners of technology could place descriptive information in the database for a filing fee, and those seeking answers to problems could gain access to it for a search fee. The owners were thus provided with a means for finding people who could use technology they were unable to employ themselves or wished to sell for some other reason, and the seekers were given a shortcut for finding what they needed. As conceived by Norris, the mission of Technotec was to make "innovation possible through market pull and technology push rather than technology push alone."[12] Both owners and seekers would benefit from the exchange, and Control Data would earn a profit by bringing the two together. Worldtech, also launched in September 1975, was intended to be an international marketing service to promote technology transfer on a worldwide basis.

Two additional ventures in the area of technology transfer were soon undertaken: Local Government Information Network (LOGIN) in late 1978, and AgTech in September 1979. LOGIN was a computerized database compiled in cooperation with the National League of Cities, the National Association of Counties, and the Council for International Urban Liaison. Intended for use by cities, counties, and other local governmental entities, LOGIN assembled information on productivity improvement, facilities maintenance, municipal services, energy management, and a wide range of problem-solving techniques.[13] AgTech, a computer data bank of agricultural technology, provides information on subjects of particular importance to family farmers, including farm machinery, energy conservation, home food processing, land development, livestock diseases, and similar topics of vital importance to the efficient management of medium- and small-sized farms.[14]

The results of these programs have been mixed. Worldtech never really got off the ground; without some form of tax incentive (a favorite Norris nostrum) to encourage owners to make technology available, the process of digging it out was much too people-intensive for a large organization. In July of 1986 the service was sold to a small company able to use it profitably. Although Technotec showed encouraging progress for a time, the failure once again of tax incentives to materialize created problems similar to those of Worldtech.

LOGIN, on the other hand, is doing very well; still a small business by Control Data standards, its database contains over 30,000 pages of useful technical information and is growing steadily as users exchange ideas and experience and add to the volume of data in the central file. Several hundred local governments across the country currently subscribe to the service, and the number of clients and frequency of use are both increasing.[15] AgTech enjoys a wide and growing clientele. The success of both LOGIN and AgTech is due largely to their focus on specific, identifiable markets and their ability to gain access to large quantities of useful information on which to build their databases.

One of the most dramatic things Norris and his associates learned from the Northside experience was that many people ordinarily considered unemployable could be converted into motivated, productive workers. In the course of opening other plants in poverty areas, the techniques originally developed for this purpose at North-side were further refined into a replicable body of skills. Meanwhile Norris was deeply troubled by the increasing numbers of education-ally and culturally deprived young people growing up with little prospect of ever finding a useful and reasonably rewarding place in society. Here was an urgent need with frightening implications, and Control Data had learned how at least part of it might be served. In keeping with his long habit of selling to others what the company had first learned to do for itself, Norris determined to package and market commercially the body of job-readiness skills that had repeatedly demonstrated their usefulness. The result was Control Data's Fair Break Program, launched in May of 1978.

Fair Break combines PLATO-based classroom work with peer-group discussions and sessions with trained counselors. Students typically spend about four months in the program, during which they learn basic reading, arithmetic, life-management, and job-seeking skills. They are also helped to identify personal problems they may have and to work out solutions for them. Many local programs are conducted in tandem with Control Data Institutes to offer a combi-nation of job-readiness and specific job-skills training.

Fair Break is typically delivered on contract with state and local government agencies and financed chiefly by federal job training funds. Advisory councils made up of local staff of the federal job training agency, educators, and representatives of community orga-nizations provide oversight and guidance to local program directors and add materially to the quality and effectiveness of the undertak-ing.

Most but not all local Fair Break programs deal primarily with the educationally and culturally disadvantaged. Many participants are high-school dropouts; others include single mothers seeking to work their way out of welfare. Most have little or no job experience, or histories of poor job performance. They are generally young, but some are old enough to have outlived the industries in which they were once employed. Almost all are poor, some are handicapped, and a few have had problems with alcohol or drug abuse. Fair Break aims to provide them with marketable skills and the self-confidence and motivation to seek, get, and keep jobs.

As of November 1986 there were 45 Fair Break centers operating in various parts of the country, each tailored to the needs of its local economy. In Atlanta training is offered in retail sales, office clerical work, and entry-level jobs in computer programming, computer repair, and word processing. In Elyria, Ohio, a program was designed to serve an area hard hit by massive layoffs at U.S. Steel and the shutdown at American Shipbuilding. In Chicago low-income residents are given opportunities to learn office technology and bank teller skills. In West Virginia displaced workers are retrained and disadvantaged people are helped to break out of the poverty cycle.

Some programs are designed to prepare physically handicapped persons for productive employment. PLATO is a particularly effective instrument for this purpose because its terminals can be fitted with a variety of devices to enable people with different kinds of disabilities to use them. The President's Committee on the Handicapped is sponsoring a pilot program in Washington, D.C. to train disadvantaged people in digital electronics, and the Veterans Administration is exploring the possibilities of using PLATO to help retrain its sizable constituency of physically disabled.

Typical Fair Break Center, 1978 (*Source*: Control Data Corporation)

An interesting variation is Control Data's Homework Program. Developed originally to provide work for some of its own employees homebound by illness or accident, it has been extended to train computer programmers for other companies. Because a trainer can give interactive instruction via PLATO—transmitting lessons to a student's terminal, watching his or her own screen to see how the student responds, and correcting as necessary—training can be delivered to students hundreds of miles away as easily as if trainer and student were seated at the same console.

The remarkable versatility of PLATO makes it useful for helping people with a wide range of disabilities, physical and otherwise, to become productive citizens. Work is done on purchase-of-service contracts with public and private agencies in accordance with agreed-upon performance standards and subject to close surveillance by the contracting agencies. Because Homework is delivered by an organization subject to the strict regimen of business, its cost-effectiveness is high.

Experience with Fair Break led to two other programs for disadvantaged youth: Advanced Career Employment Training (ACET), started in March of 1979, and Career Outreach, begun in April of 1981. ACET was designed to train young Job Corps people brought to Minneapolis from various parts of the country for work in the computer industry, and the mission of Outreach was to help disadvantaged young people get started by combining education and work experience.

Norris cites Fair Break, ACET, and Career Outreach as "examples of the types of programs that are urgently needed and should be replicated nationwide." He goes on to say, however, that implementing such programs is prohibitively expensive in the absence of purchase-of-service arrangements, and that some form of government aid is necessary to enable business "to recover the costs they incur in training students, giving them part-time jobs, and placing them in full-time jobs when their training is completed." Otherwise, he concludes, "it is doubtful that [business] will get involved to any great extent."[16]

Both ACET and Career Outreach produced significant results but proved to be short-lived because continuing government support failed to materialize. On the other hand, Fair Break (now called Job Readiness) is a well-established business earning an above-average return on investment. Norris takes great pride in what this program has accomplished.

———————

But job readiness is of no avail if there are no jobs available. Recognition of this truism kept Norris's attention riveted on the crucial role of small business in new job creation.

From his extensive reading, he learned that small businesses provide the greater part of the growth of the U.S. economy and that "between 1953 and 1973 close to half the major innovations introduced into U.S. industry came from firms with fewer than 1,000 employees—and a quarter of these originated in firms with fewer than 100." He learned further that, largely as a result of these innovations, "small business has outshone big business with respect to job-creating efficiency."[17]

His early belief in the critical role of small business in new job creation was strongly supported by a 1979 MIT study that found that small companies were responsible for 78 percent of the 9.6 million new jobs added to the U.S. economy between 1969 and 1976.[18] Control Data Corporation itself had started as a very small business, and even as it grew larger it continued to have close business relations with many small enterprises. The findings of scholarly studies simply confirmed Norris's convictions as to the superiority of the job-creating potential of small businesses. He came to the straightforward conclusion that the most effective way to provide the jobs so urgently needed was to strengthen the small business sector of the economy.

As he considered this, he was impressed by the impediments faced by those trying to start small businesses and the high rate of small business mortality. Some of the more obvious sources of difficulty were embedded in the corporate tax structure and could be relieved only by federal legislation. In 1978 he chaired a Department of Commerce committee that addressed the problem of how to make capital and management resources more readily available to small, technically oriented enterprises. The recommendations of the committee called for a variety of benefits for small firms, including a ten-year carry-forward for startup losses, reductions in capital gains taxes, shared allocation of the research and development funds of federal agencies and government contractors, and tax incentives to encourage large firms to make their technologies more readily available to others.[19] Many of these recommendations were subsequently implemented by legislative or administrative action.

With his unfailing entrepreneurial instincts, Norris by this time had come to see small business as a market Control Data was uniquely equipped to serve. There are some 14 million businesses in the United States, representing more than 97 percent of all U.S. companies, which employ fewer than 500 workers each, and these in total account for about 40 percent of the gross national product. Most new businesses created each year are small—at least at the outset—and small businesses provide by far the greater part of the growth in the U.S. economy. Norris saw this huge market as an opportunity to greatly broaden Control Data's business base while simultaneously making significant contributions to new business and new job creation.

Many companies offer products or services that are utilized by small enterprises, and many such products are designed with small businesses in mind. But no one before had visualized small business *qua* small business as an identifiable market with its own special characteristics and needs. Although the analogy almost certainly did not occur to him, the mental process Norris went through was similar to that of Julius Rosenwald, who in the mid-1890s moved Sears, Roebuck and Co. from a firm specializing chiefly in watches, jewelry, and silverware to one serving the broad spectrum of needs of rural and small-town America. The result was a catalog offering a very wide range of merchandise. No farmer could possibly use everything in the catalog, but every farmer could find in it almost anything he needed for his home and farm. In a similar manner, Norris set out to offer a broad spectrum of services to small businesses—broader than any one business could possibly use but from which virtually any small business could find most of the services essential to its success.

Norris had great expectations of the Commercial Credit Company acquisition. In addition to the financial advantages it brought, one of the things that made it especially attractive were the nearly 1,000 field offices through which he envisioned developing and marketing a wide range of both financial and computer-based services tailored to the needs of small businesses. Many of Commercial Credit's customers were small businesses, and Norris saw in them a solid potential customer base.

By the latter part of the 1970s Control Data under Norris's prodding had developed a variety of services that addressed the needs of small business for technology, training, personnel recruitment, and consulting. Data-processing facilities provided payroll and accounting services for companies too small to have computers of their own. Technotec and Worldtech were intended to facilitate technology transfer to encourage both innovation and entrepreneurship. To assist both established and would-be entrepreneurs in improving their business skills, a substantial amount of PLATO-based training material was prepared on how to start, manage, and build a business.

CYBERSEARCH, an electronic employment service, was formed in early 1977 to help small businesses recruit competent personnel for engineering, data processing, and sales positions. Control Data Temporary Personnel Services—Control Data Temps—was established in August 1980 to provide a convenient, cost-effective way for small enterprises to fill their short-term requirements for professional, technical, office, and light assembly workers. Business Advisors, Inc. (BAI), a wholly-owned subsidiary, was organized in November 1979 to distribute expertise developed originally for the company's internal purposes (again, "selling what we learn"). These include a variety of human resource management services for which the primary market is other large companies, but one BAI division is devoted exclusively to providing consulting services responsive to the needs and characteristics of small business.

These and other new services added significantly to Control Data's ability to aid the small business sector of the economy. But better means of delivery were necessary to make this wide range of services more readily available to larger numbers of small businesses. Norris saw in Commercial Credit Company's far-flung network of field offices the framework on which to build a nationwide system of Business Centers to perform this function. The Business Centers would become, in effect, a chain of "retail stores" where small business owners could examine an array of services and select what they needed, returning from time to time as other needs arose.

As noted earlier, Norris's expectations on this score were not realized. Local credit office managers, competent enough to handle credit applications and other routine chores, were not up to managing the sophisticated, multiservice operation Norris had in mind. In a sincere if misguided effort to give Norris what he wanted, the

Commercial Credit-based management of the Business Center program went too far. Instead of starting slow and gradually expanding facilities and personnel, they set up large, well-appointed quarters in twenty-six cities. "When I saw the one in Minneapolis," he later commented, "I was absolutely flabbergasted at the investment they had put in and the number of people they had hired." The Business Centers lost a lot of money and the concept was thoroughly discredited. "The whole thing got so screwed up I just said to hell with it and devoted myself to other things. Meanwhile, the security analysts had a picnic."[20]

Thoroughly frustrated with the situation, Norris turned his attention to other matters, including the Business and Technology Centers (BTCs), the first of which opened in St. Paul in July 1979. Designed specifically to provide needed support for new and developing small businesses, and located primarily in job-deficient urban areas, they provide various combinations of shared facilities and essential services to nurture the successful startup and growth of small enterprises. Each BTC consists of flexible space that is subdivided and leased to small companies. Depending on the kinds of businesses served, a BTC may house laboratory, graphic arts, office, light assembly, machine shop, or other services the tenants may require. These, too, depend on tenant needs; available facilities may comprise model shops, clean rooms, and conference rooms. Shared services usually include accounting, word processing, duplicating, drafting, telephone-answering, and purchasing, and access is afforded to small-business consulting via BAI.

Of special significance is the fact that through PLATO the BTCs offer entrepreneurs training in areas critical to their survival: financing, balance-sheet management, decision-making, tax management, inventory control, sales and marketing methods, and other essential skills. As Robert Price notes, "Economies of scale make it possible to provide . . . tenants and small companies nearby with needed facilities and services of higher quality and considerably lower cost than they could get elsewhere."[21] No two BTCs are exactly alike because each is geared to its own clientele.

Unlike the Business Centers, the BTCs have been eminently successful, in part at least because Norris gave them closer attention. His task was made easier by the fact that BTC management was based in Minneapolis as part of Control Data's corporate structure, rather than at Commercial Credit headquarters in Baltimore, and he was better able to keep an eye on things.

In 1978 Control Data embarked on an even more ambitious undertaking, City Venture Corporation, a consortium of business, professional, and religious organizations that had as its goal nothing less than the revitalization and renewal of rundown urban areas.

By now Control Data was experienced in placing new plants in high-unemployment localities and converting them into efficient manufacturing operations. But while these initiatives had been successful from the company's point of view and had provided significant numbers of new job opportunities, their impact on local economic development had been limited.

To make these facilities operational, management had had to learn, often by trial and error, to deal not only with problems at the work site but also with difficulties that originated outside the plants. Many of their employees were impoverished and poorly educated. Housing in the communities was seriously deteriorated, and workers had trouble securing decent places for their families to live.

Business and Technology Center, Baltimore, Maryland, Summer 1982 (*Source*: Control Data Corporation)

Ten years after the Minneapolis Northside plant opened, conditions in the surrounding area were definitely improved, but no other large employers had followed Control Data into that part of the city, and little in the way of new small business activity had emerged. Although Control Data had unquestionably made an important contribution to the well-being of at least a portion of the population, the plant lacked the "critical mass" necessary to generate a response capable of revitalizing the area as a whole.

As an informed citizen, Norris was well aware that decayed inner city communities represented grave social and economic problems, but placing Control Data plants in such areas brought home to him in a direct and personal way the extent to which "urban blight and decay have turned many American cities into breeding grounds for fear, anger, poverty, and despair."[22] In October of 1977 he was invited to serve as a member of the planning committee for the White House Conference on Balanced Economic Growth. At about the same time, President Carter made his highly publicized visit to the South Bronx, and on his return he asked members of the committee for suggestions on what might be done to address the tragic problems he had found there. In response, Norris, who had already been thinking along precisely those lines, prepared a paper outlining the concept for a new approach.[23]

He was convinced from study and experience that there were two primary reasons why years of costly federal, state, local, and private efforts had produced so few tangible results: fragmentation of programs, and failure to involve the business community in more than what amounted to speculative real estate investment. Norris proposed remedying both deficiencies by means of a broad-based consortium of business, government, civic, and religious organizations that would mount a concerted effort to revitalize the decayed central areas of the major cities of the country.[24] Such a consortium could not only provide the needed coordination but would also create a vehicle for the more effective participation of business in the process. Not content with simply presenting his idea, Norris proceeded to put it into action. The result was City Venture Corporation, a private, for-profit company capitalized at $3 million and launched in August of 1978.

A fundamental premise of City Venture was that "the economic activity and employment opportunities basic to urban health must come largely from the private sector."[25] It would not be a "developer" but instead would provide management and consulting services to communities, cities, states, and federal agencies on a purchase-of-service basis. Job creation would be "at the heart of City Venture's objectives . . . coupled with the fostering of innovative and responsive approaches to community enrichment including education, job skill training, health care, energy optimization, housing, security, transportation, food production and processing, and environmental conservation."[26] It was Norris's intent that the new enterprise "begin small," dealing first with neighborhoods, then sections of a city, and in due course whole cities.

City Venture was a new and exciting concept and attracted wide attention. Unfortunately, its first effort was less than successful and got the entire program off to a bad start. This was Urban East in Minneapolis, Control Data's home town, which aimed at restoring a blighted area adjacent to the city's downtown. The project became entangled with an ambitious and controversial program to build the new Metrodome sports stadium and redevelop the adjacent 200 acres of badly deteriorated property. A variety of private interests and local community organizations, as well as the city and other agencies of government, were involved in the undertaking, and misunderstandings quickly arose regarding the role of Urban East.

Local community organizations attacked the project as an effort to engineer a new economic base for the area that might or might not benefit local residents and allegedly would deprive them of a voice in the future of their neighborhood. Sharply critical newspaper accounts[27] focused on the fact that City Venture was frankly a for-profit enterprise, and local activists contacted community groups in other cities warning them to beware of City Venture's designs. One group of activists even applied (unsuccessfully) to the World Council of Churches for a grant to prepare "an organizer's handbook for use by communities faced with Control Data."[28]

Control Data and City Venture protested the publicity as biased and unfair,[29] but the damage had been done. The City Council withdrew its support for the project, and all that survived was the Business and Technology Center. It continues to serve the area, although lacking such ancillary services as training and economic development its effectiveness falls short of what was originally planned. Far more serious were the doubts cast on Control Data's motives and City Venture's methods in other cities and professional community development circles, which handicapped (but did not halt) the extension of City Venture's work.

In retrospect, it is clear that with Urban East, City Venture tried to do too much too fast. The results might have been different if the same degree of care had been used to lay a solid groundwork with local groups that had preceded the earlier entry into the predominantly black Northside. When Control Data undertook to put a new plant in that community, apprehension over the racial tensions left from the recent riot prompted management to proceed with caution. Care was taken to establish good relations with community groups and their leaders to make sure that the company understood the problems likely to be encountered, and to build strong community support in advance. Similar precautions were taken in connection with the move to Selby-Dale. The Urban East area, in contrast to Northside and Selby-Dale, was populated largely by ethnic whites and Native Americans, and those managing the project did not anticipate encountering any particular problems. They failed to understand the need for neighborhood involvement and alienated some of the influential local leaders. City Venture was accused of arrogance in its dealings with the community, but naive would be a better descriptor.[30] It was an unhappy episode all around.

The learning gained from the experience was valuable if costly. Because City Venture was careful from then on to prepare the way and ensure active community involvement,[31] projects undertaken in other cities were more successful. Especially notable were those in Toledo, Philadelphia, Baltimore, San Antonio, and Charleston, South Carolina, as well as statewide programs in South Carolina and Illinois.

City Venture focused on two basic needs: helping to start new businesses and expanding others already in existence. In Norris's words, "No program for urban renewal can be successful unless it provides job opportunities for community residents and training programs to enable people to get and keep the jobs which are created."[32] For these reasons, the physical anchor of each City Venture project was always a Business and Technology Center.[33] Whether sponsored by City Venture or directly by Control Data, it was recognized that a BTC could be successful only if it were part of a well-organized complex that Norris termed a Job Creation Network.

By this time, three components had come to be recognized as essential for a successful network: a "cooperation office," a seed capital fund, and a BTC.[34] The cooperation office was a not-for-profit entity to which would-be entrepreneurs could bring ideas for new businesses and receive assistance in preparing their business plans. The seed capital fund was a for-profit enterprise typically organized by a combination of local public and private investors whose primary interest was in strengthening the local economy and who were content with modest direct returns on their recognizably chancy investments. The BTC, managed but not necessarily owned by Control Data Corporation, was the most visible part of the Job Creation Network and helped develop public interest and support for the total undertaking.

Of these three components, Norris always considered the cooperation office pivotal because it provided the means by which people in the local community could work together to generate new jobs. By institutionalizing the process, it got large numbers of individuals and organizations around the country involved in the kinds of joint efforts Norris set out to establish. Through the Job Creation Networks, he has greatly extended the radius of his influence, and as new networks are brought into being the number of businessmen and businesswomen coming to provide the leadership and initiative he has been urging for twenty years continues to grow.

The Business and Technology Center concept has spawned many imitators. So-called business incubators were unknown before the establishment of the first Control Data BTC in 1978, but they are now common in business communities from one end of the country to the other. Few if any offer the range of service and quality of support characteristic of the Control Data BTCs, and Norris views them with scorn because they operate in isolation and not as components of job creation networks. Nevertheless, they provide a measure of assistance to small business startups that had never before been available and might not be available now were it were not for the Norris prototype.

Norris launched City Venture Corporation and embarked on the business of operating BTCs as profit-making enterprises because he wanted to make a constructive contribution to solving the jobs problem, and he saw the encouragement of new business formation as the most effective means to that end. But he also recognized that to accomplish anything substantial the means would have to be self-renewing, ongoing, and able to generate revenues in excess of costs—that is, produce a profit. He recognized, too, that he was moving into a new area, that mistakes were inevitable, that a great deal of learning would be necessary, and that substantial investments would have to be made before the point of profitability could be reached.

City Venture's initial aims were high, envisioning nothing less than a comprehensive attack on a wide range of interrelated urban ills. Unfortunately, federal support for urban revitalization began to decrease early in its history, requiring City Venture first to shrink its strategy to focus primarily on job creation, education, and training; and later, with further cutbacks in federal funding, to reduce the program essentially to job creation alone. Even so, its accomplishments were impressive. As of mid-1986 there were seventeen job-creation networks operating in ten states, fifteen others were in the process of being implemented, and over 1,000 new companies employing more than 13,000 workers had been started.[35]

Despite this record, City Venture's prospects were limited, and by 1986 it was clear that the enterprise would fare better as an independent operation.[36] Control Data decided reluctantly to divest its holdings, City Venture was reorganized, and the stock owned by Control Data and other shareholders was sold to City Venture's president, Patrick J. Gorman. In his report to the final meeting of the City Venture board, Norris voiced his conviction that "the pioneering efforts of City Venture during the past eight years will be the foundation for a massive job creation engine serving primarily the United States and developing countries. Ultimately, millions of jobs will be created."[37] A fitting valedictory, with emphasis on the future.

Although Norris has spent most of his adult life in cities, he has never pulled wholly free from his family farm origins. He has a strong philosophical commitment to small- and medium-scale family farm agriculture that antedates and is much like his commitment to small-scale business. In fact, he views the family farm as a special form of small business that is capable of creating new jobs not only for the farm family but also, through the support services it requires, for a viable farm community.

Norris is deeply concerned at the extent to which large-scale corporate farming is eliminating the family farm as a significant component of U.S. agriculture. He recognizes the gains in output that have accompanied the move to big farms but charges that these have been made at too great a cost, observing that "[little] regard has been paid to the resulting loss of jobs, damage to the environment, harmful effects on human health, and the depletion of future production capacity caused by practices that are equivalent to mining the soil."[38] Nor, to his mind, has enough attention been paid to the extent of rural poverty in the United States, much of it attributable to the precarious state of the family farm.

He is convinced that the application of new and emerging technologies, especially those providing less intensive use of fossil fuels and fertilizers, can reestablish family farming as a vital cultural and economic resource, and that information technology in particular can be adapted to the special needs of small- and medium-scale agriculture. Characteristically, he has devised a strategy in keeping with that line of thinking, with computer technology as its centerpiece. In implementing that strategy, extensive data banks of technical information have been assembled that provide through AgTech what amounts to an electronic library geared to the special needs of the family farmer. Computer-based training programs built around PLATO have been developed to cover many phases of farm operation, and computer-based management systems have been designed to maintain production and financial records and to assist farmers in reaching planting, marketing, and other decisions. A newsletter provides timely crop and marketing information, and another is geared to the needs and interests of the growing number of farmers who have computers of their own.

These various services are delivered in a number of ways, including vocational-technical schools, state university extension programs, local banks and farm supply stores, and direct subscription. Another means was Rural Ventures, Inc., a cooperative undertaking closely modeled on City Venture and popularly known as RVI.

Rural Ventures, Inc. was organized in 1979 as a for-profit corporation with eighteen shareholders, including Control Data, three other companies, two agricultural cooperatives, five religious groups, a foundation, a health services organization, several individuals, and the Institute for Cultural Affairs, a Chicago-based organization dedicated to raising the standards of living of very poor people, especially those in developing countries. In pursuit of its aim to increase the productivity and profitability of family farms, Rural

Ventures contracted with governmental agencies, groups, and individuals to provide a variety of services, including preparation of farm business plans, design and construction of farm buildings, animal and crop selection, equipment and energy utilization, consulting, timely market information, and PLATO training. Attention was also given to bettering education, health care, and housing, and to creating new small businesses to supply necessary support services for the local farming community. The first two RVI projects were in rural Minnesota and the third was in Alaska where the clients were two Eskimo villages.[39] Projects were subsequently established in other parts of the country.

Rural Ventures was successful in improving the efficiency and amenities of life of the farming communities it served, but was only marginally successful as a commercial enterprise. A major difficulty was the lack of government interest in the family farm. As one Control Data insider observed, "People at the state level do not consider the small and medium-size farms as [coming within the scope] of their economic development activities." For this reason, funding was sparse. "That's why half the revenue [of Rural Ventures] came from Native American communities because they had their own funds and could make up their own minds and set their own priorities."[40]

Norris was disappointed with Rural Ventures. He expected it to open up a new market of major proportions that would not be confined to the United States. By far the greatest need (which Norris sees as the greatest opportunity) for improving small-scale agriculture is in the developing countries of the world. A necessary precondition for the industrialization that most of these countries are trying desperately to achieve is an agricultural base capable of supporting the nonfood-producing population without which industrial development is impossible.

To Norris the investment made in nurturing family farm technology in the United States represented an investment in R&D that had vast potential not only in business terms but also in terms of human welfare on a global scale. But much the same problems were encountered overseas as at home. In Jamaica, for example, where an effort was made to establish an RVI project, the government was more interested in large-scale agriculture, an attitude reinforced by advice from the U.S. Ambassador to Jamaica, William A. Hewitt, who had formerly headed the John Deere Company and was convinced that the future of agriculture lay in the heavily mechanized big farm.

In an economy move, the administrative organizations of City Venture and Rural Ventures were combined in 1985 under Rural Ventures' president, Patrick Gorman. Some months later, when the the shareholders of City Venture sold their stock to Gorman, the shareholders of Rural Venture did likewise and the two companies were merged. City Venture was the surviving corporation.

At the final meeting of the board of Rural Ventures, Norris expressed regret at its failure as a commercial enterprise but reviewed with some satisfaction the social benefits it had conferred. He saw as most important the demonstration of "the great potential for viable small and medium-sized family farms, given appropriate technology and affordable and readily available education and training in applying it."[41] His confidence in the merits of what it set out to do remains strong, and he holds as an article of faith that "responding to the challenges of small-scale agriculture is vital to the preservation of our heritage. Equally important, it is the only way we can approach the awesome task of improving agricultural production in developing countries. If we are to meet one of the most basic of all human needs—the need for food—we must return to the small farms of the past, bearing with us the technologies of the future."[42]

Closely related to the Fair Break-type of training program were a number of programs Control Data introduced in the penal corrections area. When Wendell Anderson took office as governor of Minnesota in 1972, one of the problems he confronted was conditions within the state penitentiary system. Serious charges had been leveled about the treatment inmates were receiving, and Anderson discussed with his friend, Norbert Berg, the possibilities for establishing an ombudsman program to bring cases of abuse to light. After conferring with Norris, Berg volunteered the services of a loaned executive to aid in establishing such a program and assigned the task to Richard D. Conner, one of the young men who had played a key role in bringing the Northside plant into productive operation.

Conner visited the prisons, interviewed administrators and prisoners, and came to know something of the realities of prison life. Among other things, he was impressed by the fact that many inmates were strikingly similar to some of the disadvantaged people he had helped hire for Control Data's Northside plant, who also lacked elementary skills in reading and math.

Meanwhile, progress was being made in the development of PLATO courseware, and the notion formed in Conner's mind that PLATO could be the means for substantially upgrading the low quality of education within the prison system. He communicated his concerns and ideas to Berg and, through him, to Norris, where they found a ready reception. The upshot was the installation at Control Data's expense of a bank of PLATO terminals at the Minnesota State Prison in Stillwater.

The results were startling. Inmates who enrolled in the program became fascinated with PLATO and applied themselves enthusiastically to the computerized learning process. On average, participants gained 1.6 grade levels in reading ability and 2.16 levels in math in about twenty hours of work on PLATO, enhancing the likelihood of their being able to find and keep jobs on release from prison.

Based on this experience, Control Data in 1974 undertook a modest program to introduce PLATO into prisons, and in 1981 launched a full-fledged effort to market the complete PLATO and Fair Break programs to prison systems in various parts of the country. The timing, however, was less than optimal. PLATO was still hampered by being tied by expensive telephone lines to a central computer, and the marketing effort had only limited success. Still, by the beginning of 1986 it had been introduced into eighty prisons, and now that it is no longer dependent on a remote processing center its prospects for expansion appear promising.

One consequence of the Fair Break/PLATO prison experience was to instill in the minds of Norris, Berg, and others in the higher levels of Control Data management a lively interest in the problems of the U.S. correctional system. They were appalled by what they learned about it: its enormous and growing costs, its failure to rehabilitate, its high rate of recidivism. They came to realize that most inmates returned to society as greater risks than when they were first incarcerated. Here was an "unmet social need" if there ever was one. Why not make it a part of Control Data's business plans?

Just as the Northside experience had led to company plants being placed in other poverty areas, the early prison experience led to work being placed in prisons. As Norris commented some years later, "When you stop to think about it, there really isn't much difference between an inner-city poverty-stricken neighborhood and a prison."[43] With this thought in mind, Control Data in 1981 entered into a contract with the Minnesota State Department of Corrections to assemble computer peripheral equipment at the Stillwater prison. Many of the same policies and procedures which had worked to bring Northside on line were employed there, and the project was as successful in its way as Northside had been. Unlike the typical prison industry jobs of making license plates and doing similar unskilled work, assembling computer equipment provided training and experience on which inmates could build new lives after leaving prison.

Employee productivity at Stillwater rivaled that of the company's other plants, and the quality of work was even higher.[44] A portion of the prisoners' earnings was deducted to defray the cost of their maintenance during incarceration, thus reducing somewhat the cost of the correctional system to the state. Far more important, however, was the fact that participating inmates became qualified for good jobs in the outside world. Several were subsequently hired by Control Data itself.

In the course of the Stillwater project, Control Data became acquainted with an inmate organization called Insight that some of the prisoners had established to help one another through college extension courses. Favorably impressed, the company worked with Insight to start a telemarketing program through which carefully selected inmates learned to be effective telephone salespeople. Another group of inmates was trained to write courseware for PLATO; another to instruct homebound handicapped workers under the company's Homework program; and still another to provide computer programming for Control Data and other clients. In all cases, inmates acquired marketable skills, received individualized computer-based remedial education and training in seeking for jobs and coping with life, and were given counseling to help prepare them for their eventual return to the outside world.

Control Data's Stillwater undertaking attracted considerable attention in circles concerned with the problems of the correctional system. Among those who personally inspected the operation was U.S. Chief Justice Warren Burger. He had long been troubled by the fact that most prisons are "warehouses of convicted criminals, with few facilities for education, training, production, and recreation," and advocated the idea of building "factories with fences around them—where inmates, after training, engage in useful production." He once asked rhetorically, "Do we want prisoners to return to

U.S. Chief Justice Warren Burger at Ceremony Conferring University of Minnesota Degrees Earned Largely Through PLATO by Inmates of Maximum Security Prison at Stillwater, Minnesota, August 17, 1982 (*Source:* Control Data Corporation)

society as predators or producers?" The Chief Justice liked what he found at Stillwater. "Control Data," he wrote, has "pointed the way .... It works."[45] In Norris's words, "experience with education and training and real jobs at Stillwater state prison and elsewhere demonstrates that inmates can be trained to be a stable and efficient workforce, that they can deliver quality products and services, that their labor potential should not be lost to a life of idleness, that prison schedules can be modified to accommodate prison industry, and, as a result, that inmates when released are much better prepared to obtain meaningful employment."[46]

Work at Stillwater and at other institutions using Fair Break and PLATO brought Control Data executives into direct contact with the horrendous problems of the U.S. penal system. They were struck by what they learned of the rapid rise in prison populations, the urgent need for new prison facilities, and the escalating costs of new prison construction. As Norris and his associates weighed these worrisome issues and Control Data's own experience, they came to see corrections as a potential market not only for Control Data but other corporations as well.

This line of thought led Norris to explore with City Venture Corporation the concept of private-sector financing, construction, and management of the nonsecurity functions within prisons. A task force created to study the possibilities reported that prisons were badly overcrowded and becoming more so, that public resources were becoming increasingly overstrained, and that the public was "distressed over the high failure rate of those who go through the correctional process." The report concluded that the time was "at hand for the private sector to put together a new model of a correctional facility" that would employ education and training programs, productive work experience, and skilled prerelease counseling to prepare prisoners for their eventual reintegration into society.[47]

The report included a detailed business plan that was presented in 1983 to the board of City Venture, where it met with a cool reception. The board was reluctant to deviate from its original mission: the revitalization of inner-city communities. Norris argued that "the prison is really an extension of an urban underclass neighborhood—it just has a wall around it. It's mostly the same people, and they just go back and forth." The board was not persuaded and the plan was placed on hold.[48] The Fair Break education and training component, however, is very much alive and is being actively marketed as part of Control Data's Employment Preparation Services. Thus the company is maintaining its relationship with the correctional system, and senior management is confident that the corrections field offers attractive possibilities for future development.

━━━━━━━━━━

Also high on Norris's list of concerns were health care and the delivery of medical services. He was convinced that "society can no longer afford the cost of today's health care system, [and] that efforts at achieving better, more affordable health care must be directed toward preventing illness rather than treating it after the fact." He pointed out that "Americans bear the highest per capita health care costs in the world, yet we do not rank among the ten top nations on most common health indices."[49] Not unexpectedly, he saw in computer technology the means for dealing more effectively with the complex problems of health maintenance, medical service delivery, and cost containment.

He found it shocking that of the huge sums spent in this country on health care, very little goes toward health education and disease prevention. "As a nation," he argued, "we must learn to accept the idea that individuals and communities are responsible for their own well-being. We must also change our thinking to perceive good health as a natural condition, and illness and injury as departures from the norm. We must stop defining health as the absence of disease."[50] Disillusioned by the failure of both the medical profession and government to approach the problem from this angle, he felt that if anything constructive was to be done the initiative would have to come from business.

Employers have a major stake in the health of their employees; the cost of health insurance is a large part of the cost of doing business, and to this must be added the cost of lost time and lower productivity resulting from poor health habits. From early in Control Data's history, Norris tried to encourage good health practices among his own employees. He started years ago by having scales installed in the restrooms of all major Control Data operations as silent reminders to employees to watch and control their weight. A much more ambitious effort was undertaken in 1979 with the launching of StayWell, one of the first comprehensive employee fitness programs in the country. WellTimes, a newsletter for employees and their families, presents information about common health problems and means by which various hazards can be dealt with or avoided. Employee lunchrooms display posters and literature on diet and nutrition, and discussion sessions are held for employees who choose to participate in the StayWell program.

The heart of the program is a computerized system through which employees use PLATO to enter detailed information about themselves and their lifestyles into a computer, which then analyzes the data and generates individual health status profiles with suggestions for health-improvement goals and ways to reach them. Thereafter, individualized training programs are delivered through PLATO and seminars. Employees report back to the computer from time to time and are critiqued on their progress, with strict measures being taken to ensure confidentiality. Only with the aid of computers could this vast amount of data be recorded, analyzed, kept current, and used to prepare the personal health-improvement regimens and deliver the individualized training required.

True to form, once StayWell was established and working smoothly within Control Data, Norris took steps to market it to other corporations. "We believe," he wrote, "that PLATO will prove to be the only effective and practicable means of disseminating health education and information to a wide audience while simultaneously responding to individual user needs."[51] With employee health insurance rapidly becoming a major cost of doing business, some companies are beginning to realize that they have an important economic stake in keeping their employees healthy, and StayWell is designed for precisely this purpose.

Norris also saw the computer as a tool for keeping insurance costs under control. For some years Control Data had managed its own employee health insurance program with computers, improving the accuracy and promptness of benefit payments. This program, too, was marketed to other corporations wishing to improve the administration and control the costs of their programs. The potential exists to use the vast amount of information in the database for comprehensive analyses of health service needs and for the design of more effective means for serving them, but a program for this purpose has not yet been developed.

Norris has long been interested in the economic and social problems of the developing countries, whose needs he saw as areas of great future opportunity. One of the most acute of these, to his mind, was the need for improved health care. Because conditions on American Indian reservations are similar in some ways to those of developing countries, Control Data in the early 1970s cooperated with tribal leaders to set up a demonstration project at the Rosebud reservation in South Dakota.

Health conditions there were deplorable, with the incidence of disease far above national averages. Only one small, understaffed hospital was available to serve a population of 8,500, and many had to travel as far as 130 miles over poor roads to reach this inadequate facility. Under the overall direction of Roger G. Wheeler, vice president for personnel and public affairs, Control Data equipped a medical van that made regular trips through the entire reservation, treating over 900 patients a month, all at Control Data's expense.[52] While results were encouraging to a point, the experience, Wheeler later reported, "convinced us that we do not belong in the medical provider business. Instead, we belong in businesses that provide services to the medical provider community."[53] Before withdrawing, Control Data replaced the van with two permanent clinics staffed by trained Indian paramedics and took steps to integrate the activity back into the Indian Health Service, where it could continue to benefit the tribe.

Norris's most significant effort to improve the nation's health-care system dealt directly with the delivery of medical care and the practice of medicine itself. According to Norbert Berg, Norris's interest in medicine goes back to the 1930s when as a salesman for Westinghouse Electric he often cooled his heels in doctors' offices while waiting to sell them X-ray equipment. He used this time to read all the medical literature he could find. As a result, Berg says, "he really believes he knows a great deal about health and medicine."[54] Be that as it may, Norris has thought for a long time that the enormous capacity of computers to process and manipulate data could one day be adapted to aid in the diagnosis and management of illness. Over the years, Control Data made several forays into different areas of hospital and medical practice, with the most successful being a cooperative arrangement with the Latter Day Saints Hospital in Salt Lake City begun in the early 1970s. This led to the development of an integrated system of laboratory, patient, and hospital management which now goes by the acronym HELP for *Health Evaluation through Logical Processing.*

A key component of HELP is the processing of laboratory tests. The laboratories of large hospitals produce enormous volumes of data that must be handled with great accuracy; for this reason, the laboratory is frequently the first clinical area to be automated. Control Data has become the leader in laboratory automation, with over 160 installations to date, typically in hospitals that have the needs and the resources to be trendsetters.

With the explosion in medical knowledge, the basic information needed to practice medicine today far exceeds the capacity of the unaided human mind to manage. Even an expert dealing with a complex problem of diagnosis cannot handle more than eight or ten hypotheses at a time, whereas computer-based HELP can handle dozens. The central feature of the system is a vast and continually expanding knowledge base built up over a period of fifteen years from nearly a million case histories and some 3,000 medical decision rules drawn from them and from the expert opinions of specialists in various fields.

HELP collects and analyzes patient data from all departments of a hospital, checks and cross-checks when new data are entered, indicates treatment alternatives, and alerts the physician to potentially life-threatening situations. It processes and interprets test results and suggests further tests where indicated. It cross-checks prescriptions against patient records and warns the physician of anything in the patient's history that might indicate the unsuitability of a particular mode of treatment. The doctor makes all patient-care decisions, but HELP broadens his or her range of knowledge relevant to specific cases and improves the quality of diagnosis. It monitors the progress of patients after treatment is prescribed, automatically examines all incoming information for any change that indicates cause for concern, and alerts the responsible professional. Doctors can see what is happening at any time simply by checking the patient's file at a convenient computer terminal.

The system not only improves the quality of patient care but saves money for patients, hospitals, and insurers. Diagnoses can be made more quickly and precisely, tests processed and interpreted more rapidly, unnecessary tests avoided, records kept more accurately and completely, and charges accumulated automatically. In hospitals where HELP has been installed, the average hospital stay is reduced by about one day—a potential saving for the national health care system of many billions of dollars a year.

To work properly, all persons involved in the operation of HELP—doctors, nurses, pharmacists, technicians, administrators—must be trained for their respective roles. For this purpose, extensive training programs have been developed, some of which are delivered through PLATO—yet another example of the ubiquity of PLATO throughout the entire Control Data system.

Improved and more efficient health care is one of this country's most important social needs. On Norris's initiative, Control Data has embarked on a number of programs designed to aid in this as well as other areas. Some of these efforts have required major investments over a period of many years. Not all have been successful, but they have laid the foundations for businesses which hold attractive promise for Control Data and for service to humanity.

Without question, the most important of Norris's "societal needs" ventures has been PLATO computer-based education, initiated in 1963 in cooperation with the University of Illinois and gradually developed and refined in the years that followed. Placing an important plant in the riot-torn Minneapolis Northside in 1968 and subsequently insisting that all new plants be located in poverty areas, urban or rural, was the next major stage in the evolution of his business strategy.

Beginning in the mid-1970s, Control Data under Norris's direction embarked on many programs that at first glance may seem to have little in common: new business and new job creation, technology transfer, converting the culturally and physically handicapped into productive workers, assistance to small business, rejuvenation of decayed inner-city communities, making the family farm competitive, better health care, more effective delivery of medical services. However, all of these fields represent serious problems of twentieth-century society, and the programs Control Data developed to deal with them use computers to provide education, training, and better management services. In the words of Norbert Berg, "The common thread going through all these different projects is computer-based information."[55]

CHAPTER 9

The View from the Top

William C. Norris goes down in the history of our times as an entrepreneur who built a great modern enterprise and gave new depth and meaning to the role of business in society. His record as a manager, however, is mixed. He recognizes that he is "not a good administrator" (he prefers the title *administrator* over *manager*) but protests that this is "not because I can't administer, it just bores the hell out of me." Back in ERA days, he says, "I really was a good administrator, but I soon learned I could get other people to do that," and he was glad to let them do it. He was always "very careful about having other people associated with me who make up for my deficiencies."[1] In this he was successful in large degree.

From the very beginning of his business career, Norris's primary concern was providing strategic direction. This was critically important during the 1960s and 1970s, when Control Data grew from a small company with a handful of employees into one of the largest U.S. corporations. None of this would have happened without strong direction on his part and the support of such able lieutenants as Mullaney, Cray, Kamp, Miller, Price, Berg, and others to whom he gave broad authority and responsibility and then left largely on their own. If he erred in this respect, it was in going too far and not exercising enough control.

Norris's managerial style grew out of precisely the same traits that helped make him a world-class entrepreneur. His interests were always focused more on the future than on the present; on things that were about to be, not things that were; on developing new ideas rather than maximizing ideas already in place. In the words of Robert

Price, who succeeded him as chief executive officer in 1986, "Bill Norris has more insight and foresight than anyone I've ever known. . . . [He] sees the potential of things before others do."[2]

In fact, Norris's vision was concentrated so intensely on the future that he sometimes seemed to think of it as already here. He saw so clearly what *could* be done that he simply assumed it *would* be done—and even, at times, that it *had* been done. He displayed a marked tendency for prolepsis, for thinking of an eventual goal as if it had already been reached. The things he wanted to do were often so clear in his mind that he talked about them as though they were *faits accomplis* rather than ideas in process of development. The apocryphal silkworm story his associates told so wryly came close to expressing the literal truth. This characteristic carried with it important advantages. One was constancy of purpose.

During Norris's tenure as chief executive, his tenacity was legendary; as Mullaney says, "When [Bill] gets on a track, he stays with it."[3] Time and again he refused to drop projects because of early mishaps or stumbles, an innate habit strengthened by his experience at Sperry-Rand where management was often too quick (he thought) to kill initiatives that did not work out immediately. Norris explains, "In Control Data, when we hit adversity, we would slow down our effort, but we never cancelled a project that still made sense."[4]

But there were disadvantages to his tenacity. He often underestimated the difficulties involved in reaching goals he had set. His impatience to get new projects underway without taking time for careful advance study and analysis (his opposition to market research was proverbial) led to false starts and problems that might have been avoided. Cases in point were City Venture and Rural Ventures, whose futures were so clear in his mind that he considered them, for practical purposes, almost at hand. Even when obstacles could be foreseen, he was inclined to ignore them, go around them, or overwhelm them. Once, when lawyers objected that a feature of a plan he was proposing for multistate cooperation in economic development was unconstitutional, his quick response was, "Well, amend the Constitution."[5]

Curiously, the clarity with which he saw the future and his disdain for difficulties were at the root of one of his greatest weaknesses as a manager: He was not a good communicator. He was, in fact, a *poor* communicator at both the sending and receiving ends. He did not always bother to explain the final result he wanted to achieve, and subordinates often mistook for ultimate goals aims that to him were only interim benchmarks. Confusion was an inevitable result.

Norbert Berg, who learned better than anyone else how to work with Norris, claims it was "easy"—if you knew how. "You just find out *exactly* what he wants done, and then do it," he says. "The hardest part is the first part. A lot of people don't understand what he wants done. They don't ask him. They guess. And they often guess wrong."[6] The reason many failed to ask was that they were nervous in Norris's presence and anxious to get out of his office as quickly as they could, and they sometimes left without a complete picture of what he wanted. Actually, Norris was extraordinarily patient in explaining things if requested to do so.

He seldom laid down specific guidelines or defined limits for implementing his directions. He seemed to think that anyone could see what needed doing without having everything spelled out. He was "flabbergasted" by the lavish appointments and excess staff he found upon visiting his first Business Center; lacking a clear advance definition of what the role and character of the Business Centers were to be, those in charge had gone overboard to give Norris what they thought he wanted.

People also found it hard to communicate with him—especially if they disagreed with him. Because he saw so clearly the ends he was seeking, he tended to be impatient with those whose vision was less astute and to brush aside opposing points of view. From early in his life he had learned to have confidence in his own judgment, whether others agreed with him or not. He became known for having a "short fuse" and for being "rough" in dealing with those who didn't see things the way he did. Some people, in fact, considered it risky to deal with him at all and as far as possible avoided doing so.

Part of the problem was that Norris was painfully shy and did not relate to others in a free and easy manner unless he knew them very well. "After you get to know him," more than one longtime associate has testified, "he's a warm and friendly person, a pleasure to be with and talk to." But few reached this point in their relations with him. His top people learned how to take problems to him and discuss them with him openly, and even to counter him when they thought he was wrong, but subordinates were prone to keep silent or to say what they thought he wanted to hear. Many feared to tell him things they thought might make him angry. Norris finds it difficult to understand why people should feel this way about him, but the fact remains that many did.

Actually, Norris respected people who had command of their facts and had thought through their positions clearly, even though they might be contrary to his own. He had no respect whatever for people who changed their positions for no reason other than to agree with him. His presence, however, was so powerful that except for a handful of very strong people at the top, few ever dared to cross him. In consequence, he gained the reputation of surrounding himself with "yes men." Although understandable in the circumstances, the accusation was less than fair; "yes men" (or women) never went far with Norris.

A more important outcome of the atmosphere thus created was to close important channels of communication through which chief executives normally stay informed about the course of affairs within their organizations. This, combined with Norris's intense concentration on the goals he was pursuing, kept him relatively isolated from internal Control Data problems. The dangers inherent in such a position were relieved only by the ability of Robert Price and Norbert Berg to explain to people in the organization what Norris really wanted.

Norris's entrepreneurial style included a curious combination of patience and impatience. He was quite willing to accept that developing new markets takes time and commitment, that large risks are involved, and that quick payouts are rare. But he grew testy with opposition and delays that he interpreted as foot-dragging. His experience with the management of Commercial Credit Company is illustrative. For years he tried to infuse them with a more innovative and entrepreneurial spirit, and for years he was frustrated in his efforts. On several occasions he insisted on certain actions that Commercial Credit management opposed and that they only took reluctantly. At Control Data headquarters in Minneapolis, Norris did not have to spend much time persuading others to his way of thinking because most had learned to respect his judgment. This was not true in Baltimore, where "people resented being told to do something by someone they felt didn't know their business."[7]

Norris was not a "consensus manager." He listened to opinions and advice and then made his own decisions. To him, the future was already in view, and he was in a hurry to get there.

Norris has frequently called attention to the fact that small businesses tend to be more innovative and willing to take risks than large ones. It is notable, therefore, that Control Data remained innovative and entrepreneurial even though by 1980 it had grown to be one of the largest companies in the United States. Clearly, size is not the only determinant of organizational creativity. Much more important is the turn of mind of those who hold key positions in the enterprise, and their ability to direct its course.

Two conditions are necessary for significant risk-taking and innovation to occur: willingness to try the new and unconventional, and the capacity to move the enterprise into new and nontraditional courses. *Ability to control* is as important as *willingness to try*, and the great advantage of the smaller organization is the fact that it is easier to control. But effective control by the chief executive is not the exclusive province of small business. It is more rare in big business, but by no means unknown.

For all the years Norris was in office, Control Data, despite its very large size and widely distributed ownership, remained as effectively under his charge as if it had been an independent, owner-managed business. Few heads of other major corporations in the country had anything like this degree of autonomous power. It is instructive to examine the footing on which it rested.

Essentially, Norris's power lay in the enormous respect in which he was held by his board and by the organization he built. That in turn was based on experience. People learned to have confidence in Norris's business judgment because it proved consistently sound over a long period of years. He was right in his decisions to back Seymour Cray with his big computers, to go into peripheral products, to develop data services, to sue IBM; he was right so often that those whose support he needed (board, key executives, shareholders) were ready to go along with him even when they had doubts about particular courses of action. He was careful to use his power with integrity and restraint, and people had confidence it would not be misused.

That Norris was founder and chief executive from the outset helped greatly, of course. He did not have to work his way up through the organization; he was always the boss; nobody could remember a time when he was "just one of us" because he never was.

In the beginning, when Control Data was a small business, he ran it like one, and in a very real sense he continued to do so, at least until 1980 when he moved up to chairman and turned over operating responsibilities to Robert Price.

He was always careful to maintain good relations with the company's directors and to consult them on important issues of policy and strategy, but until his retirement the Control Data board was always *his* board. Norris himself tells a revealing story. In the mid-1960s, when the company was experiencing one of its recurrent periods of financial difficulty, the Continental Bank of Chicago suggested to Norris that he add George A. Strichman, head of Colt Industries, to the Control Data board. The idea made sense: Continental carried a large share of Control Data debt and was worried about the safety of its loans, and Control Data had always had a strong cadre of outside directors. "We think Strichman can help you," the bank said. "Fine," Norris responded, and invited Strichman to meet with him. The two had a very candid talk, which according to Norris went something like this:

Norris: I've invited you here at the suggestion of Continental.

Strichman: I know that, and I'm willing to join the board if Continental thinks I should and you want me. But I've got to have a very frank answer: Whose board is it?

Norris: What do you mean, "whose board is it?"

Strichman: Who puts people on the board, and who do they answer to?

Norris: Well, I suppose they answer to me.

Strichman: Okay. Fine. I just wanted to know, because if it's not that way I don't want any part of it.

In recounting the story, Norris added: "When the chips were down, George would support you because he was part of your board. I can't quarrel with that. I think that works better than all this so-called democracy."[8]

That the board of directors was "his" does not mean it was subservient or in any way a "rubber stamp," as critics sometimes charged. The directors were loyal to Norris in the sense that they had great respect for him but not in the sense that they felt obligated to support whatever he put before them. At board and committee meetings they asked hard questions and insisted on hard answers. It never occurred to them to conduct themselves in any other way, nor did they believe that Norris would have it any other way. He might have been short or impatient with his staff, but never with his directors.

It was not a conventional corporate board. Contrary to an opinion that became increasingly popular in the 1970s that the only insider on the board should be the chief executive officer, there was always strong insider representation on the Control Data board. Norris believes that a high-risk, high-technology company needs among its directors persons with intimate, firsthand knowledge of the business and of the resources and capabilities of the organization—knowledge only insiders can have.[9]

Norris also believed in strong nonmanagement representation on his board, and from 1966 on these were always a majority. But while the outside directors of most major corporations are drawn largely from the ranks of chief executive officers of other large companies, Norris looked much further afield and recruited directors from scientific, military, academic, governmental, and other circles. He knew the value of having other corporate chief executives, active or retired, as directors, but he took care to supplement their wisdom and experience with that of others from diverse walks of business and professional life.

Furthermore, Norris worked his board very hard, requiring of his directors a greater commitment of time and energy than many with heavy responsibilities for their own corporations could comfortably accept. All directors served on two or more board committees, many outside directors served on the boards of subsidiary corporations, and individual directors were called on frequently for special tasks related to corporate affairs. Norris consulted informally and often with those who had particular experience or competence in areas where critical decisions were required. He depended on his board to a much greater extent than is typical of most other heads of major corporations.[10]

By 1980 Norris's business strategy was essentially in place. Control Data Corporation was established as producer of powerful computers, and with over half the world market for memory devices it dominated the peripheral products field. IBM's old Service Bureau Corporation had been thoroughly integrated with CYBERNET, and with fifty data centers operating on six continents Control Data occupied an exceptionally strong position in the international data services market. Professional and engineering services were securely rooted in that profitable and growing field. Through Commercial Credit, the company had become one of the country's important financial institutions. The technology of computer-based education was well-developed, and despite ongoing marketing problems PLATO's future was beginning to look promising even to skeptics. And Norris's unconventional notion about addressing societal needs as business opportunities had progressed beyond the talking stage and was an operative reality. Norris had cause to be satisfied with the shape his work had taken.

At age sixty-nine, while not yet ready to retire, he began planning for that eventuality. Actually, he had started thinking about it at least as far back as 1968, when he had engaged Cresap, McCormick and Paget to make a preliminary assessment as to the availability of potential successors among members of his key staff. This move was in response to needling from his director and confidant, Robert Leach, who frequently demanded of him, "Bill, if you were hit by a truck tomorrow morning, who do you have to take your place?"[11] The study revealed that Norris did in fact have on his staff several outstanding young men who could be considered possible candidates, although none would be ready without further training and experience. The years that followed were rich in opportunities for growth and maturation. By the mid-1970s, the promising young men of a few years before were seasoned executives, and by 1980 the field of candidates had narrowed to two.

At the board meeting in May of that year, Norris told his directors that when the time came for him to retire (which he made clear was not yet) he would recommend that his duties be divided between two men, Robert M. Price and Norbert R. Berg, with Price to be president and chief executive officer and Berg to be chairman of the board. He pointed out that while Berg and Price had quite different profiles of ability and experience, these were mutually complementary, and together they comprised a combination of strengths Control Data would need for its next generation of top management.

Norris explained to the board that he wished the duties of the two men to be defined in such a way that Price would be CEO in fact as well as name, but certain areas would be designated as the special province of Berg. He recognized that this posed a delicate problem: how to divide the responsibilities to permit a sharing of power without compromising the role of the chief executive. He recognized, too, that any such arrangement would work only if the two men wanted it to work and that no administrative or organizational contrivance could offset any inclination to the contrary. He was confident, however, that Price and Berg, who had already worked together closely for many years, would make a good team.

Both Price and Berg had been identified in the 1968 Cresap, McCormick and Paget study as individuals of high promise. Price had emerged as one of those whose interests and capabilities could take him all the way to the top. He was recruited in 1961 at age thirty-one by the infant Control Data Corporation as a mathematical staff specialist working on linear program codes and was quickly promoted to manager of applications services. In 1963 he was named director and in 1966 general manager of the company's burgeoning international operations. Thereafter, he rose rapidly through a series of positions to president of the Systems and Services Company (a major corporate division) and to president of the Computer Company (i.e., everything except Commercial Credit). In 1977 he was elected a director of the company, and in 1980 he was named president and chief operating officer of Control Data Corporation.

Berg was hired as a Control Data supervisor in 1959 at age twenty-seven. He moved quickly to personnel manager of the computer group, to which were soon added the duties of director of administration for that group. In 1965 he was advanced to the post of director of administration and personnel for the entire company, reporting directly to Norris. Two years later he was named vice president, in 1973 senior vice president, and in 1977 a member of the board.

At the time of the Cresap, McCormick and Paget study and periodically thereafter, Berg made it clear that he had no ambitions ever to become chief executive. He had a strong preference for staff-type work and felt he could be most effective in supporting roles. He was also keenly conscious of the fact that he had been trained as an industrial relations man rather than as an engineer, mathematician, or computer scientist, and he recognized that for a long time to come Control Data would require a chief executive who was thoroughly grounded in some aspect of computer technology.

In preparation for the eventual transfer of power to Price and Berg, the by-laws of the corporation were amended at the July 1980 board meeting to create a Corporate Executive Office with Norris as chairman and chief executive officer, Price as president and chief operating officer, and Berg as deputy chairman of the board.[12] Norris continued to be responsible for overall company performance; Price, subject to that higher level of authority, was to manage the affairs of the company; and Berg was to take on certain defined functions, notably the "identification and development of business opportunities in areas of societal needs"—in other words, areas Norris placed high on his own corporate agenda and whose continuity he was anxious to assure. Berg was also charged with dealing with agencies of state and local governments, handling senior executive personnel matters, and providing "counsel and guidance to officers and senior staff."

The basic purpose of the Corporate Executive Office was "to provide opportunities for Price and Berg to acquire hands-on experience in the exercise of major corporate responsibilities and a real-life test of their capacity to work together in harmony and effectiveness."[13] In other words, Norris wanted a trial run of the arrangement he had in mind for his eventual retirement. He would remain in office for an indeterminate period, not only because he was not yet ready to leave but also to be in a position to step in if problems should arise.

Control Data operated under this arrangement for the next five and a half years until Norris's actual retirement at the beginning of 1986. From the board's standpoint, the plan worked well. Norris delegated to Price broad responsibility and commensurate authority for all phases of company management. Price kept Norris informed and sought his advice on major problems, but Norris was careful not to interfere or second-guess his decisions. Price had an opportunity rarely given to other than chief executive officers to "exercise major corporate responsibilities," and he did so in a highly competent manner. Likewise, Price and Berg demonstrated their "capacity to work together in harmony and effectiveness." The Corporate Executive Office thus accomplished its two primary objectives.

It did not, however, function as an "office" in an operative sense; that is, no actions were ever taken in the name of or on the authority of the Corporate Executive Office. As a practical matter, the arrangement simply represented a division of responsibilities between the three men, who worked well together as a functioning top management team. Price largely took over the job of running the company, Norris devoted himself chiefly to exploring new opportunities for

Members of the Corporate Executive Office, L to R: Robert M. Price, President, Norbert R. Berg, Deputy Chairman, and William C. Norris, Chairman, 1982 (*Source*: Control Data Corporation)

corporate growth, especially in the "societal needs" areas, and Berg provided counsel and support for both and handled delicate relationships with state and local governments and other key external constituencies.

The role of the Corporate Executive Office was not well understood. In the minds of people other than the three at the top, there was some uncertainty as to who was responsible for what. As long as things went along smoothly, this was of little concern, but as troubles developed in 1984 and deepened in 1985 people both inside and outside the company began to question the arrangement.

Although the three never discussed it among themselves or with others, they, too, must have experienced a degree of uncertainty. Norris gave Price full assurance of his authority to manage company affairs, and while Price never had reason to question the authenticity of that delegation, he was well aware that Norris as chief executive had both a legal right and a moral obligation to countermand any action which in his judgment was contrary to the best interests of the company. This awareness must certainly have constrained Price's thinking and action.

And Norris must have felt the reverse of these concerns. Despite the complete sincerity of his desire to give Price a wide range of responsibility and authority, he knew that in the final analysis the welfare of the corporation rested on his shoulders, and as long as he was chief executive he could not in fact make complete delegation to anyone. The fact that the relationship between the two men remained untroubled was due in large part to the good offices of Berg.

There had long been a special relationship between Norris and Berg, which had its beginnings in the early days of the company's history. Berg quickly came to Norris's attention for the orderly and effective manner with which he handled his personnel and administrative duties in Mullaney's Computer Group. Then, in 1962, not long after joining the company, Berg was hospitalized with tuberculosis for what proved to be a long absence. He had been with Control Data for only three years, and in that time had had no more than fairly casual contacts with Norris.

Nevertheless, Norris had formed such a favorable opinion of Berg that he called in the company administrative officer and told him, "Listen, I don't want some clerk to cut off Berg's pay. Keep him on the payroll until he comes back to work." At the time Berg had three children (one also afflicted with tuberculosis), a pregnant wife, and no resources to fall back on. From then on Berg's loyalty to Norris was complete and unconditional,[14] and in the years that followed the two men grew increasingly close in their working relationships.

In 1965 Berg was advanced to the position of director of administration and personnel for the company, reporting directly to Norris. The two started meeting every morning in Norris's office to organize the day's work, review problems to be resolved, and discuss ideas forming in Norris's mind, a practice they would follow for years to come.

Not long after Berg became director of administration and personnel, IBM's efforts to block the marketing of the new CDC 6600 forced the layoff of some 2,000 Control Data employees, a prospect Norris dreaded. Actual handling of the layoffs came within Berg's responsibility as director of personnel, and Norris warned him "it won't be easy." Berg performed the unhappy task effectively yet with sympathetic concern for those who had to be dropped. Norris was greatly relieved and impressed with the young man's skill.

Time and again, Berg stepped in to relieve Norris of one kind of unpleasant duty or another. For all his apparent toughness, Norris hated to fire people—a serious handicap in a chief executive. Associates ascribed his attitude to an unusual degree of sensitivity about people and a reluctance to cause pain and discomfort to a fellow human being. According to one of his senior executives, "Bill seemed to be a cold, aloof person, but underneath that hard shell was a soft heart." Berg assumed this function, which on several occasions required informing senior officers that their services were no longer needed. At one time a popular pastime in the Minneapolis-St. Paul area was naming "the thinnest book ever written"; a title that went the rounds in Control Data was *People I Have Fired* by William C. Norris.[15] Inevitably, Berg became known in some quarters as "Norris's hatchet man," an appellation Berg considered "wrong and unfair." He was, in fact, a rather sentimental person who shrank from causing pain in others but who willingly took on any task his job called for or that might be of help to Norris.

A much more important role that Berg came to fill was that of communicator. Because of Norris's personal style of managing, communications between him and his organization were especially difficult. It took great determination to build Control Data into the company it became; unfortunately, that determination included a large component of singlemindedness that discouraged people from being open with him. This created a situation dangerous for any chief executive, particularly one in an organization of the size to which Control Data had grown by the mid-1960s. Berg gradually took on a communications function without which Norris would have found it difficult to operate.

On the one hand, he kept Norris informed on things he needed to know. According to one longtime aide, "Norris is just so awesome to most people that they can't say the things to him that Berg can." Norris had such confidence in Berg's personal loyalty that he would accept from him unwelcome information which, had it come from someone else, might have evoked an angry response.

Berg took care to preserve the integrity of his own organizational relationships and would often preface a verbal report to Norris with the caveat, "I'm not going to tell you who told me this, so don't ask me." Over the years, Norris pushed him only a few times with words to the effect: "How the hell can I accept this if you won't tell me where it came from?" To which Berg would reply, "Because I won't ever tell you anything again. You can't ask me that." Norris was likely to answer, "Aw, that's bull——," but then laugh and say, "I understand, you can't tell me."[16]

There were times when Berg was able to say, when no one else could, "Bill, you can't do that." And Norris was able to say, "Norb, I can't say this to anyone but you." Berg felt that he and Norris could talk freely with each other because Norris was sure of his loyalty and knew he had no axe to grind.

On the other hand, Berg often found it necessary to interpret Norris to others in the organization, and Norris for his part would often transmit his instructions through Berg; in point of fact, he could communicate more effectively through Berg than he usually had the patience or was willing to take the time to do directly. This process had a negative as well as a positive side. In acting as interpreter and transmitter, it was necessary that Berg invoke Norris's name frequently. He always relayed Norris's instructions accurately and completely, but there was occasional uncertainty in some people's minds as to who was doing the speaking, Norris or Berg. Said one longtime aide, "When a guy's upset with the message he gets, it's natural for him to wonder where the message is coming from, but without checking with Norris, which he wasn't likely to do, there was no way to test."

The close relationship between Norris and Berg was the cause of some concern within the organization. Berg recalls that at one of their regular morning meetings in the spring of 1970, "Norris got up and closed the door and said, 'Norb, you should be aware that there is some resentment on the part of some people over you because they know that I talk things over with you and sound things out with you.'" They discussed the problem, but other than Norris agreeing to "encourage [senior executives] to work with me and . . . use my help," no change was contemplated.[17] By now Berg had simply become too essential to Norris for either man to worry too much about what others might think.

Their relationship was further enhanced by the creation of the Corporate Executive Office in 1980. With Price managing the company, Norris was able to devote himself primarily to exploring new business opportunities in the social needs areas in which he saw Control Data's greatest prospects for business growth—areas to which Berg was closely attuned by temperament and training. Here again, he was able to provide support which Norris found immensely valuable—for example, in computer-based education, urban and rural rehabilitation, new business and new job creation, and corrections.

Freed from day-to-day operating responsibilities, Norris was able to spend more time pursuing long-range strategic interests and ideas for improving the economic, social, and political environment of business in general and Control Data in particular. There were elements of that environment that he found deeply disturbing: the perennial problems of joblessness, the precarious state of family farming, the threat of hostile corporate takeovers, the need for more effective technological cooperation, and the continued erosion of U.S. strength in international markets. In an effort to deal with these and related matters, he embarked on what amounted to a one-man crusade to alert people in leadership positions to the dangers and to outline the courses of action he considered essential for the good of the economy and the country.

Beginning as far back as 1967, he had been urging business leaders to play a more active role "to assist in solving social problems such as those of the underprivileged, pollution, and urban congestion,"[18] and in the years that followed he had spoken before many different audiences on one aspect or another of the same general theme. With the establishment of the Corporate Executive Office the pace of these activities mounted significantly, and between July 1980 and December 1985 he delivered a total of 238 public addresses—an average of almost one a week.[19]

He also authored numerous articles for newpapers and magazines, dealing with the same themes as his addresses but aimed at wider audiences. In 1982 he commissioned Dr. Harold F. Williamson, professor emeritus of economics at Northwestern University, to combine his speeches and papers on related topics into chapters for a book titled *New Frontiers for Business Leadership*; published in 1983, it received interested attention in business and academic circles.

He sustained an incredibly busy pace. In one four-day period in early 1983 he attended a Monday evening reception at the home of the chairman of the Government Research Corporation in Washington, D.C., followed by dinner with the Minnesota congressional delegation; the next day he breakfasted with representatives of a group of high-technology companies at the Shoreham Hotel, attended a meeting at the Office of Technology Assessment, lunched with editors of *The Washington Post*, met that afternoon with Senator Howard Metzenbaum in his office in the Capitol, and flew to New Haven, Connecticut, where that evening he delivered an address to the Yale Business and Economic Forum. On Wednesday he had breakfast in New York with a representative of the medical profession to discuss Control Data's work in the health-care field, followed that with a meeting with the president of the Carnegie Corporation and the governor of North Carolina, and went from there to meet with David Rockefeller at the Chase Manhattan Bank. That afternoon he flew back to Washington, where he had dinner with the director of the Administration for International Development (AID) and the president of Control Data Caribbean at the home of Control Data director Lois Rice. After dinner he flew to Orlando, Florida, where the next morning, Thursday, he attended a meeting of the Conference on International Economic Cooperation. He arrived back in Minneapolis that afternoon, utterly weary but proud of all he had been able to accomplish.[20] Altogether it was a remarkable agenda for a man in his seventies.

Norris's efforts to influence the course of affairs were not limited to speaking and writing. He also—and perhaps more importantly—assisted in setting up organizations to deal with specific problems, a process he referred to as "institutionalizing" the endeavors in which he was interested. Under this heading, the job creation networks occupy a special place. In addition, he devoted a substantial amount of his personal time to Minnesota Wellspring, a public/private partnership founded in 1981 to foster new business and job creation by expanding the development and application of technology and improving education. Wellspring is a broadly based organization embracing state government agencies, business corporations, organized labor and agriculture, and universities. It was Norris's idea, and from the beginning he has provided a large share of its leadership.

One of Norris's most creative accomplishments was the establishment of the Microelectronics and Computer Technology Corporation (MCC), incorporated in January 1983. Located in Austin, Texas, and headed during its first four years of operation by retired Admiral Bobby Inman, MCC is engaged in advanced long-term research in microelectronics and computers. MCC is a consortium of high-technology companies, now twenty-one in number, who pool certain portions of their research efforts and share in the results. Each member is responsible for developing its own products from those results, but the pooling of costly basic research speeds the rate of progress and provides a far higher rate of return on the research dollar. Norris estimates that each dollar invested in MCC produces ten dollars worth of results of interest to Control Data.[21]

MCC was Norris's brainchild, but the task of recruiting participants and putting the organization together he left largely to Price. The undertaking originally met with considerable resistance because of apprehensions over the possibility of running afoul of the antitrust laws, but this was overcome chiefly by keeping the Department of Justice informed at each stage of the process and making sure that no meetings were held without a member of the Anti-Trust Division in attendance.

For years Norris had been concerned with the inhibiting effects of antitrust anxieties on efforts to promote cooperation in technological research, and the difficulties encountered in establishing MCC spurred him to action. The result was enactment of the National Cooperative Research Act of 1984, which cleared away antitrust uncertainties with respect to this type of intercompany cooperation.

Norris lobbied both houses of Congress intensively over a two-year period, talking with individual legislators in their offices and testifying before committees. He convinced Congress that cooperation, based on the MCC model, is the only effective way for the United States to respond to the Japanese challenge. He even sat through meetings of the Senate subcommittee staff drafting the bill and helped define the term "research and development" for purposes of the act, which was passed unanimously by both houses and signed into law in October 1984.

Some of the other supporters of the legislation later claimed credit, but the bill as finally passed was based squarely on Norris's proposals, and he was the first witness quoted in the Senate Judiciary Committee's report on the bill. As of the end of 1985, some thirty cooperative R&D ventures had been registered under the provisions of the act, working on problems as widely diverse—and as important—as cancer research, artificial intelligence, automobile emission control, fossil fuels, and nuclear technology. In terms of scale of impact, passage of this legislation stands as one of the most significant accomplishments of Norris's long and fruitful career.

In a somewhat different context, the establishment in 1985 of the Midwest Technological Development Institute (MTDI) was another major achievement whose benefits are likely to reach far into the future. This, too, was Norris's brainchild, a brilliant embodiment of the concern for cooperative effort that has characterized his thinking since the days of his deep personal involvement in cooperative technological endeavors during World War II.

Where MCC is a consortium of private companies, MTDI is a joint venture of nine midwestern states. Norris is the moving spirit behind MTDI and chairman of its board of directors. Members of the board are appointed by the governors of the participating states, and the entities most directly involved in the actual work of MTDI are state universities and economic development agencies. The organization has three primary purposes: expanding technological cooperation between industries and domestic and foreign universities; providing a mechanism to improve the access of industry—especially smaller companies—to the fruits of technological research; and promoting an equitable transfer of technology between the midwest and the world at large.[22] MTDI is still in its early stages of development, but its aims are high and its promise is great.

From 1980 through 1985, Norris was engaged in many other activities with long-range implications for the company and the economy. These included serving as a member of President Reagan's Private Sector Initiatives Task Force in 1981 and chairman of its subcommittee on employment, and as a member of the U.S.–Jamaica Business Committee in 1982 and chairman of its subcommittee on small business and agriculture. Opposition to hostile corporate takeovers occupied yet another considerable portion of his time. This was a matter of special concern to Norris, partly because of Control Data's vulnerability on that score but also because of his visceral revulsion to the idea of forcible acquisition by corporate raiders whom he repeatedly denounced as "white-collar thugs" engaged in "looting corporate treasuries, cheating shareholders, and undermining America's ability to compete in world markets."[23] No other subject had the capacity to raise Norris's blood pressure to like degree. He was able to secure legislation in the state of Minnesota designed to make hostile takeovers more difficult but despite dogged persistence failed in his efforts at the federal level.

Norris used to good advantage the time he gained by turning company operations over Price. It was an enormously productive period for him, and one in which he took full advantage of his prodigious energies and capabilities.

Norris had never been close to the organization (even in ERA days he had not been a "shopwalker"), but until the establishment of the Corporate Executive Office he had been fairly readily available at least to his principal aides. This changed, however, after mid-1980. With Price for all intents and purposes running the company, and with his newly acquired freedom to devote himself to matters he saw as important to the company's future, he came to rely almost wholly on Price and Berg for all communications between him and the organization.

Norris had always been held in awe by the men and women of Control Data Corporation. From this time on, that awe increased, and he became virtually a figure of myth and legend.

CHAPTER 10

A Time of Troubles

During the early years of the Corporate Executive Office, things seemed to go very well. Revenues grew from $3.8 billion in 1980 to $4.1 billion in 1981, with further increases in each of the three following years to $5 billion in 1984. Net earnings rose from $150.6 in 1980 to $170.6 million in 1981, dropped to $155.1 million in 1982, and recovered to $161.7 million in 1983. Considering the problems the computer industry in general was facing at this time, this falloff in earnings appeared temporary and no cause for alarm.

Many who had been critical of Norris's ventures into unorthodox fields began to be more optimistic about the company and its future, and by 1982–83 even investment analysts who had long been skeptical of PLATO as a drain on earnings were viewing it positively. In mid-1982, one highly respected market newsletter observed, "We do not believe that investors fully recognize the intrinsic value and uniqueness of the component software and systems technology of [Control Data], which is augmented by the financial and marketing support of Commercial Credit." Early in 1984 another newsletter noted that "PLATO's revenue and pre-tax profit could be sizeable in 1985 and beyond," an opinion that by then was becoming fairly widespread in informed investment circles. The same newsletter went on to predict that Control Data earnings would increase by about 30 percent in 1985 and realize further increases of 28 percent in each of the five following years, a prospect that if realized would have justified Norris's most optimistic expectations. This euphoria was reflected in the market, where Control Data's common stock, after adjustment for a two-for-one split, more than doubled from $28 in July 1980 to $64 in July 1983.

As early as 1982, however, things had begun to go wrong. The trouble started in the peripheral products area.

The decision to enter the OEM and plug-compatible markets had appeared for some years to be very well-grounded, and by 1980 the peripherals group was being hailed by the trade press as "turning in the stellar performance on the corporate balance sheet."[1] By 1983 Control Data peripheral products were a $1.5 billion business, and with 47 percent of the OEM disk-drive market, the company dominated the peripherals industry.

But problems had started surfacing in 1982, when there was a slowdown in the peripherals business. Although 1983 appeared to show improvement, gross margins deteriorated. The business began to come apart in 1984 and crashed resoundingly in 1985. That year began with forecasts of $1.7 billion in peripherals revenue and $100 million in pretax profit. At midyear these figures were revised drastically downward, and the year-end actuals were revenues of $1.3 billion and a staggering pretax loss exceeding $300 million. Control Data's former money machine had become a major drain on resources.

In late 1984 the company withdrew suddenly and completely from the plug-compatible disk-drive business, taking a $130.2 million writeoff in the process. The story behind that painful move is illuminating.[2]

A key reason behind Control Data's going into plug-compatibles in the first place was the assumption that it would be an incremental business. It was at the outset, but it did not stay that way. The first plug-compatible drive and its controller were relatively simple devices, but as time passed the two became increasingly sophisticated. By 1982, when work began on designing a drive equivalent to the one IBM was expected to bring to market in 1984, the product had grown far more complicated and its development time and costs far more extensive than anything the company had previously experienced. Conservative estimates called for a $75 million investment to develop the new drive and another $75 million to design the controller it required; the controller, in fact, would itself have to be a powerful computer. The ante to stay in the game had jumped to $150 million.

Actually, the ante was much higher. Over the years, IBM's new product introductions had become more difficult to predict, and

Control Data was caught short when in 1984 it became known in the marketplace that IBM had another disk drive in the works with twice the capacity of the one it would bring out next. Control Data was faced with the prospect of making a huge investment in a drive that would have only a limited market life, and an even greater investment to be ready for the next turn of the competitive wheel—the medieval rack comes to mind. It was a hard choice, but Norris and Price decided to cut their losses and get out of the plug-compatible business altogether. Thomas Kamp, whose idea it had been to enter the plug-compatible market, objected strenuously from the sidelines; in early 1983 he had been promoted to vice chairman of the board and was no longer directly involved in operations.

Additional difficulties soon compounded this major setback. Control Data had seen other computer manufacturers and assemblers of computer systems as a major market for its products, and for some years it had proved to be one. The flip side of the coin was the vulnerability of the OEM business to slowdowns in that market, and the year 1985 marked one of the most serious downturns in the industry's history. Some of Control Data's customers went to the wall, and others, including some of the industry's largest operators and Control Data's best customers, cancelled or sharply reduced their orders.[3] "We weren't sleeping," Norris later commented, "but we didn't react quickly enough. Sometimes success is your greatest enemy."[4]

To further complicate matters, an explosion of new technologies yielded superior products that competitors were selling at sharply lower prices, and to meet those prices resulted in correspondingly lower income margins for Control Data. A number of important new products the company announced in the 1982–83 period were late in actually getting to market, and some of these had quality problems that were difficult and costly to correct. With benefit of hindsight, it is now clear that by 1983 in peripherals Control Data's costs and quality were out of line with competition. In mid-1985 Price and his staff calculated that to realize revenues and profits by 1987 equivalent to those of 1984, it would be necessary to produce and ship twice as many peripherals units with half as many people and half as much plant capacity.[5]

Along with the explosion in technology came a sharp rise in competition in a shrinking market. The challenge from domestic competitors was serious enough, but to this was added the threat posed by the Japanese, who saw disk drives as the key to the worldwide computer market. As the only large-scale independent manufacturer left in the peripherals business (other U.S. companies are essentially bit players), Control Data bore the brunt of the Japanese onslaught.

Any of these problems alone—timing, market slowdowns, development costs, technology, or competition—would have created serious difficulties for the company; in combination they were awesome.

Peripheral products were not the only part of the business in trouble. The company's data services divisions had also seen better days. Remote data processing was losing money in Europe, partly as a result of several acquisitions that turned sour but also because of difficulties inherent in maintaining economies of scale on a continent divided by many national boundaries. Because borders cannot be crossed easily in the remote data processing business, it had been necessary to establish separate processing centers in each country. A master center in Belgium helped provide some economies of scale, but operations in individual countries remained essentially national. When business turned down in 1982–83, the European processing operations began to record sizable losses, imposing an added drain on company assets.

The advent of microcomputers in the early 1980s had a serious impact on the data services business. Many customers found that they could now use desktop computers to handle on-site many of the tasks for which they had formerly used Control Data timesharing services. The new technology presented opportunities as well as problems, but the company was slow in responding to them. The limited storage capacity of microcomputers was a handicap for certain kinds of work; however, by linking "intelligent" desktop computers with large central computers the potential existed not only for preserving the remote processing business but for raising it to new levels of effectiveness. This required major system and software changes that were not undertaken with the promptness or pursued with the vigor the circumstances called for. "The major problem," Norris later observed, "was that [data services management] didn't move fast enough to adjust to the implications of the microcomputer, even though I used to review it with them."[6]

For Engineering and Professional Services, microcomputers opened up a broad new field that they entered immediately: helping large users of the new small machines to plan the most effective configurations of equipment for their special needs and providing reliable maintenance services. A large organization needing many computers for a variety of functions has a multiplicity of equipment to choose from, some suited for certain purposes and some for others; competent professional assistance in making the best selection is a significant advantage. And companies with several different kinds of equipment, especially those with widely dispersed operations, are likely to experience servicing and maintenance difficulties if they must rely on individual vendors who are reluctant to service equipment not their own or at locations inconvenient to their service centers.

As previously noted, the Control Data Institutes had also lagged in meeting the challenges posed by microcomputers. The new machines could, for example, deliver instructional materials via floppy disks, but they were lacking in ability to store programs and knowledge bases and to manage the instructional process. Only when it became possible to link "intelligent" terminals with central mainframes did the institutes and the PLATO system in general start moving into the new technological environment.

There were parallel problems and opportunities in the technical applications area, traditionally the province of CYBERNET. The potential existed here for developing sophisticated applications programs to combine the convenience of customers' on-site computers with the great backup resources of central supercomputers and provide a kind and level of service previously unknown. But this, too, could not be accomplished quickly or without considerable cost.

Control Data's tardiness resulted in a rapid loss of customers and a serious decline in data service revenues in the 1983–84 timeframe, setbacks that coincided with the grave problems encountered by peripheral products and contributed importantly to the financial crisis of 1985–86.

While peripherals were floundering and remote data processing services were having problems, other parts of Control Data's service business were doing well. Arbitron, Ticketron, and Engineering Services were thriving, as were government systems and, for a time, the computer mainframe business. Revenues and profits from these operations largely masked to the outside world what was happening elsewhere in the company.

From the latter part of 1984 onward, however, sharply intensified price competition brought on by the general malaise of the computer industry significantly lowered the profit margins of computer mainframes, adding materially to the company's mounting woes. IBM and Digital Equipment Company moved aggressively into the scientific and engineering market. Complicating the competitive situation in mainframes were difficulties encountered by the sales force in overcoming anxieties about the company's future. The users of such equipment are heavily dependent on vendor support, and any doubt as to the vendor's continuity is a matter of acute concern. Also, beginning about 1982, Cray supercomputers cut deeply into that important part of Control Data's business. Control Data no longer had the supercomputer field virtually to itself, although it held high hopes for the ETA-10 due to reach the market before the end of 1986.

By the fall of 1984 Control Data was facing a growing liquidity problem. In peripheral products, the downturn in the computer industry had resulted in excess inventories, and sharply intensified competition had created the need for costly improvements in manufacturing facilities. The CYBERNET and timesharing businesses had had to be restructured, also at considerable expense, and research and development dollars were being spent to keep the new ETA-10 supercomputer on schedule.

Selling Commercial Credit seemed a logical way way to raise the needed cash. That business was profitable, but its rate of return was low by finance industry standards, and it was losing market share in the fiercely competitive conditions that followed deregulation of that industry. Because of Commercial Credit's failure to implement successfully some of his most cherished plans, Norris had long since lost interest in it, and Price, for his part, was deeply involved in the harassing problems of the computer business. The need had long since passed for the lease-financing function Commercial Credit had originally been acquired to serve, and the Baltimore-based subsidiary had become an increasingly worrisome distraction to its Minneapolis-based parent.

Commercial Credit had a net worth of more than $800 million, and a selling price anywhere near that amount would solve Control Data's liquidity problems overnight. The company's investment bankers, Goldman Sachs & Co., strongly recommended this course, and in November of 1984 Control Data announced that Commercial Credit was for sale.

Unfortunately, the task of finding a suitable buyer proved harder than predicted by the company's investment bankers, chiefly because the company was engaged in so many different businesses: consumer and business finance, life and health insurance, vehicle leasing, real estate, banking, mortgage lending, and a variety of other activities potential buyers found difficult to accommodate. Finding it impossible to negotiate a sales agreement on acceptable terms, Control Data took Commercial Credit off the market in June of 1985.

Meanwhile Control Data's financial problems had grown worse than when Commercial Credit was first put up for sale.[7] In light of this deteriorating condition and foreseeing the possibility that a buyer might not be found in time, work had been started earlier in the year on the prospectus for a public securities offering of $200 million in bonds and $100 million in preferred stock. In July 1985, after the Commercial Credit sale had fallen through and before the securities had been placed on the market, a letter was received from the Securities and Exchange Commission challenging the accounting treatment of certain portions of the company's 1984 earnings report.

The SEC took exception to a tax benefit that had been recognized in connection with the 1984 plug-compatible write-off, and the accounting treatment of losses incurred by Earth Energy Systems, a company in which Control Data had invested because of Norris's interest in wind power as a renewable energy resource. Both were technical accounting matters and the company's handling of them had been fully approved by its public accountants, Peat, Marwick, Mitchell & Co., one of the nation's prestigious accounting firms. On August 6 the company restated its 1984 year-end earnings from $31.6 to $5.1 million, and at the same time recognized the effect of updated financial information and restated its second quarter 1985 figures from a $3.8 million profit to a $4.8 million loss.

The restatement was quickly followed by a series of stockholder suits alleging that company officers and directors, with the connivance of the outside auditors, had manipulated statements to give a misleading picture of the company's business performance and financial condition. The suits charged that the company and its auditors had "tried to maintain an artificially high market price for the common stock," and that investors who bought stock had paid higher prices than they would have paid had the true facts been known. Hard on the heels of the restatement of earnings and the filing of the suits came notice from the insurance carrier that the company's officers and directors liability policy would be cancelled after the ninety-day period required by the contract.

The new earnings figures had the further consequence of placing the company in technical default on its bank indebtedness. Urgent negotiations resulted in temporary waivers of loan covenants, giving the company until September 15 to bring itself back into compliance. The new $300 million securities issue had been important before; it now became imperative.

Still worse was to come. Work proceeded apace on the new issue, but continued deterioration of the company's business had by this time made it clear to insiders that the company would suffer a far larger than expected loss for the year. Remote processing services continued to lose money in Europe, computer systems profitability dropped sharply, and the bottom fell out of peripherals. These unhappy developments were cause for increasing concern to both Control Data and the managers of the offering, Goldman Sachs and Merrill Lynch.

The night before the scheduled closing on September 17, Price and his chief financial officer, Marvin Rogers, and representatives of the two investment firms debated in a lengthy telephone conference whether or not to go ahead. According to Rogers, "Everyone agreed that, despite the language of the prospectus, perceptions in the business community did not cover the range of loss which now appeared probable. It was going to be worse than we thought anyone expected." After painful review of all the facts, the wrenching decision was made to cancel the offering—literally, almost "two minutes before midnight."[8] The next day Price issued a press release announcing the decision and explaining that "Despite the fact that we had descriptive language about our performance in the prospectus, it was not absolutely clear that our financial position was fully understood by prospective investors."[9]

The eleventh-hour cancellation sent shock waves through Wall Street and rocked the already damaged confidence of many in Control Data's future. Standard and Poor promptly lowered Control Data's and Commercial Credit's credit ratings, sharply raising the cost of money for both. The market price of Control Data's stock dropped six points to under $17 a share, down a full one-fourth from the level at which it had been selling.

Business Week headlined an article, "Has the Street Given Up on Control Data?"[10] and *USA Today* ran a story, "Control Data Seen Out of Control."[11] Doomsayers had a field day, and journalists stretched to find colorful words to describe Control Data's plight: "financial hemorrhaging," "sea of red ink," "beleaguered Control Data," "deepening financial crisis," "worst troubles in decades," "ailing computer company." *The Economist* of London sympathized with the "ragged trousered" unfortunate.

Added to all of management's other concerns was acute anxiety over the possibility that the company's difficulties had made it ripe for a hostile takeover. *The Wall Street Journal* speculated that "[on] paper, at least, it can be argued that Control Data's assets, if better managed or sold, would be worth substantially more to shareholders than currently indicated by the price of its stock." The article pointed out that after cancellation of the securities offering, company shares were trading at one-third to one-half of book value, and that the market value of Control Data was less than the net worth of Commercial Credit alone. One unnamed investor was quoted as saying that at the current stock price, "I don't see any way that the company doesn't attract the attention of a corporate raider who could acquire it, and quickly pay off his investment by selling only a few units."[12]

But more immediate troubles mounted swiftly. A short-term moneymarket debt outside the bank agreement was due to mature in a few days, and the company expected to meet it by drawing on approximately $100 million still available under revolving fund agreements that were not in default. The company's bankers, however, refused to advance additional funds and as a result Control Data defaulted on the short-term debts, which in turn placed it in default on its principal bank indebtedness. The situation was critical.

There was panic on the part of the banks. Less than a year before, on Halloween of 1984, Storage Technology had filed for Chapter 11 protection under the federal bankruptcy code and many banks had been badly burned. Control Data was now seen by some as "another Storage Technology," and the banks were determined to avoid repetition of that previous loss experience. However, they soon learned from Control Data's books that the company's asset values were far more than enough to repay all bank indebtedness, and that this was not a situation in which creditors would get back only a few cents on their dollars; if worse came to worst they could be repaid in full from the sale of Commercial Credit, Arbitron, Ticketron, and other readily separable assets that were valued at well over twice the total amount of bank indebtedness.

Finding that they were under no real threat of losses, the bank representatives with whom Control Data was dealing at the working level showed little of the concern creditors normally feel for protecting their debtors to help assure repayment of their loans. Daniel Pennie, the company's senior legal officer, described the resulting behavior as "a feeding frenzy." There was considerable friction among the numerous domestic and foreign banks involved, all of them scrambling to improve their positions *vis-à-vis* the others. Not having to worry about keeping the business going, they felt free to nitpick and haggle until they got the best possible terms. And because no bank wanted to fare less well than any other, the result was what Rogers called a "least common denominator syndrome," by which he meant the harshest terms on which all the banks could agree.

After months of tortuous negotiation, in June of 1986 the sale of $125 million in accounts receivable was completed and the defaults were cured by a new override agreement. Control Data was no longer in default, but the new covenants were tightly restrictive. With its financial house in order, Control Data went to market on July 31, 1986—nearly a year after the earlier abortive effort—with a new securities offering of $200 million of senior notes and $150 million of convertible debentures. The investment community, its confidence returning, oversubscribed the two issues by a total of almost $50 million. The company could now breathe easier.

=====

By mid-1986, progress had been made in restructuring company operations as well as finances.

Peripherals presented the thorniest problems, and in February of 1985 Lawrence Perlman was given the demanding responsibility of pulling that business back from the brink of disaster. He found the business in desperate shape. An "enormous bow wave of plant and equipment" had been built up at the same time prices were falling; inventories were not only much too high but badly overvalued, and the sudden slackening in demand resulting from the downturn in the computer industry "hit with enormous impact." Plants had to be closed and thousands of workers laid off, and this had to be done quickly.[13]

With full support from Price and Norris, Berg and Frank Dawe, vice president for human resource management, worked with Perlman to devise means for making these painful adjustments as easy as possible to those adversely affected. In disposing of plants, efforts were made to do so in ways that would preserve the maximum number of jobs in the communities involved. Working with state and municipal authorities, some plants were sold to local plant management or other community groups.

Where entire plants were not divested but substantial reductions in personnel were necessary, a variety of measures were employed to ease the impact; these included reduced overtime, temporary leaves of absence without pay, and formation of employee placement centers to help displaced employees find jobs elsewhere. Workforce action teams were formed to utilize surplus employees at many levels to do everything from raking lawns to painting walls. Especially significant were the efforts made to inform employees in advance of company problems likely to affect them and to alert them to the possible personal consequences. Despite their necessary harshness, the measures taken by the company to deal with its crisis were remarkably well accepted by employees.

The basic problem Perlman found was that peripherals had too many product lines and was not concentrating sufficiently on those in which it had market share and competitive advantages. In a rapid series of excisions, he reduced the number of lines from fifteen to seven. Steps were taken to speed up the process of modernizing manufacturing technology, tighten quality controls, strengthen marketing, and accelerate research and development to regain Control Data's traditional position at the leading edge of storage technology. By late 1986, the time of this writing, peripheral products were well along on the comeback trail.

International data services were still a problem, but significant headway was being made in the domestic data services business. Whereas in the past these had been largely confined to payroll and accounting applications, offerings were now expanded to other business functions, with particular emphasis on marketing information services such as the highly successful Arbitron. Business Services extended its operations to include credit union, legal, and human resource services, and has had particular success with its "yield management" programs that are used by airlines and hotels to maximize revenues by monitoring their seat and room utilization. In these and other business applications, Control Data has combined the increased power of microcomputer technology with (where appropriate) the speed of more powerful central mainframes.

In the area of scientific and engineering services, traditionally the province of CYBERNET, parallel efforts are being directed to the development of sophisticated applications programs combining the convenience of customers' on-site workstations and computers with the backup resources of central supercomputers to provide a level of service previously unavailable. Early examples of the potentials of this approach are applications in the areas of structures, piping, electronic design, and power distribution systems.

Perhaps more important are organizational changes that have been made to enable the company to capitalize on its services capabilities. Managerial responsibilities have been realigned according to market opportunities rather than technology employed. There is no longer an organizational entity known as data services. Instead, services are now grouped into four separate businesses: Technical Support Services, Business Services, Scientific Information Services, and Economic Development Services, each headed by a senior officer and engaged in addressing the special needs of its own markets.

From the early days, applications programs to deal with customer problems have been an essential feature of Control Data strategy. If the company had continued to rely primarily, as it did originally, on simply selling computer time, it would long since have been out of that business. Instead, the objective had been that of delivering *solutions* to its customers. Therefore, providing ever more complete information and applications by the most appropriate means available became integral to company strategy and was now recognized as a requirement for restoring the company to sound economic health. Those privy to what is planned have confidence that services in a variety of forms will reemerge as a central thrust of Control Data's business and a pillar of the company's strength. In the words of Robert M. Price, "Computer services offer Control Data its best chance for above-average growth and profitability."[14]

It was Price who played the leading role in seeing the company through this difficult period and restructuring its finances and operations, initially as president and chief operating officer and from

January 1986 on as chairman and chief executive. In this he had the strong support of Berg, particularly when it came to dealing with the delicate human and community relations problems involved. Price consulted with Norris and kept him informed, but Norris gave him a free hand and backed him fully.

Norris had never pretended to be an expert in corporate finance. In the early days of the company's history, he demonstrated considerable persuasive power in securing loans from skeptical bankers, but the crafting of financial strategy was outside his range of interests and he was quite willing to leave it to others in whom he had confidence, as he had in Price. And no one who knows Norris could imagine his having the patience to endure the months of haggling negotiations that were an unavoidable part of the process. Norris followed events closely but was content with Price's management of the day-to-day course of events.

CHAPTER 11

Changing the Guard

Although Price managed the company during the critical 1984–85 period, it was Norris who attracted the most public attention. He became, in effect, the lightning rod for complaints about Control Data's poor performance. There was widespread belief that the company's problems were rooted in Norris's unconventional notions, that he was "frittering away resources on offbeat social schemes and letting grand visions overcome the day-to-day details of running a business for profit."[1]

This attitude reflected a serious misunderstanding of the facts. Control Data's problems did not lie in the unconventional programs associated with Norris's name but in the company's basic businesses: peripheral products, data services, and computer systems. It was here that the drastic losses were occurring. Less than 5 percent of the company's assets were employed in the so-called societal needs areas, and while some of Norris's projects had not yet reached profitability, their losses (other than those incurred in the ill-starred Earth Energy Systems investment) were minuscule in relation to those of the company's strictly standard activities. Yet they bore the brunt of the blame.

The explanation lies not only in their unconventionality but also in the prominence they had been given for a dozen years by Norris himself in his numerous public statements. Norris was a colorful and enigmatic figure and by far the most visible member of the Control Data organization. Because he so often talked about societal needs, they were what he and Control Data had come to be most closely identified in the public mind. And when troubles arose it was these that were presumed to be their cause.

Although this perception was wide of the mark, it was generally and stubbornly held. Charges of "involvement in trivial projects" and "using Control Data assets to pursue social ideas at shareholder expense" were frequently leveled, often by writers who did not take the trouble to check their facts. Norris was accused of "neglecting the business to pursue exotic humanitarian projects," a complaint that had often been made when the company was doing well but was now repeated with an accusatory "we told you so." One investment analyst wrote in a newsletter to subscribers that "Control Data has got to eliminate the garbage and get back to basics." A favorite whipping boy was PLATO, which many critics saw as a "side project, unrelated to the core of the business" and "a serious diversion of company resources." Norris had stated several times that Control Data had spent $900 million on PLATO; now business journalists used this figure with telling effect.

Throughout, Price's position generated considerable interest and sympathy. Early in the critical period, *Business Week* commiserated with him for having been "unable to stop profits from plummeting under the burden of Norris's heavy investments in these mostly unprofitable services."[2] And again: "Price appears to be walking a tightrope. If he angers Norris by pushing too zealously to trim favored but unprofitable operations, he could fall out of grace with the chairman, who has a reputation for elbowing aside any executive who challenges him. On the other hand, Price will be blamed, as chief operating officer, if corporate profits remain low. By serving Norris, Price could become inextricably linked to the problems that have driven down the stock price."[3]

Reporters in the Minneapolis-St. Paul area were especially critical of both Control Data and Norris—as were many local business leaders, if more privately. For some years the extravagant attention given the company and the man had been a source of irritation among those with whom he had never established warm personal relations. There were some who took satisfaction in the turn of the screw.

━━━━━━━━━━━━━━━

Both in the press and in private conversation, reference was often made to Norris's age—seventy-four in July of 1985—and to the fact that he had overstayed the time chief executives customarily retire. He was prominently featured in a *Business Week* article entitled, "Chief Executives Who Won't Let Go,"[4] and speculation became general that the time had come for him to step down. Amid stories of Control Data divesting unneeded assets, one critic suggested that Norris was one of the "assets" that the company ought to divest. Another was so unkind as to say, "Bill Norris is living proof of the need for a mandatory retirement policy."

There is no question but that Norris was reluctant to let go of the reins. He frankly enjoyed the status of chief executive of a major corporation, not for the social standing, for which he cared little, but for the voice it gave him in the worlds of business and government (Norris's version of President Theodore Roosevelt's "bully pulpit"). He still had goals to achieve, and he wanted an effective base from which to pursue them. Not least important, he did not want to leave while the company was in trouble—"I don't like to walk away from a fight." He was in vigorous health, with an energy level higher than that of many who were years his junior. While his father died at an early age, his mother lived until well past ninety, and at seventy-four he was confident he still had many productive years ahead. He was in no mood to throw in the towel.

Even so, he was not unaware of the inexorable turning of the calendar pages, and of the fact that the time would come when he would have to retire. But he was determined to make sure that that event, when it came, would be accomplished in an orderly fashion. He had begun preparing nearly twenty years earlier, when he retained my old firm to review the availability and degree of readiness of possible successors within the Control Data organization. More recently, in 1980 the board at his request had created the Corporate Executive Office to test his plan of having Price and Berg succeed him. He was pleased with the way that arrangement was working. Price was handling the company's problems with confidence and skill, and Price and Berg together had demonstrated their ability to function as a first-class management team.

One thing that Norris found especially reassuring was the systematic manner in which Price had set about reviewing and evaluating all phases of Control Data's businesses. Starting in November of 1984, Price had begun holding strategy meetings on the afternoons and evenings before regular board meetings. At these sessions, the officers responsible for each business of the company appeared before the directors and presented detailed analyses of where their particular businesses stood, the problems they faced, and their assessment of future prospects. The pros and cons of alternative courses of action were discussed, and management measured its conclusions against the judgment of the directors. By this means the directors were kept informed on the directions management proposed to go, and management had the benefit of the directors' counsel. Norris was satisfied with the course of these meetings and the resulting clarification of the company's strategic directions.

Nevertheless, as Control Data's troubles continued to snowball all through 1985, board members were uncomfortably aware of their penultimate responsibility. As they followed the course of events and made sure that management knew what was going on and were taking all appropriate measures to conserve the company's assets and protect its future, it was never far from their minds that the single most important responsibility of a board is to select the chief executive officer and, if necessary, to relieve an incumbent of his duties and appoint a successor.

There were those on the outside who questioned whether the Control Data board had the courage and capacity to handle the task when faced with so awesome a character as Norris. Considering his age and the problems the company was having, more than one person assumed that the only reason Norris was able to stay was because he had the directors under his thumb.[5]

This was far from true. The board was "his" in the sense that the directors were personally loyal to him, but not in the sense that they had surrendered any of their responsibility for independent judgment. The directors were deeply concerned about the course of company affairs and growing indications that year-end results would be considerably worse than had been anticipated. They were also worried by the increasingly negative press the company was receiving and began themselves to consider the need for a near-term change in leadership.

Sometime during the week of October 21, Norris had a long talk with Berg during which they discussed frankly the mounting tide of public criticism and the growing uneasiness among some of the outside directors. They also reviewed the progress being made to bring company affairs under control. With business strategy now firmly in place as a result of the systematic reviews Price had been conducting, Norris felt confident that he could turn over to Price and

Berg the responsibility for implementing that strategy and retire in good grace. The time to do this, Norris and Berg concluded, was at the annual stockholders' meeting the following May.

However, Norris's carefully laid plans and timetable were soon overtaken by events. At this meeting in late October Berg raised what would prove to be a critical issue. He suggested that perhaps the time of Norris's retirement would be a good time for him to leave also. In view of his close identification with Norris, he argued, there was a strong likelihood that his becoming chairman would be perceived as an effort on Norris's part to retain *de facto* control. Norris firmly vetoed the idea.

He later discussed with Price his decision to retire and the timing he had in mind. In the course of the next few days he checked his thinking further in separate conversations with some of the non-management directors.

A meeting of a committee of the board had previously been scheduled for November 5 and 6, and Norris took this opportunity to meet informally with five of the company's eleven outside directors. He told them in confidence of his decision to retire and his intention to recommend that Price succeed him as chief executive officer and Berg as chairman, in accordance with the plan originally put in place over five years before. Several of those present expressed reservations about dividing the office of chairman from that of chief executive, but as this was an informal, *ad hoc* meeting no effort was made to reach a conclusion.

Subsequently Norris invited all the outside directors to have dinner with him alone at Bluff House on November 13, two evenings before the November board meeting. (The outside directors usually gathered this far in advance of board meetings for committee meetings and other company business.) At that time he distributed a memorandum in which he reminded the directors that "starting in July of 1980, and periodically since then," he had advised the board of his intention to recommend that his responsibilities be divided between the two men. The memorandum went on to detail the manner in which he proposed that the two offices work and the reasons he considered the arrangement to be in the best interests of the company.[6]

There followed a heated discussion in which Norris, supported by two directors, argued strongly for the plan. Most of the others, however, were opposed, some vehemently so, objecting that while the original plan may have been sound under normal circumstances, the company's critical condition made it essential that there be no ambiguity as to the chief executive's authority. If the chief executive were not also chairman, they argued, people would question who was really in charge. The point was also made that if Berg were chairman, his close relationship with Norris (which would undoubtedly continue) might handicap Price. Berg's premonition on this score proved all too accurate.

The opposition to Berg had nothing to do with his qualifications for the chairman's office. The board was quite willing—in fact, anxious—that he remain as deputy. But they wanted to make sure that both the authority and the responsibility of the chief executive would be absolutely clear and that a change in management would take place in fact and not merely on paper.

Views were exchanged freely at this session, but no conclusion was reached, and Norris asked the outside directors to meet with him again the following evening. In advance of that meeting, Norris and Berg had a long talk during which Berg urged Norris to drop his request that Berg be named chairman. Norris argued that his proposal was in the best interests of the company but finally bowed to Berg's insistence that it would be a mistake to push further. At the meeting that evening, Norris agreed reluctantly to accept the judgment of his outside directors. Nothing was said at the full board meeting the next day, but for all intents and purposes the decision had been made. The details of the retirement arrangements were worked out in the weeks that followed.

Both Norris and Berg were deeply disappointed by this outcome. Each had considered the matter settled long before, and it came as a shock to find it was not. Berg felt he had been dealt with unfairly because the promotion he had been led to expect—not only by Norris but by individual members of the board—would not be forthcoming. Norris believed that Berg's special skills would be needed to handle the internal and external problems that lay ahead and that Berg could support Price more effectively from the position of chairman than deputy.

But Norris's point of view found little support among the outside directors. Berg's effectiveness over the years had stemmed not only from his relationship with Norris but from his ability to get things done smoothly and without fanfare—the mark of a good staff man. He had a knack for resolving conflicts in such a way that few people other than those who were directly involved even knew they existed, but while this was evidence of his skill, it had the ironic consequence of keeping his work from being appreciated outside a close inner circle. When the time came for the promotion he had expected, the support he needed from directors outside that circle was not there. Characteristically, he took his disappointment in good grace and turned his hand immediately to aiding Price as loyally and faithfully as he had long aided Norris.

At the time of a special board meeting called in mid-December to consider, among other things, problems arising from the imminent cancellation of the company's directors' and officers' insurance, Norris formally advised the outside directors of his intention to retire as of the January board meeting rather than wait until the annual meeting in May. He had come to the conclusion that as long as the decision had been made, it would be a mistake to delay the action beyond the January meeting. The local and business press were already speculating about his imminent retirement, and now that the decision had been made the story was likely to leak at any time. If it became public knowledge that he was leaving but would not actually step down for another four months, both he and Price would be severely hampered in their ability to provide the decisive leadership the company needed. The directors agreed and approved the retirement arrangements that had been worked out in committee following the November board meeting.

To add to the mounting perceptions of disarray at the top, Control Data lost five of its directors in the next two weeks. Three outside directors stepped down when Control Data was unable to secure new liability insurance for its officers and directors at an acceptable price to replace the coverage that had been cancelled effective December 19, and two officer-directors retired at the end of the year. Continued board membership now carried a substantial personal financial risk, in addition to the heavy time burden it had come to entail.

The actual transfer of power was accomplished matter-of-factly at the regular meeting of the board on January 10, 1986. The meeting opened with Norris presiding. The first order of business, as always, was a review of financial and operating statements, followed by Norris's customary oral report on the state of Control Data affairs.

That completed, Norris formally made his decision to retire a matter of record and presented resolutions naming Price chairman, president, and chief executive officer and renaming Berg deputy chairman. The necessary actions were moved, seconded, and carried with no further comment.

Without either Norris or Price changing their places at the table, Price assumed chairmanship of the meeting and presented resolutions accepting Norris's decision to retire, expressing appreciation for his services, and electing him chairman of the board emeritus and chairman of a newly formed committee on Innovation and Long-Range Opportunities. Other than these actions, taken in *pro forma* fashion, there were no speeches and no ceremony, and Price conducted the remainder of the meeting routinely. Despite the calm facade, everyone present was aware of being party to a historic event.

Immediately after the meeting, Norris, Price, and Berg faced a battery of press and television cameras and journalists from national and local news media who had gathered for the event. In a prepared statement, Norris expressed confidence that "the company's basic strategy is sound." He confirmed that "a number of assets essential to that strategy" had been redeployed and that "certain organizational and operational changes [had] been made in response to changed conditions in the company's business environment." He emphasized that he had "confidence in Bob Price's capabilities to implement the decisions that have been made" and that he was pleased that Berg would "continue his active involvement in the company as deputy chairman of the board."

Price, for his part, paid graceful tribute to Norris and confessed that it would not be "easy to follow a legend." He went on to sketch the progress being made in restructuring the company's finances and outlined in broad terms the strategy he proposed to follow. "Control Data," he concluded, "is a company with great pride in its past and great confidence in its future . . . [Armed] with that pride and that confidence and the legacy of Bill Norris's vision, we are eager to move into a new era."[7]

After months of highly critical comment, the reaction of the press to Norris's retirement was predominantly complimentary. The day before the public announcement of his retirement, a columnist for the *Minneapolis Star and Tribune* mused on the rumor that Norris was about to step down with, "That means we're about to lose a congenitally opinionated, wonderfully outspoken and everlastingly

William C. Norris at Press Conference Announcing His Retirement, January 10, 1986 (*Source*: Minneapolis Star and Tribune)

imaginative corporate curmudgeon."[8] *Time* magazine headed its story of the official announcement "A Visionary Exits."[9] Under the heading "A Good Corporate Citizen Steps Down, Not Out," the *Minneapolis Star and Tribune* in its lead editorial on the day of his retirement paid tribute to Norris as "a man with many visions" and concluded with a stirring encomium: "Because Norris wasn't afraid of mistakes, he made them. Because he was a man of vision, he sometimes went too far. Because he was a self-confident leader, he wouldn't be second-guessed. As a result, some promises weren't delivered. But because of that courage, vision and leadership, many promises were. Minnesota and America are richer in many ways because of him."[10]

CHAPTER 12

Creating the Future

On his last day in the office he had occupied for fifteen years, Norris confessed to Berg that he "felt a tug in the belly" that reminded him of the feeling he had when he left the farm in Nebraska to take the job with Westinghouse.

On Monday morning, January 13, 1986, following the announcement of his retirement the preceding Friday, he settled into his new quarters in Bluff House. Over the weekend, Berg had personally supervised the moving of his desk and personal belongings—the bust of Plato, books, fishing trophies, wall decorations, mementos. For many years Norris had had two full-time personal secretaries, but he felt that he would now need only one, and this morning she was at her desk in the outer office with filing cabinets and office equipment all neatly in place, ready for Norris to start his day's work.

Bluff House is a three-story, Tudor-style residence that was on the property when it was bought by Control Data. An attractive home across the road from the Tower, on a wooded bluff overlooking the Minnesota River, it had since been used as a guest house, for small private meetings, and for the entertainment of distinguished visitors. It was now converted into a comfortable office for Norris. His office windows have a magnificent view over the trees to the river, and just outside these windows is a feeding trough for deer that is kept supplied with grain through the harsh winter months; during his few idle moments, Norris enjoys watching them. On quiet days with few visitors coming and going, they wander about on the lawn in front of the house. All in all, it's an idyllic setting where Norris came quickly to feel very much at home.

William C. Norris in His Bluff House Office, February 1986 (*Source*: Control Data Corporation)

The only overt sign that his days are somewhat more relaxed is the fact that he arrives for work a half-hour later than was his custom for years. He still leaves for home at about the same time but carries with him only one briefcase instead of two. It is always filled with papers for evening work. His daily agenda is as tightly scheduled as ever, and as closely adhered to; lunch is still served to him in his office where he usually eats alone, his current reading propped before his plate and notepad at hand. He keeps current on Control Data affairs through regular sessions with Berg and periodic visits from Price.

He maintains his busy speaking schedule. During the first eight months of his retirement, he made twenty-one public addresses before a variety of governmental, business, professional, and academic groups—including one in Switzerland, one in Belgium, and two in Canada. One of the reasons he had been reluctant to retire was concern that he would no longer have an effective base from which to pursue his work; that concern has proved unwarranted. He remains in popular demand as a speaker, and his calendar is filled with commitments for the months ahead. Apparently his public position is so secure that his name alone is platform enough. He continues to testify before legislative committees, to meet with members of Congress and governors, and to confer with business, professional, and governmental committees in connection with the projects on which he is working.

As in the past, his speaking and meeting schedule requires a fair amount of travel, but his itinerary is no longer as hectic as it used to be. On a trip to New York soon after his retirement, he and his wife, Jane, took time off to see two plays and to visit the Metropolitan Museum of Art; it was the first time in over twenty years that they had seen a play together and his first visit ever to the Museum. In October of 1986 he traveled to Japan for a Conference on Advanced Technology and the International Environment and stayed over with Jane for a few days of sightseeing. In his years as chief executive he had usually raced home from his out-of-town meetings and was at his desk early the next morning. On several occasions since the move to Bluff House Berg has said, "I've never seen Bill as relaxed and happy as he is now."

Norris speaks with enthusiasm about his "new career," and in many ways he acts like a young man just getting started on his life's work: He sees a lot of things he wants to do and is anxious to get at them.

Throughout his career, two themes have dominated Norris's thinking: the advancement of technology and the application of technology to the solution of practical problems. Both themes find their penultimate expression in the activities in which he is now engaged.

He has blocked out four areas of concentration: (1) working on long-term projects for Control Data, (2) strengthening the competitive position of U.S. industry in world markets; (3) providing aid to developing countries through improved education, job creation networks, and higher agricultural productivity (with emphasis, of course, on small-scale farms); and (4) assisting some of the members of his family in their business ventures.[1] Control Data Corporation benefits directly or indirectly from his activities in all areas except the last, which presents no conflict.

There are few distinct boundaries between the first three areas, and many of his activities relate in one way or another to at least two and often to all three. For example, as chairman of the company's Committee on Innovation and Long-Range Opportunities created by the board at the time of his retirement, he is working to identify future strategic directions in which Control Data is most likely to prosper. In his mind, these have to do chiefly with matters like computer-based education, job creation, technological cooperation, and agricultural productivity, all of which he considers important to Control Data's future and essential both to rebuilding U.S. competitive strength and aiding the developing countries of the world.

There is a holistic quality in Norris's way of thinking that enables him to see the interrelatedness of seemingly divergent problems and processes. While for purposes of discussion he divides his work into three discrete areas, these primarily concern the *channels* through which he has organized his activities, not the *content* of the areas themselves. Thus the first deals with the work of Control Data Corporation, the second with efforts exerted through various combinations of organizations in which Control Data plays an important but not the central role, and the third with tasks that require the active involvement of this country's foreign aid programs and the cooperation of governments of the developing nations.

This high degree of interrelatedness is apparent in the work of the Midwest Technological Development Institute (MTDI), created in late 1984 at Norris's initiative. A consortium of nine Midwestern states (Illinois, Indiana, Kansas, Michigan, Minnesota, Nebraska, North Dakota, Ohio, and Wisconsin), its goal is to expand technological cooperation by promoting technology transfer between universities and industry, and between the Midwest and the rest of the world. The board of MTDI consists of thirty-six members—four each appointed by the governors of the participating states—drawn principally from business, the universities, and state agencies involved with scientific affairs and economic development. Norris is board chairman and "chief energizer."

His interest in MTDI arises directly from his concern for the decline in the competitive strength of American industry. He cites a *Business Week* article stating that "In current dollars, the [manufacturing] sector has plunged from a peak of 30% of gross national product in 1953 to about 21% in 1985, with much of the decline coming within the last decade."[2] He warns that "Pressured by fierce international competition, the U.S. is abandoning its pre-eminent status as an industrial power by increasingly obtaining its manufactured parts and products from abroad, exporting its precious technology and jobs in the process."[3]

Norris sees "increased industrial/university/government cooperation in R&D" as one response to the challenge this trend presents,[4] and MTDI as an instrument for this purpose. He explains that MTDI "will promote cooperative technology development through the establishment of a series of consortia, each focussing on a single area of technology which is significant to the Midwest, builds on strengths of the participants, and has potential for the commercialization of results." Consortia are now being organized in four fields: (1) advanced engineering polymers, (2) ceramics, (3) advanced manufacturing, and (4) technology for family farms and smaller-scale food processing.[5]

Currently Norris is devoting special attention to the advanced manufacturing project. "There's a lot of research going on in advanced manufacturing in places like the National Bureau of Standards, Purdue, Michigan Institute of Technology, and Northwestern," he says, "but they're *research* plans, they don't take that technology out and do something with it. They expect industry to do that, and industry doesn't have the resources except for the very large companies like IBM, General Motors, and General Electric." The investment required to create advanced manufacturing systems which incorporate CIM (for Computer-*I*ntegrated Manufacturing) is enormous and a strain on the resources of even the largest and most prosperous corporations.[6]

Despite the cost, Norris sees this as the only means for restoring U.S. industrial strength, and for that reason believes that the technology must be made available and affordable to manufacturing organizations of *all* sizes, not just the giants. He frequently calls attention to the fact that "Cash-strapped small companies, our principal creators of jobs and innovation, are particularly threatened. . . . "[7]

Norris's plan for dealing with this problem is an ambitious one: creating advanced manufacturing center networks to do manufacturing on a contract basis for companies of all sizes in a wide range of industries. Manufacturing technology has reached the point where it is potentially generic in the sense that "with the same equipment . . . it's possible to do a lot of different things. The central control system can store data instead of parts, and when you need a part you make it; you don't have to have a lot of components lying around, you make them as you need them."

A perceptive article in *Business Week* explains the process in these terms: "The basic premise behind CIM is that by totally automating and linking all the functions of the factory and the corporate headquarters, a manufacturer would be able to turn out essentially one-of-a-kind products—at the lowest cost and almost overnight. With a CIM factory . . . companies would have the ability to respond instantly to changing market conditions, tailor products for each buyer, cultivate a wider mix of customers, and introduce new products at will."[8]

There is an interesting parallel here with the history of computers. The early computers were single-purpose machines, able to perform only a limited number of functions; to do anything else, they had to be rewired or another machine had to be built. With the coming of improved programming capabilities it became possible to design machines able to perform many different functions. Similarly, the traditional factory can produce only those products for which it was specifically designed; to make anything else, it must be equipped with different machinery ("rewired") or a new factory must be built. CIM, in effect, is a "programmable factory."

A computer program is an organized body of data designed to instruct the machine to perform certain operations in a defined sequence. In CIM the computer can tell the plant's machines what to make, how many to make, and in what order to make them. As Norris points out, this is "an enormous data handling matter." The hardware needed is already at hand in the form of workstations, mainframes, and supercomputers, but a great deal of work remains to be done to develop the software—the programs—required.

Once that task is accomplished, a CIM-based factory will be able to produce many different things and change with ease from making one product to making another. Long runs will not be necessary for productive efficiency, and economies of scale will lose much of the importance they now command. Even small companies using terminals on their own premises will be able to design a product and have it manufactured in the facility Norris envisions. With the other advantages small companies have—flexibility, creativity, lower overhead—small-scale manufacturing can come into its own again.

Under the aegis of Minnesota Wellspring, Norris is in the process of organizing a consortium of state government, universities, and industry in Minnesota to build one of the advanced manufacturing center networks he has in mind. At the outset this will be a not-for-profit undertaking, but he intends for it to evolve over time into a straightforward commercial enterprise. Although this appears to run contrary to what he has stood for for many years, Norris recognizes that the cost and risk involved make any other approach impractical. "The cost is uncertain. You don't know when the damned thing is going to work. This is probably a three- or four-year time span in order to actually turn out production in a meaningful way. There aren't many companies that can stand that."

He estimates that somewhere in the neighborhood of $75 million will be needed just to get the Minnesota network started. Setting up satellite networks in nearby states and connecting them to the central facility—another part of his plan—could cost from $20 to $25 million each. "There's not much through-put hooked to that," he says, "and the cost will be increased substantially when a full compliment of equipment is assembled." He estimates that this will take five or six years and perhaps longer, but he is confident that when it is "actually in operation it can operate like a business." Revenues will come from larger companies who send representatives to the center for training in preparation for installing their own CIM systems and from contract manufacturing for smaller firms. Norris expects that when this point is reached, the centers will be profitable and fully self-sustaining.

Norris hopes that states with sufficient resources, such as Illinois, Ohio, and Michigan, will build their own advanced manufacturing centers and add them to the network, and that these centers will lead in turn to the establishment of satellites in nearby states. This, he is confident, will go a long way toward restoring the industrial strength of the U.S. Midwest and of the nation as a whole.

The alternative is grim, not only in terms of competitive strength but of economic structure as well. As things now stand, computer-integrated manufacturing requires capital investment of a magnitude possible only for very large companies with vast financial resources. Unless practical ways can be found for making CIM available to the 100,000 job shops that now account for three-fourths of the nation's manufacturing output, most of these will be forced to the wall and what remains of the country's industrial production will be concentrated in the hands of a few giants able to make very large investments in state-of-the-art equipment. At present, the inherent disadvantages of giantism—bureaucracy, red tape, weakness in creativity, "corporation man" culture, and the like—are offset in some degree by the presence in the economy of small-scale enterprise. If this is lost, more will go with it than a large number of companies and a large number of jobs. Important human and social values are at stake.

Norris sees ways these dangers can be avoided and the promises of modern industrial technology realized. Characteristically, his vision is a large one; he has never thought small.

———

Equally high on Norris's list of concerns is competition with Japan, a major problem for Control Data Corporation and for much of the rest of U.S. industry.

He maintains that industry in this country must find a way to work with the Japanese, and he acknowledges that it won't be easy. "People have learned from experience that joint ventures in product areas don't often work out well with the Japanese," he says. "They're so damned aggressive, and they're willing to take a longer-range viewpoint than we are." On the other hand, "what does make sense is cooperative research, where the goal is far enough out so they're not stealing your technology nor are you stealing theirs, but they're making a contribution that's equivalent to yours. That's the only way we're ever going to be able to resolve this goddamned situation with Japan, where they're getting a cheap ride on our technology."[9]

The imbalance in the flow of technology between this country and Japan has troubled Norris for a long time. He is incensed that the Japanese have free access to the research laboratories of U.S. universities, while Americans are denied similar access to work being done in Japan. He is particularly angry that "the Japanese send their best graduate students to the U.S. to obtain Ph.D.s," in many cases with partial U.S. support.[10] In 1983 he went so far as to publicly float a proposal to close the doors of university laboratories in this country to the Japanese.[11] It aroused howls of protest here and abroad and nothing ever came of it.

But Norris does not give up easily. He considers the deterioration of this country's once dominant position in technology a grave threat to its future, and he sees the threat from Japan as especially menacing.

He ascribes our decline in technological strength *vis-à-vis* Japan to an "enormous disparity in technology flows" between the two countries, and cites statistics showing that "in the 1980-83 time period, the Japanese have enjoyed a five-to-one advantage over the U.S. in electronics technology exchange and a seven-to-one advantage in machine tools." He attributes this "major cause of our trade deficit with Japan" to a number of influences, chiefly the fact that most U.S. research is conducted openly and published freely while most Japanese research is conducted in industrial and governmental laboratories closed to Americans.[12]

Norris is seeking to establish a more balanced flow of technology by means of federal legislation and for that purpose has several projects in work. "The first thing we have to do," he says, is "know what's going on, which we do not; we have to get our statistics from Japan." He proposes to include in a bill now before Congress a provision making the Department of Commerce and the National Science Foundation responsible for monitoring and reporting the flow of technology in both directions across U.S. borders. A second proposal would deny access to the work of any national laboratory, such as Argonne or Los Alamos, to "any foreign entity that does not provide similar access to U.S. citizens and organizations."

Finally, and most important, he is seeking to have included in the Omnibus Trade Bill a section entitled "Negotiating Objectives Regarding High Technology Access" calling for "the elimination of policies and practices which deny equitable access by United States persons to foreign technology or contribute to the inequitable flow of technology between the United States and its trading partners."[13] Once this is done, he says, "it has to become a part of the trade talks, and we can begin to make some progress."[14]

Norris is working hard on legislation in these three areas, and he is optimistic about the outcome. Through his years of advocacy in Washington, he has ready access to congressional legislators, among whom he reports growing recognition that "the United States has a serious problem" in the area of technology flows. He was successful in securing passage of the National Cooperative Research Act of 1984; he expects to be successful in this effort, too.

━━━━━━━━━━

Early in the first year of his "retirement," Norris began work on organizing a Farm Technology Consortium under the Midwest

Technology Development Institute. Its purpose will be "to foster technological cooperation among businesses, universities, and government to more efficiently create the right kind of technology for viable farms and related industries," with special attention to the needs of medium- and small-size family farms.[15]

Four projects are now in the planning stages: (1) improved collection and dissemination of existing cost-effective technologies; (2) a series of "farm systems" to aid farmers in the selection and proper use of the technologies best suited to their purposes; (3) "expert systems" using artificial intelligence techniques as tools of farm management; and (4) small-scale food processing.

Norris explains that although a large body of knowledge about farming techniques is available, most of it deals with large-scale farming. Much is known about techniques useful to smaller-scale operations, but it is widely scattered and hard to come by. Norris proposes to assemble and organize this information and make it more easily accessible to those who need it.

He further explains that the objective of the farm systems project is to design business plans that are economically sound and suited to family farm management. Expert systems consist of large-scale databases with "rules of thumb" compiled from the experience of experts to aid in decision-making on such matters as financial management, crop production, choices of farm equipment, and the treatment of livestock diseases. Norris proposes to develop expert systems for family farmers that will function in much the same manner that expert systems in the medical field aid doctors in diagnosing and treating illness. Work has begun on systems for dairy herd management and family farm financial management.

Norris is especially intrigued with small-scale food processing, where he sees "a whole host of possibilities." He cites the $100 million wild rice industry in Minnesota as an example of the kind of lucrative "niche market" that could be developed by family farmers as a supplementary source of income. He notes that the University of Nebraska's institute for small-scale food processing is doing good work but that its impact could be greatly enhanced if it were part of a multistate program like the one he is in the process of organizing.

A fifth project still in the early planning stage involves research and development in the field of biotechnology, using genetic engineering techniques to create new forms of plant and animal life.

Future products of genetic engineering have major economic potential in areas such as viral infections, cancer, cardiovascular disorders, and other human ills; market opportunities will be measured in billions rather than millions of dollars. Agricultural applications offer even greater economic potential, although further down the road. Specialists already envision the possibility of inserting the nitrogen-fixing genes of clover into the DNA of corn to increase crop yields and reduce the world's dependence on fossil-fuel fertilizers. Norris sees in genetic engineering "enormous potential to really change the face of agriculture."

The successful development of biotechnological products will most likely be the province of smaller firms. A complicated procedure requiring many steps, skills, and bodies of knowledge, it is better suited to firms that are not inhibited or slowed by the red tape and bureaucratic structure that go hand-in-hand with large size. Genetic engineering is a fast-moving technology, and the ability to move quickly to take advantage of new research and change directions without losing momentum is critical.

Norris insists that in all projects the Farm Technology Consortium plans to pursue, biotechnological and otherwise, care will be taken to proceed "on a basis that's at least scale-neutral. Let the present forces go, and it'll get driven again in the damned large-scale direction that agriculture has always been driven. Very large-scale agriculture is environmentally destructive, and has a lot of other bad characteristics. Why not manage this damned process for a change and at least make it scale-neutral? I think we can get support for that."

It will require federal funding, "but I've learned from experience that there are a lot of people in the U.S. Congress who are just crying to get out in front and lead something that makes sense for the country. Several of them have told me, 'Just get me a program that makes some sense and I'll lead it. I want to do something meaningful.' "[16]

The urge to "do something meaningful" aptly describes the driving force behind Norris's own career. The strength of that drive has not diminished with time and continues to underlie the busy schedule he maintains to this day. "I don't believe in retirement in the sense of sitting around and not doing useful things," he recently told an interviewer in his office in Bluff House. "Strictly speaking, I didn't retire."[17]

He is still fighting for his grand ideas: advancement of technology, computer-based education, job creation networks, family farming, industry/government/university partnerships. Something of the scope of the tasks he has now set for himself is suggested by his statement to another interviewer that he "had accomplished maybe 10 percent of the work he plans to do in this world."[18]

His eyes are still fixed on the future, as they have been through his long career. For him, the past is important only for the learning it gave and the present only as a step toward tomorrow. At the climax of a career rich in achievement, Norris is still busily engaged in creating the future.

Epilogue

In his forty years in the computer industry, William C. Norris racked up a remarkable record of achievement. He was one of the founders of that industry and the last to retire from active service. With a handful of engineers and technicians and paper-thin resources, he built a globe-spanning business. He was a leader in the development of top-of-the-line computer technology and greatly broadened the applications of that technology to serve the needs of modern industrial society. By any measure, he is one of the giants of the computer industry.

Throughout its history, every new business venture on which Control Data embarked was in a new and unexplored field: more powerful computers than the world had ever known, peripheral equipment for competitors, scientific and engineering data services. Moves subsequent to 1967 into the so-called "unmet societal needs" areas were no less—and no more—pioneering than the company's earlier undertakings whose "traditional" status were never in question.

Ventures into new fields are inherently risk-laden. There are few guideposts to mark the way; it takes time to "learn the territory" and how to serve it. False starts and mistakes are common and sometimes fatal. Dangers such as these were especially prevalent in the new and untried fields Norris chose to develop.

A great deal of comment has recently appeared in the press and investment analysts' reports on the drastic cutbacks Control Data is making to eliminate unprofitable operations. Much of the comment assumes that these are the programs which have acquired the pejorative label "social." This assumption is very wide of the mark. Almost all of these cutbacks have been in the company's "traditional" businesses, notably peripheral products and international data services.

As of this writing (late 1986), Control Data Corporation appears to have turned the corner and to be headed back to normal levels of revenue and profit. There is acute irony in the fact that this turn in the company's fortunes is being widely attributed to the elimination of Norris's so-called "frivolous" and "unbusinesslike" programs. A typical current remark goes, "As soon as Norris was pushed aside, the company started to do okay."

This misconception is unfortunate because it discredits Norris's whole philosophy. Central to that philosophy is the notion that a primary function of business is to serve major unmet needs of society (in cooperation, Norris always emphasized, with governments and other institutions). Control Data's troubles are seen by many as conclusive evidence that that notion is a dangerous delusion. Norris's critics have been predicting for years that in trying to implement that philosophy Control Data was headed for trouble. The company's near-disastrous recent difficulties are seen as confirming these predictions and as a warning to other business leaders who might be tempted to follow Norris's lead.

This line of thought is doubly unfortunate. First, as already noted, it is based on false assumptions. Second, so far from Norris's "social programs" being the cause for Control Data's troubles, they may very well prove to be the foundation for its future.

Time and again, Norris has voiced his conviction that major unmet social needs represent potential markets of vast magnitude. He may have made false starts in his efforts to penetrate the education market, but there is no question about its immense size. Nor can he have been far wrong in believing that the revitalization of decayed inner cities could be the basis for a new industry rivaling automobiles and steel. If the greatest business opportunities lie in the areas of greatest unmet needs, the "social markets" offer opportunities unmatched by any other sphere of enterprise.

Control Data is not the only computer company going through a time of troubles. The 1980s have been hard for the entire industry, including IBM with its enormous resources and commanding competitive position, and more than one previously prosperous electronics company is no longer among the alive and well. The 1990s promise to be just as difficult. Continued rapid technological advances and increasingly sharp competition from Japan and other East Asian countries are bound to pose new threats, especially in the hardware segment of the industry where the Asians have demonstrated remarkable manufacturing skills.

From early in its history, much of Control Data's strength has been in the problem-solving applications areas. The unmet social needs markets in which Norris has been so keenly interested are essentially markets for applications. Education, economic development, technology transfer, and advanced manufacturing technology are all areas where the demand for applications will far exceed that for hardware. Norris's grand design called for strengthening Control Data's position in its existing markets while establishing new and impregnable positions in these vast untapped applications markets.

But the significance of Norris's work goes beyond Control Data Corporation and the computer industry. Few business leaders, in this country or elsewhere, have thought as long and as deeply about the role of business in society. Norris was impatient with prevailing notions that "corporate social responsibility" consists of such things as avoiding environmental contamination, participating in civic activities, and contributing generously to local charities. His vision was far wider.

Norris saw business as an institution responsible for serving not only the material needs of society but many of its less tangible needs as well. Most significantly, he saw this as a task to be accomplished as an integral component of business strategy and not as a peripheral concern to be served when and if the profitability of the company's main lines of business permitted.

Norris articulated a philosophy that calls for applying the massive resources of the corporate world to providing better opportunities to those for whom doors to the good life have been closed. He may not be the only big businessman who has shown a genuine concern for the neglected and forgotten of society, but he is certainly one of the few who tried deliberately to fashion business policies to help lift them into the mainstream of American life.

Long after the details of his business career have been forgotten, William C. Norris will be remembered for his vision of the part business *as business* can play in building a more humane society. He showed the way to give capitalism a human face. That is his enduring legacy.

Notes on Sources

Much of this book is written from direct personal knowledge gained from working with William C. Norris and Control Data Corporation for some twenty years, first as a consultant and subsequently as a director, which latter position I still hold. In both capacities, I have had an opportunity to become well acquainted with the key people in the organization and to follow company affairs at close hand; with respect to some of the critical policies and events recorded in this book, I have been a participant and not merely an observer.

To knowledge gained in this manner has been added an extensive body of information gained from interviewing present and retired directors, officers, and executives of Control Data and informed outside persons. These interviews, seventy-four in all, were conducted over the seven-year period in which I gathered data for this book. The interviews were tape recorded and most were transcribed in full; in some instances, however, I merely took notes from the recordings on points directly relevant to particular matters. When this book is safely off to press, I intend to deposit the tapes, transcriptions, and notes in the Control Data Archives.

These archives are already a rich mine of information. Norris and his senior associates have a sense of history all too rare in business circles, and this led some years ago to the establishment of what is without doubt one of the better archives on the contemporary corporate scene. An especially valuable feature of the archives is a series of histories of Control Data's early years prepared in 1980 on instructions from Norris by the men and women directly responsible for developing and managing important company programs; as references in the text indicate, I have made extensive use of these materials.

Norris and Control Data have been the objects of keen press interest for years, and Norris himself has given many interviews and published articles of his own; there is thus a considerable body of public information fairly readily available, and some of this I have found quite useful.

Norris has maintained an incredibly complete record of his own activities and thinking. As recounted in the book, the largest single stockholder in the original Control Data Corporation, next to Norris himself, was a physician-friend from Waterloo, Iowa, whom he had come to know while he was a salesman for Westinghouse. Because this friend was located at a distance, Norris felt obliged to keep him informed on the state of his investment, and for that purpose wrote him a weekly letter giving a detailed account of current company affairs: problems encountered, alternatives considered, and actions taken. In similar fashion, he wrote frequently to his twin sister Willa, a professor at Michigan State University. And as head of Control Data Corporation, of course, his business correspondence was substantial. Copies of these voluminous records are still in Norris's personal files.

Over the years, Norris made literally hundreds of speeches, many of them public and others to stockholders, employees, investment analysts, and various special groups. Some of the more important of these were reprinted in booklet form for distribution to stockholders and other interested parties (see Part II of accompanying Bibliography). His verbal reports to his board of directors were always written out in advance. Whenever he had an important meeting—say, with a member of Congress or another business leader—he prepared a detailed outline of the points he wanted to cover. Copies of all of these have been carefully preserved, and some of them (notably the speeches) have been deposited in the archives.

I doubt that any other business leader in history has left as complete a documentary record of his thinking and the development of his company as has Norris. It is a uniquely valuable and irreplaceable record, and suitable provision should be made for its permanent preservation.

As a business historian, it gives me considerable pleasure to think of the opportunities future scholars will have to study from original documentary materials the life and work of a man who left so large an imprint on his times.

Notes

Chapter 1: Celebration

1. Harvey Brooks, Lance Liebman, and Corinne Schelling, eds., *Public-Private Partnership: New Opportunities for Meeting Social Needs* (Cambridge, MA: Ballinger, 1984).
2. Vianney Carriere, "No One Laughs at William Norris Now," *The Globe and Mail: Canada's National Newspaper*, 31 October 1981.
3. William C. Norris, "A Risk-Avoiding, Selfish Society," *Business Week*, 28 January 1980, p. 20.
4. Carriere, "No One Laughs."
5. Thomas Barr, quoted in "Lawyer Backs IBM Success," *St. Paul Pioneer Press*, 21 May 1975.
6. Unless otherwise noted, this account of Norris's personal characteristics is based on firsthand knowledge and on interviews with close associates and members of his family.
7. *E.g.*, Robert M. Price, address to Control Data Twenty-Fifth Anniversary Conference, Control Data Archives.
8. Interview with Norbert R. Berg, 19 September 1981.
9. *Ibid.*
10. Interview with Norbert R. Berg, 20 January 1986.
11. David Seligman, "The Norris Enigma," *Fortune*, 23 January 1984, pp. 191–192.
12. "America's Most Admired Corporations," *Fortune*, 9 January 1984, p. 61; *Fortune*, 6 January 1986, pp. 16–17.

Chapter 2: Preparation

1. Unless otherwise indicated, this account of Norris's early years is based on interviews with his sister Willa and wife Jane in Jamaica, 14 January 1984, and with William C. Norris in his office in Minneapolis, 3 March 1986.

2. Transcript of interview of Norris by Jeannye Thornton of *U.S. News and World Report*, 14 May 1984 (Control Data Archives).
3. "Editor's Roundup," *Beef*, August 1979, p. 25.
4. Interview with Norris at Bluff House, 3 March 1986.
5. *Ibid.*
6. Transcript of interview of Norris by Carol Pine, not dated, but probably 1980 (Control Data Archives).
7. This account of Norris's work and events in the Navy Cryptological Unit is based on the following three sources: Interview with Norris at the Hotel Sans Souci, Ocho Rios, Jamaica, 13 January 1984; interview with Joseph M. Walsh at Control Data headquarters in Minneapolis, 14 November 1983; and Erwin Tomash and Arnold A. Cohen, "The Birth of an ERA: Engineering Research Associates, Inc. 1946–1955," *Annals of the History of Computing*, October 1979, pp. 83–97.
8. Interview with Norris, 13 January 1984.
9. Tomash and Cohen, "The Birth of an ERA," p. 92.
10. Interview with Jane Norris, 14 January 1984.
11. For a more detailed account of the transition from government agency to private corporation, see Tomash and Cohen, "The Birth of an ERA."
12. *Cf.* "Computers and Commerce: A History of the Role and Influence of ERA." (This is a proposal submitted to the National Endowment for the Humanities by the Charles Babbage Foundation of the University of Minnesota. A copy of this proposal was sent to Norris with a covering letter dated 15 April 1985 from Arthur L. Norberg, director of the foundation. Copy in Control Data Archives.)
13. Interview with Joseph M. Walsh, 14 November 1983. Walsh subsequently became a director of Control Data Corporation and served in that capacity for many years.
14. Conversation with Joseph Walsh at Control Data headquarters, 15 March 1985.
15. Interview with James E. Thornton in his office at Network Systems, Inc., Brooklyn Park, Minnesota, 3 March 1986.
16. Letter from John W. Lacey to W.W. Jackson, 22 May 1969 (Control Data Archives).
17. Tomash and Cohen, "The Birth of an ERA," p. 94.
18. Interview with Norris, 13 January 1984.
19. Interview by Pine with Norris, *ca.* 1980.
20. Interview with Leroy F. Stutzman at Control Data headquarters, 26 January 1984, supplemented by a conversation with Norris in his office, 15 March 1985. Stutzman later served for many years as a director of Control Data Corporation.
21. Interview with Stutzman, 26 January 1984.
22. *Ibid.*
23. Interview with Norris, 13 January 1984.
24. *Ibid.*
25. *Ibid.*
26. Interview with Norris, 3 March 1986.

Chapter 3: Building the Company

1. Carol Pine and Susan Mundale, *Self-Made: The Stories of 12 Minnesota Entrepreneurs* (Bloomington, MN: Dorn Books, 1982), p. 114.
2. Age and employment data furnished by Corporate Personnel Department, Control Data Corporation.
3. Houns, Mollie P., "A History of Control Data's Founding and First Year of Operation," not dated (Control Data Archives), p. 8.
4. *Ibid.*
5. *Cf.* Katherine Davis Fishman, *The Computer Establishment* (New York: Harper & Row, 1981), p. 198.
6. B.R. Eng, M.G. Rogers, and J.J. Karnowski, "Control Data Financial History July 8, 1957–December 31, 1979," Control Data Narrative History Project, p. 40 (Control Data Archives). Eng was controller of the company, Rogers was financial vice president, and Karnowski was treasurer.
7. Interviews with Jane and Willa Norris in Jamaica, 14 January 1984, and with William C. Norris at Bluff House, 3 March 1986.
8. Houns, "A History," p. 1.
9. Interview with Norris at the Hotel Sans Souci, Ocho Rios, Jamaica, 13 January 1984.
10. Interview with Norris, 3 March 1986.
11. Interview with Norris, 13 January 1984.
12. Prospectus dated 29 July 1957 (Control Data Archives).
13. Interview with Frank C. Mullaney at his home in Naples, Florida, 21 February 1984.
14. Interview with Norris, 13 January 1984.
15. This thumbnail sketch of Seymour Cray is based on interviews with present and former Control Data executives who worked closely with him and knew him well.
16. Interview with Norris, 3 March 1986.
17. "Worldwide Census of Control Data Computer Systems," memorandum prepared by the company's Market Analysis Department, 22 May 1970 (Control Data Archives).
18. The contract with the Bureau of Ships set the price of the first 1604 at $600,000. In 1960, the same year that machine was delivered, the navy signed contracts for six more 1604s at $1.5 million each. Mollie P. Houns, "A Snapshot of Technology," not dated (Control Data Archives), pp. 7, 10. *See also* R.W. Allard, "History: EDP Systems," 2 July 1980, p. 2 (Control Data Archives).
19. Interview with Robert D. Schmidt, Control Data headquarters, 12 November 1985.
20. Interview with Norris, 3 March 1986.
21. "Computers Get Faster Than Ever," *Business Week*, 31 August 1963, p. 28.
22. Quoted in Rex Malik, *And Tomorrow . . . the World? The Inside Story of IBM* (London: Millington, 1975), p. 485.
23. Interview with Norris, 13 January 1984.
24. A detailed account of the Control Data–IBM suit is found in Elmer B. Trousdale, "History of CDC v. IBM," 11 July 1980 (Control Data Archives). Trousdale is a partner in the Oppenheimer law firm and played a major role in the prosecution of the Control Data case. A memorandum in Norris's personal files dated 8 May 1968, "IBM's History as Indicative of IBM's Future

Actions and the Pending Confrontation in Large Computers," gives a summary account of Control Data's experience with IBM in connection with the 1604 and the 6600; the "Pending Confrontation" refers to the soon-to-be-introduced CDC 7600. R.W. Allard, "History: EDP Systems," 2 July 1980 (Control Data Archives), written as part of the company's Narrative History Project, reviews the technical characteristics and market results of the several series of Control Data computers, beginning with the 1604.

25. Memorandum from S.R. Cray to W.C. Norris, 14 February 1972 (Control Data Corporation, W.C. Norris files).

26. Interview with Thomas G. Kamp in his office at Centronics Corporation, 19 April 1985.

27. Interview with Mullaney, 21 February 1984.

28. Information supplied by Marvin G. Rogers, former chief financial officer, Control Data Corporation.

29. Quoted in Donna Raimondi, "From Code Busters to Mainframes: The History of CDC," *Computerworld*, 15 July 1985, p. 98.

30. Interview with Norris, 3 March 1986.

31. "Seymour Cray, Reclusive Researcher Works to Shape Own Future," *St. Paul Dispatch*, 7 December 1981, pp. 1, 4–5B.

32. Interview with Norris, 3 March 1986.

33. Interview with Edward E. Strickland in his office at Control Data headquarters, 6 January 1984.

34. Interview with Mullaney, 21 February 1984.

35. William H. Fuhr *et al.*, "Peripherals History Narrative," 7 July 1980, Control Data Narrative History Project (Control Data Archives).

36. Interview with Mullaney, 21 February 1984.

37. Eng *et al.*, "Control Data Financial History," p. 40.

38. William C. Norris, *New Frontiers for Business Leadership* (Minneapolis: Dorn Books, 1983), pp. 173–174.

39. Interview with William R. Keye in his office at Control Data headquarters, 3 September 1981. Keye's association with Norris goes back to ERA days. He was one of those who left Sperry to help found Control Data Corporation, was for many years a senior executive of the company, and advanced to the position of vice chairman of the board.

40. Interview with Strickland, 6 January 1984.

41. Eng *et al.*, "Control Data Financial History," Table IV following p. 153.

42. Interview with Strickland, 6 January 1984.

43. Norris, *New Frontiers*, p. 174.

44. This account of the company's military work is based on "History of the Military Division, Control Data Corporation," Control Data Narrative History Project (Control Data Archives).

45. This account of Control Data's moves into the international marketplace is based on interviews with Robert W. Duncan, 21 June 1985, Eugene L. Baker, 4 October 1983, and Robert D. Schmidt, 12 November 1985.

46. Interview with Norris, 3 March 1986.

47. Interview with Duncan, 21 June 1985.

48. *Ibid.*

49. This account of the move to Bloomington and subsequent development of the property, and the anecdotes recounted, are from an interview with Norbert R. Berg, 20 January 1986.

50. Information provided by Roland M. Cauldwell of the Control Data Real Estate Department.

Chapter 4: Broadening the Base

1. This account of Control Data's entry into the peripheral products business is based on W.H. Fuhr, "Peripherals History Narrative," 7 July 1980, Control Data Narrative History Project (Control Data Archives), as well as interviews with William C. Norris, 13 January 1984 and 3 March 1986; Frank C. Mullaney, 21 February 1984; Thomas G. Kamp, 19 April, 21 June, and 29 August 1985; Robert L. Perkins, 30 April 1985; and John W. Lacey, 22 May and 4 and 5 November 1985.

2. Interview with Perkins, 30 April 1985.

3. Interview with Eugene L. Baker in his office at Control Data headquarters, 4 October 1985.

4. For a detailed discussion of the decision to enter the OEM business, see W.H. Fuhr, "Peripherals History Narrative," pp. 13–16. See also interview with Mullaney, 21 February 1984.

5. Interview with Kamp, 19 April 1985.

6. Fuhr, "Peripherals History Narrative," pp. 50–51.

7. Interview with Kamp, 19 April 1985.

8. Interview with Kamp, 29 August 1985, and W.H. Fuhr, "Peripherals History Narrative," pp. 50–51.

9. "CDC Maps Broader Peripherals Tack," Electronics Business, January 1980, p. 76.

10. Interview with Norris, 3 March 1986.

11. Robert R. Burns, "Control Data Corporation: Data Services Business Segment, 1961–1970" (Control Data Archives). Burns headed the Data Center operations during much of the period covered by this report. See also memorandum from R.C. Gunderson to William C. Norris, "Input to the Control Data History File," 11 July 1980 (Control Data Archives), and the interview with Gunderson, 11 July 1985. Gunderson, now retired, was product manager for the new 1604 computer and in the early 1960s was responsible, among other things, for running the in-house service facility from which the company's data services business began.

12. Interview with Norris, 13 January 1984.

13. Interview with Robert M. Price in his office, Control Data headquarters, 27 June 1985.

14. Interview with Frank C. Mullaney at his home in Naples, Florida, 21 February 1984.

15. Interview with Norris, 13 January 1984. See also Elmer B. Trousdale, "History of CDC v. IBM" (Control Data Archives), pp. 1–2, 5, 15–16, 20.

16. Transcript of interview with journalist Carol Pine, ca. 1980 (Control Data Archives).

17. Interview with John W. Lacey, Control Data headquarters, 19 November 1985. See also interview with Norris, 13 January 1984.

18. Estimate furnished by Control Data Legal Department. See also Elmer B. Trousdale, "History of CDC v. IBM," p. 13.

19. Interview with Norris, 13 January 1984.

20. Telephone interview with Jack Ryan, 16 October 1985. Ryan is a partner of McBride & Baker, Control Data's Chicago law firm in the IBM case.

21. Interview with Norris, 13 January 1984.

22. The account of this meeting is based on the interview with Lacey, 19 November 1985.

23. For details of the settlement, see Elmer B. Trousdale, "History of CDC v. IBM," pp. 51–55.
24. Conversation with Richard G. Lareau, Control Data board room, 13 September 1985. Lareau, a partner in the Oppenheimer law firm, was present at the meeting in his capacity as Norris's legal counsel.
25. Interview with Ryan.
26. Elmer B. Trousdale, "History of CDC v. IBM," pp. 54–56.
27. Letter from Richard G. Lareau, 20 September 1985.
28. *Wall Street Journal*, 29 July 1985.
29. This account of the origin and development of IBM's data services business and the subsequent integration of the Service Bureau Corporation into Control Data is based in large part on a group interview conducted with Henry J. White, Robert W. Kleinert, Stephen W. Beach, and John P. Gougoutris, 27 June 1985. All were members of the Service Bureau Corporation at the time of its acquisition by Control Data, and all subsequently advanced to major positions in their new parent company.
30. *Ibid.*
31. Rex Malik, *And Tomorrow . . . the World? The Inside Story of IBM* (London: Millington, 1975), p. 66.
32. *Cf.* Elmer Trousdale, "History of the IBM Lawsuit" (Control Data Archives), pp. 78–79.
33. Interview with Norris, 4 March 1986.
34. Interview with Norris, 13 January 1984.
35. For a detailed account of the acquisition of Commercial Credit Company by Control Data Corporation, see W. Bruce Quackenbush, "Commercial Credit Company Merger," 15 July 1980 (Control Data Archives).
36. "Marrying for Money," *Business Week*, 22 June 1968, p. 37.
37. Interview with Lacey, 19 November 1985.
38. Memorandum, 4 November 1986, from W.R. Olson, manager, External Financial Reporting, Control Data Corporation.
39. Interview with Lacey, 19 November 1985.
40. Unless otherwise specified, this account of the efforts to integrate the operations of Commercial Credit Company with those of Control Data is based on interviews with William C. Norris on 4 March 1986, Lawrence Perlman on 16 May 1986, and Paul G. Miller on 23 May 1986, and on the author's personal knowledge as a director of Commercial Credit Company for the period 1975–1982.
41. Interview with Miller, 23 May 1986.
42. Interview with Norris, 4 March 1986.
43. *Ibid.*

Chapter 5: The PLATO Story

1. This account of Norris's early interest in computer-based training and the beginning of Control Data's association with the University of Illinois is drawn from an interview with William C. Norris in his office at Bluff House on 12 August 1986.
2. This account of the early development of the PLATO system is based on an interview with Dr. Donald Bitzer in his laboratory at the University of Illinois

on 2 November 1981, and on discussions over the years with various Control Data executives involved in PLATO affairs.

3. This sequence of events was confirmed by a telephone conversation with Dr. Bitzer on 19 March 1986.

4. Interview with Roger E. Arent, Control Data headquarters, 28 June 1985.

5. This account of the startup of the Control Data Institutes is based on an interview with Layton Kinney at Control Data headquarters on 28 June 1985. Kinney was the executive in charge of the institute program during its early years.

6. Interview with William C. Norris, 12 August 1986.

7. Interview with Arent, 28 June 1985.

8. Interview with John W. Lacey, Control Data headquarters, 4 September 1986.

9. Interview with Dr. Walter H. Bruning, Control Data headquarters, 27 June 1985.

10. Interview with Norris, 12 August 1986.

11. This assessment is based in part on a discussion with Robert M. Price on 31 July 1986.

12. Interview with Norris, Bluff House, 4 March 1986.

13. Data supplied by Roger E. Arent and Eric W. Peper, Control Data Corporation.

14. Interview with Norris, 12 August 1986.

15. This discussion of the difficulties encountered during the early years of PLATO in the marketplace is based on interviews with John W. Lacey on 22 May 1985, Dr. Walter H. Bruning on 27 June and 18 July 1985, Roger E. Arent on 11 July 1985, and William J. Ridley on 18 July 1985. Several additional interviews with Lacey contributed materially to the contents of this chapter.

16. William C. Norris, *New Frontiers for Business Leadership* (Minneapolis: Dorn Books, 1983), p. 75.

17. Jonathan Kozol, *Illiterate America* (New York: Doubleday, 1985), p. 5.

18. Dr. Walter H. Bruning, quoted in Rick Steelhammer, "Illiteracy is Expensive," *Charleston Gazette*, 6 September 1985.

19. Interview with Norris, 12 August 1986.

20. "PLATO History," Control Data Archives. Also interview with Lacey, 19 November 1985.

21. Interview with Norris, 12 August 1986.

22. Interview with Robert W. Duncan, Control Data headquarters, 21 June 1986.

23. *Ibid.*

24. Shohei Kurita, "CAI: The Boom Is On in Education-Conscious Japan," *Electronic Business*, 1 August 1986, pp. 112–113.

25. Vianney Carriere, "No One Laughs at William Norris Now," *The Globe and Mail: Canada's National Newspaper*, 31 October 1981.

26. Quoted in Charles I. Mundale, "Bill Norris: The View from the 14th Floor," *Corporate Report Minnesota*, January 1978.

27. Valena White Plisko and Joyce D. Stern, eds., *The Condition of Education: A Statistical Report* (Washington: National Center for Educational Statistics, 1985), p. 141.

28. Interview with Norris, 12 August 1986.

29. Interview with Robert M. Price, 4 June 1979.

30. "Education Revenue," Memorandum from C.L. Horton to R.W. Duncan, 9 January 1986.

31. Interview with Norris, 4 March 1986.

32. *Ibid.*

Chapter 6: The Northside Story—and Its Sequel

1. This account of events leading up to the decision to locate a plant in the Northside area of Minneapolis and problems encountered in bringing the plant into operation is based on interviews at various times with Norbert R. Berg, Roger G. Wheeler, Eugene L. Baker, Richard D. Connor, and Gary H. Lohn.
2. Interview with Norbert R. Berg, 20 January 1986.
3. Interview with Roger G. Wheeler, 24 November 1985.
4. *Ibid.*
5. Addresses by William C. Norris before Houston Minority Group Symposium, 18 February 1969, and Chicago Industrial Relations Association, 26 May 1969 (Control Data Archives).
6. Interview with Robert M. Price, 4 June 1979. Price was not personally involved in the startup of the new plant, but is recounting here the feelings of colleagues who were.
7. Interview with Norbert R. Berg, 3 September 1981.
8. Interview with Gary H. Lohn, 3 April 1979.
9. Interview with Berg, 3 September 1981.
10. Interview with Wheeler, 24 November 1985.
11. *Ibid.*
12. Interview with Robert Weinstein, 12 September 1979.
13. Interview with Richard D. Conner, 4 April 1979.
14. Interviews with Lohn, 3 April 1979, and Connor, 4 April 1979.
15. Interview with Wheeler, 24 November 1985.
16. Interview with Berg, 3 September 1981.
17. Interview with Barbara Dugar, senior personnel administrator, Northside plant, 3 May 1979.
18. Interviews with Berg, 9 September 1981 and 28 January 1986.
19. Interview with The Honorable George Latimer, Mayor of St. Paul, 4 June 1979.
20. Information on the startup and work of the Selby–Dale Bindery is drawn chiefly from an interview with its manager, Richard Mangram, 13 August 1981.
21. Interview with Latimer, 4 June 1979.
22. Interview with Berg, 9 September 1981.
23. This account of the startup of the plant in Campton, Kentucky, is drawn from interviews with Norbert R. Berg on 3 September 1981 and 20 January 1986.
24. Interview with Latimer, 4 June 1979.
25. Roger G. Wheeler, "Memorandum to the Public Policy Committee" 9 March 1983 (Control Data Archives).
26. Transcript of remarks of the Honorable Henry Cisneros, mayor of San Antonio, in introducing William C. Norris as keynote speaker at a meeting of the Texas Association of Private Industry Councils, San Antonio, 30 June 1986 (Control Data Archives).

Chapter 7: Evolution of a Strategy

1. The concept, "converting social needs into business opportunities," was first enunciated by Peter F. Drucker in 1973. Adoption of this phraseology by

Norris has an interesting history. I was elected a director of Commercial Credit Company in 1975, and at my first meeting of the board Norris outlined a series of PLATO-related projects for improving education and reducing hard-core unemployment for which he wished Commercial Credit to assume responsibility; he took pains to emphasize that he expected these to be pursued as business ventures and not as corporate philanthropies. During the course of the discussion that followed, I made a comment to the effect, "Bill, as I hear you talking you sound very much like Peter Drucker who says that the best way to deal with social problems is to convert them into business opportunities." Norris does not recall my comment, but Drucker's concept seems to have struck a responsive chord; in any event, I was interested to note that from about this time forward that particular wording began to appear more and more frequently in Norris's conversation and writing. Norris had arrived at the business strategy independently, but the phraseology with which he came to describe it was apparently an unconscious borrowing from Drucker. Drucker's classic statement of the concept was as follows: "Social problems are dysfunctions of society and—at least potentially—degenerative diseases of the body politic. They are ills. But for the management of institutions, and, above all, for business management they represent challenges. They are major sources of opportunity. For it is the function of business—and to a lesser degree of other main institutions—to satisfy a social need and at the same time serve their institutions, by making resolution of a social problem into a business opportunity." Peter F. Drucker, *Management: Tasks, Responsibilities, Practices* (New York: Harper & Row, 1973), p. 337. The concept is further explicated on pp. 337–342.

2. William C. Norris, letter to The Honorable Harold LeVander, Governor of Minnesota, 15 April 1968 (Norris files).
3. Interview with Eugene L. Baker, 4 October 1985; also, memorandum dated 23 May 1975 from G.H. Lohn to the company's Corporate Social Responsibility and Concerns Committee (Control Data Archives).
4. Robert M. Price, response to a question at the press conference on the occasion of William C. Norris's retirement, 10 January 1986 (Control Data Archives).
5. American Academy of Arts and Sciences and Control Data Corporation, *Transcript, Conference on Social Problems and Business Opportunities*, Session V, 29 June 1982, pp. 45–46 (Control Data Archives).
6. William C. Norris, *New Frontiers for Business Leadership* (Minneapolis: Dorn Books, 1983), p. 53.
7. Quoted in James O'Toole, *Vanguard Management* (New York: Doubleday, 1985), pp. 367–368.
8. Norris, *New Frontiers*, p. 49.
9. William C. Norris, "Profit-Driven Response to Societal Needs," statement before the Intergovernmental Relations Subcommittee of the Senate Governmental Affairs Committee, Washington, D.C., 30 July 1981 (Norris files).
10. Quoted in O'Toole, *Vanguard Management*, p. 368.
11. William C. Norris, "Responding to Society's Needs," Essay for Aspen Institute for Humanistic Studies, August 1978 (Norris files).
12. For a detailed explication of these two kinds of decisions, see Ted Kolderie, "Business Opportunities in the Changing Conceptions of the Public Sector Role," in Harvey Brooks, Lance Liebman, and Corinne Schelling, eds., *Public-Private Partnership: New Opportunities for Meeting Social Needs* (Cambridge, MA: Ballinger, 1984), pp. 89–110.
13. Norris, "Responding to Society's Needs."

14. *Ibid.*
15. Norris, *New Frontiers*, p. 55.
16. Interview with Norbert R. Berg, 9 September 1981.
17. Interview with Jane and Willa Norris, 14 January 1984; also interview with William C. Norris, 12 August 1986.
18. Interview with Berg, 9 September 1981.

Chapter 8: Serving Society's Unmet Needs

1. Robert M. Price, "Developing Organization Policies and Structure to Facilitate Profitable Relationships with Entrepreneurs," GMI Engineering and Management Institute, 30 September 1985 (Control Data Archives).
2. Interview with Norbert R. Berg, 9 September 1981.
3. William C. Norris, *New Frontiers for Business Leadership* (Minneapolis: Dorn Books, 1983), p.90.
4. *Ibid.*, pp. 60–61.
5. Interview with William C. Norris, 12 August 1986.
6. For example, in his *New Frontiers*, p. 61.
7. *Ibid.*, p. 64.
8. Memorandum dated 26 February 1976, "Millions of New Jobs Program" (Norris files).
9. *Cf.* memorandum, "Jobs Program," 16 July 1976 and notes of meetings with Senator Humphrey, 14 September 1976 and 6 September 1977 (Norris files).
10. Discussion with Norris in his office, 13 March 1986.
11. Interviews with Norris, 4 March and 12 August 1986.
12. Norris, *New Frontiers*, p. 63.
13. *Ibid.*, p. 115.
14. Control Data Corporation, "AgTech Data Base," May 1980 (Control Data Archives).
15. Telephone interview with Benjamin F. Kilgore, 22 May 1986.
16. *New Frontiers*, p. 100.
17. *Ibid.*, p. 101.
18. *Ibid.*, p. 102.
19. *Ibid.*, pp. 103–104.
20. Interview with Norris, 4 March 1986.
21. Price, "Developing Organization Policies."
22. *New Frontiers*, p. 111.
23. Norris, "Technology and Full Employment," presentation to White House Conference on Balanced Economic Growth, 12 January 1978 (Control Data Archives).
24. Norris, "Millions of New Jobs Program."
25. *Ibid.*
26. "City Venture Corporation," Control Data Corporation press release, not dated, 1978 (Control Data Archives).
27. *Cf.* "City Venture is Coming! City Venture is Coming!" *Disclosure*, January/February 1981; Karen Branan, "The Venture Barons and the Metrodome Land Grab,"*Twin Cities Reader*," 17 October 1981; and Jeff Brown, "The Dome Deal," *Minneapolis Star*, 9 October 1981.
28. A copy of this proposal, not dated, 1981 is in the files of Norbert R. Berg.

29. *Cf.* William C. Norris, "Dome Series Half-Truths Set Back Civic Progress," *Minneapolis Star*, 16 October 1981.
30. Conversation with Norbert R. Berg, 25 June 1986.
31. Interview with Herbert F. Trader, 18 August 1985.
32. *New Frontiers*, p. 113
33. Interview with Trader, 18 August 1985.
34. For a description of the Minnesota Network for Small Business Innovation and Job Creation, the prototype for the Job Creation Networks that have been established elsewhere, see Norris, *New Frontiers*, pp. 108–110.
35. William C. Norris, "Report to City Venture Board of Directors," 23 June 1986 (Norris files).
36. Interview with Norris, 12 August 1986.
37. *Ibid.*
38. *New Frontiers*, p. 123.
39. These three projects are described in *New Frontiers*, pp. 128–133.
40. Interview with Trader, 18 August 1985.
41. William C. Norris, "Report to Rural Ventures Board of Directors," 23 June 1986 (Norris files).
42. *New Frontiers*, pp. 137–138.
43. William C. Norris, "Improving America's Prisons," Factories with Fences Conference, George Washington University, Washington, D.C., 18 June 1984 (Control Data Archives).
44. Norris, draft of speech, "Improving America's Prisons," 19 January 1984 (Control Data Archives).
45. Warren E. Burger, "Ex-Prisoners Can Become Producers, Not Predators," *Nation's Business*, October 1983, p. 38.
46. Norris, draft of "Prisons" speech.
47. Control Data Corporation, *Final Report, Task Force on Prisons*, 20 March 1983 (Norbert R. Berg files)
48. Interview with Norris, 12 August 1986.
49. *New Frontiers*, p. 139.
50. *Ibid.*, p. 144.
51. *Ibid.*, p. 147.
52. William C. Norris, "Small Rural Enterprise," 11 September 1979 (Norris files).
53. Roger G. Wheeler, transcript of Riverwoods Conference, Session 5, 29 June 1982, p. 78 (Control Data Archives). The Riverwoods conference, conducted jointly by Control Data Corporation and the American Academy of Arts and Sciences, was held in preparation for the company's twenty-fifth anniversary celebration the following September.
54. Interview with Berg, 20 January 1985.
55. Berg, Riverwoods transcript, pp. 27–28.

Chapter 9: The View from the Top

1. Interview with William C. Norris, Bluff House, 12 August 1986.
2. Interview with Robert M. Price, 4 June 1979.
3. Interview with Frank C. Mullaney, 21 February 1984.
4. Interview with Norris by Carol Pine, *ca.* 1980 (Control Data Archives).
5. Conversation with Lois D. Rice, 15 July 1986.

6. Interview with Norbert R. Berg, 20 January 1986.
7. Interview with Paul G. Miller, 23 May 1986.
8. Interview with Norris, 3 March 1986.
9. William C. Norris, *New Frontiers for Business Leadership* (Minneapolis: Dorn Books, 1983), p. 189.
10. My own view on this point is supported by interviews with Joseph W. Barr on 23 June and 9 July 1980, Dr. Russell A. Nelson on 9 July 1980, and Joseph M. Walsh on 10 July 1980. Barr, Nelson, and Walsh were long-time non-management directors of Control Data Corporation. These interviews were conducted in connection with an earlier study of corporate governance.
11. Interview with Norris, 3 March 1986.
12. This account of the formation of the Corporate Executive Office and the thinking behind it is based on personal knowledge, refreshed by notes of discussions with Norris during the period May-July 1980, copies of correspondence in my files (specifically, memoranda from me to Norris dated 14 and 23 May 1980), and minutes of the July 1980 meeting of the board of directors.
13. *Cf.* my memorandum to Norris dated 10 May 1980 (my personal file, with copy presumably in Norris files).
14. The layoff and hospital stories were related to me by Berg in our 20 January 1986 interview.
15. This story and other descriptions of Norris's personal character and behavior are based on interviews and discussions with a number of Control Data people in positions to speak from firsthand knowledge.
16. Interview with Berg, 20 January 1986.
17. Norbert R. Berg, memorandum for file dated 8 May 1970 (Berg personal files, Control Data Corporation).
18. William C. Norris, address to St. Paul Junior Association of Commerce, 25 January 1967.
19. Over the years, Norris's secretaries have carefully maintained a list of all his speeches and papers, noting dates, occasions, and titles. The list includes internal matters such as talks to employee groups, reports to the board of directors and stockholders, etc., but the 238 figure given is the count of public statements only. A voluminous file, now in the Control Data Archives, contains copies of all speeches, public and private, as well as copies of papers he has published from time to time.
20. Information derived from Norris's schedule for the period 31 January-3 February 1983 (Norris files).
21. William C. Norris, "Comprehensive Economic Development and Job Creation," address to Industrial Development Association of North Dakota, 7 August 1986.
22. *Ibid.*
23. *E.g.* Norris, "Remarks," 1986 Financial Outlook Conference, The Conference Board, 27 February 1986.

Chapter 10: A Time of Troubles

1. "CDC Maps Broader Peripherals Tack," *Electronic Business*, January 1980, p. 76.
2. This account of difficulties of the plug-compatible business is drawn from a telephone interview with Thomas G. Kamp on 4 October 1985.

3. This account of general difficulties in the OEM business is drawn from a presentation by Lawrence Perlman, president of the Peripherals Company, to the Control Data board on 12 September 1985 (Control Data files).
4. Interview with William C. Norris, 3 March 1986.
5. Discussion with Norbert R. Berg, 16 October 1985.
6. Interview with Norris, Bluff House, 12 August 1986.
7. This discussion of Control Data's financial problems is based on personal knowledge, supported by interviews with Marvin G. Rogers, the company's former chief financial officer, on 26 June 1986, and with Robert M. Price on 11 September 1986.
8. Interview with Rogers, 26 June 1986.
9. Cf. David E. Sanger, "Control Data Cancels Offering," New York Times, 18 September 1985.
10. Gordon Bock, "Has the Street Given Up on Control Data?" Business Week, 30 September 1985, pp. 48–49.
11. "Control Data Seen Out of Control," USA Today, 3 October 1985.
12. Dean Rothbart, "Heard on the Street," Wall Street Journal, 20 September 1985, pp. 48–49.
13. This discussion of peripheral products and its problems is based on an interview with Lawrence Perlman in his office on 16 May 1986.
14. Statement to the board of directors, 11 July 1985 (Control Data Archives).

Chapter 11:   Changing the Guard

1. Patrick Houston and Gordon Bock, "Can a Gentleman Farmer Get Control Data Out of the Ditch?," Business Week, 27 January 1986, p. 45.
2. "Chief Executives Who Won't Let Go," Business Week, 8 October 1984, p. 39.
3. "Control Data Starts a Painful Retrenchment," Business Week, 22 October 1984, p. 96.
4. "Chief Executives Who Won't Let Go," p. 39.
5. Cf. "Control Data Starts a Painful Retrenchment," pp. 94, 96.
6. William C. Norris, "Management Succession and Related Matters," memorandum to The Outside Directors, 13 November 1985 (Norris files).
7. These quotations are from the transcript of the January 10 press conference (Control Data Archives).
8. Dick Youngblood, "Norris Made Social Responsibility a Priority and a Dispute," Minneapolis Star and Tribune, 9 January 1986.
9. "A Visionary Exits: Norris Leaves Control Data," Time, 20 January 1986, p. 44.
10. Minneapolis Star and Tribune, 10 January 1986.

Chapter 12:   Creating the Future

1. Unless otherwise specified, the information on Norris's current interests and activities is drawn from direct personal knowledge and several conversations and interviews with Norris during 1986; for this purpose, my interview with him on 11 September 1986 was especially useful.

2. Norman Jonas, "The Hollow Corporation," *Business Week*, 3 March 1986, p. 58.
3. William C. Norris, address to the Industrial Development Association of North Dakota, 7 August 1986.
4. Brochure, "Midwest Technology Development Institute," (St. Paul, MN: Midwest Technology Development Institute, not dated but probably 1986), p. 1.
5. "Advanced Manufacturing Centers—Minnesota Wellspring Proposal," 15 August 1986 (Norris files).
6. Interview with Norris, 11 September 1986.
7. "Advanced Manufacturing Centers."
8. Richard Brandt and Otis Post, "How Automation Could Save the Day," *Business Week*, 3 March 1986, p. 12.
9. Interview with Norris, 11 September 1986.
10. William C. Norris, "Remarks," address before the 1986 conference of the American Society of Mechanical Engineers, Chicago, 21 July 1986.
11. William C. Norris, "Limiting Japan's Access to Our Research," *New York Times*, 24 July 1983.
12. Norris, "Remarks."
13. *Ibid.*
14. Interview with Norris, 11 September 1986.
15. William C. Norris, address before Midwest Farm Technology Consortium, Chicago, 7 March 1986.
16. The quotations in this and the preceding two paragraphs are from the interview with Norris, 11 September 1986.
17. Interview with David Finn, "A Computer Pioneer's Deals and Ideals," *Across the Board*, April 1986.
18. Betsy Teter, "Leaving a Legacy—Control Data's Norris Has Much Left to Do," Spartanburg, SC *Herald Journal*, 10 April 1986.

Bibliography

Part I
Published Materials
(Listed in Chronological Order of Publication)

Bob Hughes, "Control Data Corporation, One of Minnesota's Newest Firms," *Minnesota Technology*, April 1958.

William C. Norris, "The Upper Midwest Needs a Research Institute," *The Minnesota Engineer*, August 1960.

Roy Wirtzfeld, "Control Data: From Mystery to Legend," *Upper Midwest Investor*, November 1961.

"Corporations: A Bead on Excellence," *Time*, 24 November 1961.

"Small, Smart, Sharp," *Business Week*, 25 May 1963.

"Computers Get Faster Than Ever," *Business Week*, 31 August 1963.

"Control Data: Big Success, Big Gamble," *Forbes*, 1 June 1964.

"Poor Man's IBM," *Time*, 14 August 1964.

"Control Data Unruffled by the Competition," *Investor's Reader*, 4 November 1964.

"We're Buying Brains," *Forbes*, 15 January 1965.

Stephen Quickel, "Is Control Data in Trouble?" *Forbes*, 15 September 1965.

"Slow Down and Live," *Forbes*, 1 March 1966.

T.A. Wise, "Control Data's Magnificent Fumble," *Fortune*, April 1966.

"When a Whiz Kid Grows Up: Growth Pangs," *Business Week*, 30 July 1966.

"Faces Behind the Figures: William C. Norris, Narrow Escape," *Forbes*, 1 March 1967.

"CDC Takes 'Peripheral' Road to Growth," *Business Week*, 5 August 1967.

Edward J. Menkaus, "Control Data Builds on Business," *Business Automation*, September 1967.

Gregory H. Wierzynski, "Control Data's Newest Cliffhanger," *Fortune*, February 1968.

"Marrying for Money," *Business Week*, 22 June 1968.

"Control Data Digs Its Gold Mine," *Business Week*, 28 September 1968.

"Computers: Tackling IBM," *Time*, 20 December 1968.

"Computers: Challenging the Giant," *Newsweek*, 23 December 1968.

"Control Data Tackles the Computer Giant," *Business Week*, 28 June 1969.

William C. Norris, "Enlightened Users Challenge Computer Industry," *Automation*, June 1969.

A.A. Butkus, "Control Data's Bold Design," *Dun's*, July 1971.

"Can Control Data Make It?" *Forbes*, 15 June 1972.

"The IBM Deal: A Windfall for Control Data," *Business Week*, 20 January 1973.

"SBC, CYBERNET Services Expected to Fit Together Especially Well," *Computerworld*, 24 January 1973.

"David and Goliath," *Newsweek*, 29 January 1973.

"Settlement for IBM," *Time*, 29 January 1973.

"Why Bill Norris Is Smiling," *Business Week*, 10 November 1973.

"CDC Stressing Services: Norris," *Electronic News*, 24 December 1973.

"A Corporate Moby Dick," *Forbes*, 15 November 1974.

Rex Malik, *And Tomorrow . . . The World? The Inside Story of IBM* (London: Millington, 1975).

"CDC's Norris Cites Positive Aspects of Multinationals," *Electronic News*, 12 April 1976.

"CDC: Big in Services—But in Systems Too," *Datamation*, September 1976.

Harry Savage, "Don't Count Us Out!" *Forbes*, 15 September 1976.

B. Barna, "Share Technology Says CDC's Norris," *Computer Decisions*, March 1977.

"CDC's Norris Calls for Global Pooling of Technology," *Computerworld*, 18 April 1977.

David Clutterbuck, "Making Social Responsibility Pay," *International Management*, July 1977.

Arthur Darack, "Yes . . . Computers Can Revolutionize Education," *Consumers Digest*, September/October 1977.

"Bill Norris: The View from the 14th Floor," *Corporate Report Minnesota*, January 1978.

William C. Norris, "High Technology Trade with the Communists," *Datamation*, January 1978.

M. Loeb, "Planting in the Ghettos," *Time*, 3 April 1978.

Keith W. Bennett, "Control Data Transforms Social Ills Into Profit," *Iron Age*, 26 March 1979.

"Social Strategy Aimed at Profits," *Business Week*, 25 June 1979.

William C. Norris, "Business Must Seek Remedies for Adverse Effects of Mergers," *Financier*, July 1979.

Erwin Tomash and Arnold A. Cohen, "The Birth of an ERA: Engineering Research Associates, Inc. 1946–1955," *Annals of the History of Computing*, October 1979.

William C. Norris, "A Small Business Benefactor Speaks Out," *Corporate Report*, November 1979.

D. Seligman, "Shuffling Along with Social Responsibility," *Fortune*, November 1979.

William C. Norris, "A Risk-Avoiding, Selfish Society," *Business Week*, 28 October 1980.

"Minnesota . . . Technology Wellspring," *Scientific American*, October 1980.

Meg Cox, "Control Data Puts Its Computers to Work Helping Farmers Make It on Small Plots," *Wall Street Journal*, 14 October 1980.

"William Norris, Chairman and Chief Executive Officer, Control Data Corporation," *Industry Week*, 27 October 1980.

Katherine Davis Fishman, *The Computer Establishment* (New York: Harper & Row, 1981).

"City Venture Is Coming! City Venture Is Coming!" *Disclosure*, January/February 1981.

"Tomorrow the World: Control Data Programs the Future," *Corporate Report Minnesota*, February 1981.

W. David Gardner, "CDC's Scrappy Chairman," *Datamation*, February 1981.

William C. Norris, "A Society Transformed by Microchips," *Christian Science Monitor*, 24 February 1981.

Willard C. Rappleye, Jr., "William C. Norris: Making Money by Creating Jobs," *Financier*, February 1981.

Don Clark, "Norb Berg: He's the Guiding Force of Control Data's Innovative People Programs," *St. Paul Sunday Pioneer Press*, 15 February 1981.

William C. Norris, "Computer-Based Education in New Areas, and Partnership in Productivity," *Computers and People*, May/June 1981.

Judson Bemis and John A. Cairns, "In Minnesota, Business Is Part of the Solution," *Harvard Business Review*, July-August 1981.

William C. Norris, "Developing Corporate Policies for Innovation: A Program of Action," *Long-Range Planning*, August 1981.

William C. Norris and Myron Tribus, "Business and the Other Spigot," *Enterprise: The Journal of Executive Action*, September 1981.

William C. Norris, "Business Can Profit by Filling Unmet Social Needs, *U.S. News and World Report*, 21 September 1981.

Jeff Brown, "The Dome Deal," *Minneapolis Star*, 9 October 1981.

William C. Norris, "Dome Series Half Truths Set Back Civic Progress," *Minneapolis Star*, 16 October 1981.

Karen Branan, "The Venture Barons and the Metrodome Land Grab," *Twin Cities Reader*, 17 October 1981.

William C. Norris, "Business-Government Partnership for Meeting Social Needs," *Financier*, November 1981.

"Norris Calls for Public/Private Partnership," *Minnesota Business Journal*, December 1981.

Carol Pine and Susan Mundale, *Self-Made: The Stories of 12 Minnesota Entrepreneurs* (Minneapolis: Dorn Books, 1982).

Ronald D. Levine, "Supercomputers," *Scientific American*, January 1982.

Ray Connolly, "U.S. R&D Consortium Takes Shape," *Electronics*, 10 March 1982.

William C. Norris, "Doing Well—and Doing Good—in the Inner City," *Christian Science Monitor*, 12 March 1982.

Larry Gauthier, "Norris Out to Prove Small Is Better," *The Business Farmer*, 19 March 1982.

Chris Benson, "Getting Down to Business: Control Data Corporation Programs Provide Jobs with Dignity," *Ebony*, June 1982.

Leonard Inskip, "Control Data's Norris: After Twenty-Five Years, He's Still a Prime Component," *Minneapolis Tribune*, 30 September 1982.

William C. Norris, "Opportunities for Profit in Meeting Social Needs," *Financier*, October 1982.

Calvin Bradford and Mihalio Temali, *The Politics of Private Sector Initiatives: The Case of City Venture Corporation* (Minneapolis: University of Minnesota Hubert H. Humphrey Institute of Public Affairs), 30 October 1982.

William C. Norris, *New Frontiers for Business Leadership* (Minneapolis: Dorn Books, 1983).

Robert Sobel, *I.B.M.: Colossus in Transition* (New York: Bantam Books, 1983).

James C. Worthy, "An Entrepreneurial Approach to Social Problem-Solving: William C. Norris and Control Data Corporation," in *Business and Economic History*, Jeremy Atack, ed. (Champaign, Illinois: University of Illinois, 1983).

William C. Norris, "R&D Cooperation Must be Fostered," *Electronics*, 24 March 1983.

"Computerized Training May be About to Take Off," *Business Week*, 28 March 1983.

William C. Norris, "How to Expand R&D Cooperation," *Business Week*, 11 April 1983.

William C. Norris, "Limiting Japan's Access to Our Research," *New York Times*, 24 July 1983.

George Harrar, "An Interview: William C. Norris, Control Data's Maverick Chairman," *Computerworld*, 12 September 1983.

William C. Norris, "Keeping America First," *Datamation*, September 1982.

Warren E. Burger, "Ex-Prisoners Can Become Producers, Not Predators," *Nation's Business*, October 1983.

"Control Data: Is There Room for Change After Bill Norris?" *Business Week*, 17 October 1983.

Ronald Rosenberg, "High-Tech Do-Gooder Speaks Up," *Boston Globe*, 29 November 1983.

Lawrence Ingrassia, "Seeking to Aid Society, Control Data Takes on Many Novel Ventures," *Wall Street Journal*, 22 December 1983.

Harvey Brooks, Lance Liebman, and Corinne Schelling, eds., *Public-Private Partnership: New Opportunities for Meeting Social Needs* (Cambridge, MA: Ballinger Publishing Company, 1984).

Stephen T. McClellan, *The Coming Computer Industry Shakeout: Winners, Losers, and Survivors* (New York: Wiley, 1984).

David Seligman, "The Norris Enigma," *Fortune*, 23 January 1984.

Don Clark and Linda McDonnell, "Control Data: A Special Report," *St. Paul Pioneer Press*, 24 September 1984.

William C. Norris, "Bringing the World of High Technology into Rural Schools," *American Education*, October 1984.

"Chief Executives Who Won't Let Go," *Business Week*, 8 October 1984.

"Control Data Starts a Painful Retrenchment," *Business Week*, 22 October 1984.

M. Doan, "Social Needs and Profits," *U.S. News and World Report*, 22 October 1984.

Richard Gibson, "Control Data Intends to Sell Its Credit Unit," *Wall Street Journal*, 8 November 1984.

James O'Toole, *Vanguard Management* (New York: Doubleday, 1985).

Eric N. Berg, "Control Data's Fall from Grace," *New York Times*, 17 February 1985.

Richard Gibson, "Control Data Plans to Sell Some Businesses," *Wall Street Journal*, 1 April 1985.

William C. Norris, "Norris Calls for International Collaboration," *Government Computer News*, 24 May 1985.

Richard Gibson and Brenton R. Schlender, "Control Data Decides to Keep Finance Unit," *Wall Street Journal*, 13 June 1985.

Richard Gibson, "Control Data Unit to Close Consumer Lines," *Wall Street Journal*, 21 June 1985.

Richard Gibson, "Control Data's Comeback Faces Rough Road: Slide Raises Questions on Chairman's Once-Magic Touch," *Wall Street Journal*, 27 June 1985.

Donna Raimondi, "From Code Busters to Mainframes: The History of CDC," *Computerworld*, 15 July 1985.

William C. Norris, "Are Mergers Hurting U.S. Economy?" *U.S. News and World Report*, 22 July 1985.

David E. Sanger, "Control Data Cancels Offering," *New York Times*, 18 September 1985.

Gordon Bock, "Has the Street Given Up on Control Data?" *Business Week*, 30 September 1985.

Dwight B. Davis, "R&D Consortia: Pooling Industries' Resources," *High Technology*, October 1985.

"Control Data Seen Out of Control," *USA Today*, 3 October 1985.

M.L. Goldstein, "Control Data Corporation: Picking Up the Pieces," *Industry Week*, 9 December 1985.

F.S. Worthy, "Does Control Data Have a Future?" *Fortune*, 23 December 1985.

Ralph Nader and William Taylor, *The Big Boys: Power and Position in American Business* (New York: Pantheon Books, 1986).

Dick Youngblood, "Norris Made Social Responsibility a Priority and a Dispute," *Minneapolis Star and Tribune*, 9 January 1986.

"A Visionary Exits: Norris Leaves Control Data," *Time*, 20 January 1986.

Patrick Houston and Gordon Bock, "Can a Gentleman Farmer Get Control Data Out of the Ditch?" *Business Week*, 27 January 1986.

Richard Broderick, "Corporate Culture: Norris at Colonnus," *Corporate Report*, February 1986.

David Finn, "A Computer Pioneer's Deals and Ideals," *Across the Board*, April 1986.

William C. Norris, "Government Must Back Development," *Computers and Technology*, 3 November 1986.

Part II
Technology Series
(Reprints of addresses by William C. Norris prepared for distribution to stockholders and the public and available from the Public Relations Department of Control Data Corporation)

No. 1 "Technological Cooperation for Survival" (February 1977)

No. 2 "Via Technology to a New Era in Education" (June 1977)

No. 3 "A Policy for Export of Products and Technology" (September 1977)

No. 4 "Technology and Full Employment" (November 1977)

No. 5 "Back to the Countryside via Technology" (January 1978)

No. 6 "Harnessing Technology for Better Urban Living" (April 1978)

No. 7 "Technology for Improving the Image of Business" (July 1978)

No. 8 "Technology for the Inner City—Experience and Promise" (September 1978)

No. 9 "Technology and the Investor—Facing Up to Society's Urgent Problems" (November 1978)

No. 10 "Rebirth of Technological Innovation via Small Business" (March 1979)

No. 11 "Pathway to Better Health via Technology" (March 1979)

No. 12 "Technology and the Handicapped" (May 1979)

No. 13 "Technology and Corporate Governance" (June 1979)

No. 14 "Technology and the Humanities" (October 1979)

No. 15 "Optimizing World Technological Resources for Mankind" (February 1980)

No. 16 "Technological Innovation and the Prudent Man" (October 1980)

No. 17 "Technology for Company-Employee Partnership to Improve Productivity" (December 1980)

No. 18 "Responding to the Technological Challenges of Small-Scale Agriculture" (November 1981)

No. 19 "Human Capital: The Profitable Investment: (October 1982)

Index

About the Author

James C. Worthy has been closely associated with William C. Norris and Control Data Corporation for two decades, initially as a management consultant and in recent years as a director.

He was formerly a vice president of Sears, Roebuck and Co., Assistant Secretary of Commerce in the Eisenhower Administration, and partner of the international management consulting firm, Cresap, McCormick and Paget. He has served as a corporate director for a number of major companies and has written and lectured extensively on business, government, and public policy.

His published works include *Shaping an American Institution: Robert E. Wood and Sears, Roebuck*, a book written from direct personal knowledge of his subject as is this book on William C. Norris.

A fellow of the U.S. and International Academies of Management, Worthy currently is professor of management at the J.L. Kellogg Graduate School of Management, Northwestern University.